By Dr. Peter L. Benson and Dorothy L. Williams
for Search Institute

Determining Needs in Your Youth Ministry

D1404062

Dear Lutheran Youth Leaders,

Lutheran Brotherhood is pleased to give you this volume as part of our RespecTeen program, a new effort designed to heighten the respect teens and adults have for each other—and themselves. We believe this book will be a practical tool for you as you seek to meet the needs of youth. If you have questions about other dimensions of RespecTeen, please call 1-800-888-3820.

Sincerely,

Paul Ramseth

Paul Ramseth
Lutheran Brotherhood

Group *Books*

Loveland, Colorado

Determining Needs in Your Youth Ministry

Copyright © 1987 by Search Institute

Fifth Printing

Edited by Eugene C. Roehlkepartain
Designed by Judy Atwood

Library of Congress Cataloging-in-Publication Data
Benson, Peter L.
  Determining needs in your youth ministry.

  Bibliography: p.
  1. Church work with youth. 2. Church work with young adults. I. Williams, Dorothy Lowe, 1926-
II. Title.
BV4447.B47   1987   259'.23   87-19774
ISBN 0-931529-56-5 (pbk.)

Printed in the United States of America

TABLE OF CONTENTS

TABLE OF DIAGRAMS

BY GEORGE GALLUP, JR.

FOREWORD

The church sometimes acts like Chicken Little. An acorn falls, and—before stopping to find out what actually happened—the church panics. "The sky is falling! The sky is falling!" it shouts, rushing to make plans based on the shaky prediction.

Fortunately, survey research is beginning to change the story. Chicken Little is learning to gather more accurate information before jumping to conclusions. As a result, the church's plans grow out of a more realistic assessment of people's needs and concerns.

With *Determining Needs in Your Youth Ministry*, Dr. Peter L. Benson and Dorothy L. Williams have given youth workers an excellent resource to help them avoid the Chicken Little syndrome. By administering, interpreting and applying this survey as the authors direct, youth workers will gain valuable insight into who their teenagers are, what they believe and how they act.

Survey research replaces arbitrary assumptions and preconceptions with hard, useful data. Thus it helps focus and set priorities in your youth ministry. Until you know your teenagers and their needs, chances are good that you will waste valuable time, energy and resources on irrelevant programming. I can only imagine the contortions some youth groups go through to attract crowds to meetings on church doctrine, only to learn that the young people really want help with understanding their sexuality.

There is also a deeper theological reason for using survey research in youth ministry. If a central goal of your ministry is to strengthen teenagers' relationship with God, then examining that relationship with all available tools is an important task. By learning how your young people understand God, you can discover ways to enhance their faith through your ministry.

The material in this book is carefully crafted, well-organized and easy to use. Because the questions focus on the teenager's own feelings, beliefs and behaviors, the exhaustive survey is particularly useful. Aside from the obvious benefits of the data, utilizing this tool in a local congregation will also unify the teenagers through their common experience of taking the survey. At the same time, it will give them a chance to sound off—which everyone likes to do.

Of course, no book can guarantee that a survey will succeed. Why? Because the project's value will ultimately be determined by how the results are applied. Some of the findings may jump out at you, suggesting immediate steps to take. Others will require putting several pieces together before you can identify specific concerns to address through your ministry.

Some survey data may surprise you. You might not have known, for instance, how concerned your kids are about drug and alcohol abuse or social injustice. In this case, the survey will have rattled your assumptions and challenged you to consider some new emphases in your youth ministry.

On the other hand, some of the data may not surprise you at all. For example, you may have already known that some of your kids have trouble with self-esteem. If the survey reveals this same problem, then it will have confirmed your preconceptions, encouraging you to continue working with the problem.

In either case, *Determining Needs in Your Youth Ministry* will open some of the closed doors to teenagers' lives. Then, as you step through those doors, you can minister to your teenagers' deepest needs, hopes and fears. Such an opportunity repays many times the investment of time and energy needed to conduct the survey.

INTRODUCTION

Most teenagers live two lives. One life is open to public view—the 16-year-old who is crazy about motorcycles; the freshman who wears too much makeup; the quiet, awkward junior higher; the outspoken and domineering senior.

But there are also secret lives hidden behind teenagers' masks. You catch glimpses of those private worlds when a young person opens up on a retreat or camping trip, or perhaps in the church kitchen when everyone else has gone home after a dinner theater. In such moments, you discover that a seemingly superficial teenager is infinitely more thoughtful and compassionate than anyone would have guessed. Or you find out that a young person who has always seemed self-confident and strong is actually struggling to stay emotionally afloat in a stormy home situation.

Such encounters remind you that your youth ministry could be much more effective if you only knew about group members' hidden lives.

Determining Needs in Your Youth Ministry is based on a survey designed to give you a well-rounded picture of your junior and senior highers' hurts, fears, worries and interests, pointing you toward programming paths that touch the teenagers' deepest needs, problems and concerns.

A simple process

If conducting a survey seems like a terribly complex chore requiring long-forgotten mathematical skills, relax. We have developed a simple, straightforward process for all your calculations. All you'll need are a couple of simple pocket calculators and a group of teenagers and adults to help with the process. Everything else is in this book. Here's what we've included:

■ Step-by-step instructions for planning the survey, including how to choose a steering committee and what decisions to make in advance.

■ Suggestions for publicizing the survey so it will be supported, well-attended and taken seriously.

■ Detailed instructions for administering the survey, including a complete meeting plan.

■ Twenty youth surveys and answer sheets.

■ Worksheets for tabulating, simplifying and summarizing the results.

■ Suggestions for analyzing and interpreting the results without having to rely on an expert.

■ Ideas for sharing the information with parents and the church.

■ Suggestions of ways to rethink your youth ministry program based on what you learn from the survey.

■ Follow-up meeting ideas for your group.

What you'll learn

The survey probes teenagers' feelings and thoughts about themselves, their families, church, school and moral values.

You'll discover several things:

■ What your kids worry about.

■ Whether they are as seriously involved in alcohol and other drugs as the media would have you believe.

■ What your teenagers think of your congregation.

■ What kind of future they anticipate.

■ Their most important values.

■ Why church is—or isn't—important to them.

■ Where they go for help when they run into trouble.

■ Their moral standards.

■ What programming interests them most.

The survey consists of 160 questions in 16 parts (plus 2 general information questions). The teenagers will need approximately one hour to complete the survey. Following are brief descriptions of the different sections:

A. What I Want in Life (24 questions). This section nearly always contains some surprises. It lists 24 values—from popular values such as wealth and popularity to more mature values such as family life and self-understanding—and asks the teenagers what is most important to them.

B. What I Worry About (20 questions). These questions cover a list of concerns that has been widely reprinted, probably because some of the results are surprising. One of the best pieces of news that emerged from the list in national use was that children care about humanitarian concerns—hunger, violence—much earlier than previously thought.

C. My Family (13 questions). Besides giving an overall sense of the quality of home life for your group members, this section asks several "I wish my parents would . . ." questions that make for a wonderful program of parent-child dialogue. A follow-up conversation between teenagers and parents about schedules, responsibili-

ties and other issues will likely enhance parent-child relationships.

D. How I Feel About Myself (5 questions). This section should confirm or refute your assumptions about your teenagers' self-esteem.

E. My Future (6 questions). Many people attribute problems such as suicide and teenage pregnancy in part to a lack of hope among young people. These questions will help you assess your group members' hopes for the future.

F. My Friends (7 questions). How do your teenagers feel about their friends? Are their friendships generally positive, or are there negative sides to their friendships?

G. Where I'd Go for Help (6 questions). Teenagers go to different people for advice. This section reveals whom your group members trust, and whether they take different problems to different people.

H. My Christian Faith (13 questions). These questions explore religion's impact on the teenagers' daily lives. A set of 6 questions lets you know whether your group concentrates on the vertical dimension of faith—the connection between God and self—or the horizontal dimension, which impels Christians to serve others.

I. What I Do (13 questions). How pervasive in your group are such negative behaviors as shoplifting, excessive TV watching, drinking, drug abuse, vandalism and physical violence? These are difficult questions to ask in person. The survey allows you to learn the information without threatening the teenagers' privacy. The section also includes information about some positive behaviors.

J. School (5 questions). This short section conveys how your kids feel about their school environment and how they behave in it.

K. Right and Wrong (6 questions). This central and powerful set of questions delves into issues such as premarital sex, discrimination and drinking. The results will likely stimulate serious discussions about morality among your kids. The responses may also include some good news for parents.

L. Male-Female Relationships (7 questions). These questions give clues to a very important set of feelings and behaviors related to the opposite sex. The responses will confirm or contradict your own perceptions.

M. and **N. My Church** and **My Feelings About My Church** (11 questions). Taken together, these two sections communicate whether your teenagers feel at home in the church and whether they sense the support of adult church members.

O. and **P. What I Want From My Church** and **How Well My Church Is Doing** (24 questions). These two sections provide invaluable help with program planning. The first 12 items assess your young people's interest in particular areas of church life, and the second set is like a report card on those same topics. Discrepancies between the two lists highlight areas of interest that are not being met.

Determining Needs in Your Youth Ministry is a valuable tool for you as you seek to minister more effectively to the teenagers in your group. Whether the results surprise you, please you, upset you or challenge you, they will lay a solid foundation on which to build plans and programs that more effectively meet the needs and interests of your young people.

CHAPTER ONE

ADMINISTERING THE SURVEY

Imagine trying to build a house without plans or preparation. No one would know what to build, where to start or what the house is supposed to look like. None of the materials would arrive when they were needed. And the roofing crew might show up before the foundation is poured. The project would be a disaster.

The idea of building a house without a blueprint is admittedly quite ludicrous. Yet the resulting chaos is similar to the chaos leaders find in their youth program when, for one reason or another, they don't plan adequately.

Conducting this youth survey requires particularly thorough planning and coordination. If you fail to develop a team to plan, conduct and interpret the survey, you may find yourself buried under unmanageable stacks of papers and statistics. And if the leaders have not prepared adequately for interpreting the survey, then results may be manipulated to fit preconceived agendas, thus shedding no new light on your group.

On the other hand, if you carefully prepare the teenagers, leaders and church members, the survey will provide fresh insight into your youth ministry program. Moreover, by dividing the work among several responsible and interested people, you not only ease your own load, but you ensure enthusiastic support for the process.

This chapter will lead you through the whole youth survey planning process. Here are the steps you will follow:

■ Select a steering committee;
■ Make preliminary decisions;
■ Publicize the youth survey;
■ Conduct the survey during a special meeting; and
■ Tally and summarize the results.

The steering committee

A strong steering committee is vital to the youth survey's success. You will work with this group in planning, administering, tabulating and summarizing the survey. The committee should include the following people:

■ **Committee leader.** Begin by selecting a committee leader who is enthusiastic, detail-oriented and a good teamworker. Then, together with this leader, choose a committee of at least three more adult leaders. Depending on the size of your youth group, each of these leaders will need other adults to help with their assigned tasks. The committee leader should work with the people responsible for each task to choose helpers.

■ **The administration leader.** Select someone to oversee the survey administration. This person will do everything possible to ensure good participation, and will see that the youth survey is administered under the best possible circumstances. He or she will need to recruit a number of young people and adults to help with publicity, food and activities for the youth survey meeting.

■ **The tally leader.** The tally leader should be a detail-oriented person. He or she will supervise the tally teams, who will transfer the data from the answer sheets onto the tally sheet and then prepare the summary.

Enlist two adults for every 10 young people who take the youth survey to serve on tally teams. These teams should be able to record scores for 10 tests in about one hour. This assignment is good for people who cannot commit themselves to long-term projects, since this work involves only a limited time commitment.

To ensure confidentiality, we strongly recommend that only adults serve on tally teams. If youth group members know that their peers will be examining their answer sheets, they may hesitate to be candid. Moreover, tallying and summarizing the scores increase interest among adults as they discover interesting or surprising data in the tally process.

■ **Presentation leader.** This person will be responsible for presenting the youth survey results to various interested groups and for working with them in taking action based on the findings. This person should be good at helping groups work together—a facilitator who listens well and doesn't need to talk a lot. In larger churches, this leader may want to coordinate teams of articulate young people and adult leaders to share the survey results with the rest of the congregation.

■ **Others.** The steering committee should also include four or five other people to help study, interpret and build on the youth survey results. These people can also contribute valuable insights as you

plan for the youth survey.

■ **Young people.** Include several young people on the steering committee. They can be particularly useful with publicity through phone calls, personal contacts, etc. They will also have important insights for interpreting the data. If you decide to use only a portion of the youth survey, the young people may be able to tell you some sections that are particularly appropriate to them. As mentioned earlier, young people should not be included on the tally teams.

Preliminary decisions

Once the steering committee is in place, it must make several decisions that will guide the rest of your planning. Your choices will depend on your youth group's size and the specific information you want to gather.

■ **When and where.** If possible, give the youth survey to all the teenagers simultaneously. But if you must include some people who cannot be present for the first administration, arrange for a single "makeup" session. Some teenagers will inevitably ask to take the survey home. Do not give in, since surveys taken home rarely return.

■ **The entire group or a sample group.** We urge you to survey everyone. However, if your group is so large that this approach would be unrealistic, choose a random sample by following this procedure:

Start with a complete alphabetical list of your group members. Decide what percentage of the group you want to survey. If you decide on about 30 percent, count down the list, choosing every third person. If you want to survey 20 percent, choose every fifth person. If 50 percent, every second person. Resist the temptation to skip names of less active people. If the system works correctly, you will end up with a mixture of committed kids and those who show up only occasionally—an accurate representation of your group.

■ **Every question or selected sections.** Decide whether to ask the young people to answer all the questions or only some of them. Having them answer all questions is generally best. After going through all the work of planning, notifying, persuading and administering, you might as well get all the information you can. Then the data will be available when questions arise later.

If your administration time is limited, however, the steering committee should decide which sections are most crucial to your group. For example, if the major goal of conducting the survey is to learn how the youth group feels about the church, you would include the last four sections of the survey. But if you are most interested in what the group thinks about the future, you would administer the first section, What I Want in Life, together with the six questions under My Future (section E).

Completing the whole survey will take about one hour. Therefore, if you have only 45 minutes available, you would have to cut approximately 40 questions.

Publicizing the survey

Invitations to take surveys usually don't attract hordes of enthusiastic participants. The secret to overcoming this lack of enthusiasm is to publicize the event in creative and attractive ways that tell each young person that he or she is an important part of the youth group.

Try centering the event around the theme "Our Puzzling Youth Group." Use the theme to say that the youth survey will answer some "puzzling questions" about the group and that the puzzle will not be complete unless every "piece" (person) is included.

This theme lends itself to numerous publicity ideas:

■ **Posters.** Invite group members to a poster party. Explain the puzzle theme, and encourage the kids to be creative. Here are two ideas:

1. Draw a puzzle in the shape of your church and then blacken one of the pieces. Underneath write: "Don't be the missing puzzle piece. Participate in our youth group survey at (time) on (date) at (place). Bring your favorite pizza topping!"

2. Draw miscellaneous puzzle pieces all over a sheet of posterboard. Then write: "Come help us figure out how the pieces of our youth ministry fit together. Participate in our youth group survey at (time) on (date) at (place). Bring your favorite pizza topping!"

■ **Buttons.** Cut out buttons from posterboard in the shape of puzzle pieces. Then write on them: "My piece will be there. Will yours?" Distribute these buttons on Sunday mornings or at youth group meetings. They're bound to invite questions from other teenagers and church members and help build interest in and enthusiasm for the survey.

■ **Invitations.** Mailing invitations to each young person will ensure that everyone knows about the youth survey, and a personalized invitation always attracts more attention than a flier. On the front of the invitation, draw a small puzzle. On the inside write: "We're taking a survey to see what our youth group looks like, and the picture won't be complete unless you are there. Please join us for this important meeting at (time) on (date) at (place). We'll be building pizzas after the survey, so bring your favorite (or most exotic) topping!"

You can easily duplicate the invitation on any 8½ × 11 paper by following the pattern in Diagram 1. After the invitations are copied, fold them so that the puzzle is on the front and the details are inside. Then

Diagram 1

INVITATION (SAMPLE)

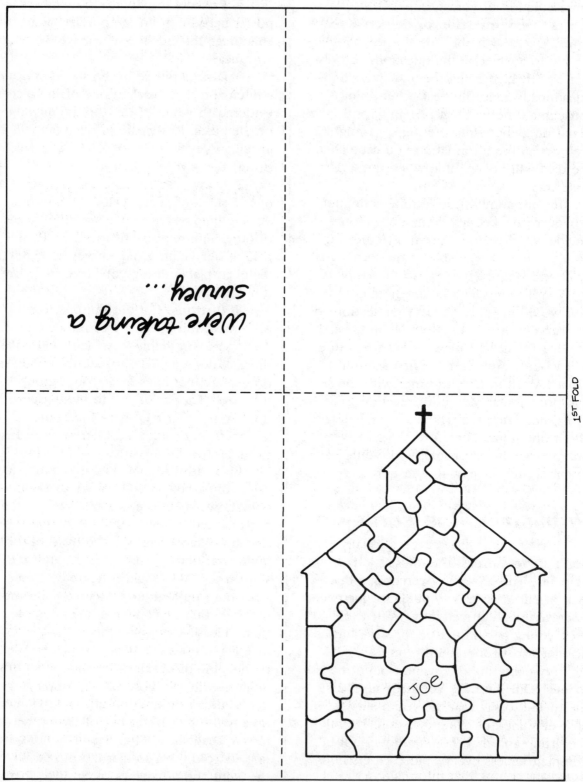

We're taking a survey...

JOE

1ST FOLD

2ND FOLD

personalize each invitation by writing the name of a young person on one of the puzzle pieces and mail the invitation to that person. The invitations will fit in A-2 envelopes (5¾×4½ inches), which are available at most stationery and paper-supply stores.

■ **Announcements.** Begin announcing the survey to the youth and the congregation several weeks before the meeting. Ask teenagers to take the lead on the announcements; their peers and their parents will enjoy—and notice—their creativity. Here are two suggestions:

1. Cut six huge, interconnecting puzzle pieces out of posterboard (one puzzle piece from each board), then write out the word S U R V E Y with one letter on each piece. Give the pieces to six different people and have them each make part of the announcement. Each person remains seated until it is his or her turn to speak. Then he or she goes forward and connects his or her puzzle piece with the previous one.

2. Have the kids do a skit in which they sit at a table and put together a puzzle. They could discuss the picture that is developing, and then suddenly stop and say:

Person 1: "Do you have the piece that fits here?"

Person 2: "No, I thought you had it."

Person 1: "Maybe that's Tom's piece."

Person 2: "But Tom is not here."

Person 1: "I guess we'll never really know what the puzzle looks like. I wish we had all the pieces."

Then the actors could explain how everyone contributes to the puzzle by participating in the youth survey. They could finish by telling all the details about the survey.

■ **Letter to parents.** In addition to building interest among the teenagers, be sure that parents are aware of and support your plans. Most parents would like to know what kind of information is being sought and how that information will be used. Volunteering this information builds trust and lets parents know that the youth program receives serious attention. See Diagram 2 (page 14) for our suggested wording for an informational letter to parents.

Creative publicity will not ensure that everyone will participate in the survey. In fact, some people probably never would, no matter what you try. But by using several different methods, you can capture the attention of as many people as possible.

The survey meeting

Administering the youth survey does not have to be a dull experience for the teenagers. Though you could simply distribute the survey and then let the young people go home when they're finished, you can also make the survey time enjoyable and enriching.

Teenagers may not take the survey as seriously if it is merely tagged on to a regular group meeting. Therefore, plan a special meeting with activities and discussions that revolve around the survey.

Any time that the teenagers have several hours to spend at church is appropriate for conducting the youth survey. You may even want to expand the meeting into an all-day meeting on a Saturday.

The following meeting would last approximately four hours, including a pizza lunch or supper. Adapt it to fit your own needs and time restrictions.

■ **Preparation.** Prepare the following for the survey itself:

1. Gather enough pencils with erasers for each young person.

2. Arrange to have enough tables and chairs available for all the teenagers to sit comfortably in one room to take the survey. Minimize nearby distractions such as noise or other groups' activities. Have the young people sit as far apart as possible during the survey to preserve their privacy.

Diagram 2
PARENTS LETTER

Dear Parent:

In our continuing effort to minister effectively to teenagers, (church) is asking our young people to complete a short survey. The data from the youth survey will help us plan for their Christian growth and learning.

Prepared by Search Institute and Group Books (two national youth-serving organizations), the survey will gather a variety of information. Youth group members will have a chance to tell their leaders what they are thinking on these and other related topics:

* What our group members value most in life.
* What they worry about.
* Their views on some tough moral questions.
* Their experiences in school and at home.
* Discussion topics or programs that interest them.

All survey answers will be completely anonymous. Nothing on the survey form will identify the answers with a particular individual. Instead, the answers will be summarized in a report on the total youth group. That report will be used to tailor our youth ministry to the specific needs and enthusiasms of this youth group.

The survey is to be given at (time, date, place). Please return enclosed card (or notify a named person) that your teenager will be present for the survey.

We have also planned a pizza-building party and other activities along with the survey. We are asking each young person to bring a favorite pizza topping. We expect to be finished by (hour).

Thanks for your cooperation.

In Christ's service,

Youth pastor

If the kids will sit around tables, seat half as many as usual around each table. If the kids use individual desks, spread them out.

3. Be sure you have enough copies of the youth survey and answer sheet (page 65) for each young person. (Twenty copies of each are included in this kit.) You have permission to photocopy pages from this book (for local church use only) if you need additional copies.

Bring a few extra copies of the youth survey, since visitors may surprise you. If some of the young people bring guests, issue surveys to the visitors and ask them to write "Visitor" on their answer sheet. Then when the surveys are being tabulated, remove the visitors' sheets from the process.

4. Give the survey administrator one or two large envelopes into which young people can put their folded answer sheets when they turn them in. This approach will preserve anonymity better than simply stacking the answer sheets on a desk or table.

Make name tags by cutting out a puzzle in the shape of a church. Each piece will be a name tag for a young person, so calculate how many you'll need beforehand.

If you use the "census" crowdbreaker (this page), create and copy enough "census sheets" for everyone to have two or three. You can save paper by printing four census sheets on one piece. The sheet should ask the following questions (or others that seem more appropriate for your group):

1. Name.
2. Grade and school.
3. Hobbies.
4. Most recent movie seen.
5. Favorite music group.
6. The funniest thing he or she has ever seen.

Gather the following supplies for your meal: ingredients for pizza dough, pizza sauce and cheese (you can buy frozen dough, or make it from scratch. Figure one pizza for four kids); and tea, soft drinks or other beverages.

■ **Crowdbreaker.** As the young people arrive, distribute puzzle-piece name tags to each person. Then when everyone is present, announce that the group is going to use the name tags to put together a puzzle of the church. Each person must figure out where his or her piece fits. There are some restrictions, however: No one is allowed to talk, and no one can take a piece from someone else. Teamwork and cooperation are the goals. After the puzzle is together, you may want to ask the teenagers to discuss the experience.

If your group is too large for this crowdbreaker to be practical, try this alternative:

Distribute two or three census sheets to each person. Tell the group members to complete the census by interviewing two or three people they don't know well and filling out the information on the sheets. Make sure everyone in the group is surveyed. Then, if you have time, ask some of the teenagers to tell something they learned that was particularly interesting about their fellow group members.

■ **Opening prayer.** After the crowdbreaker, ask the kids to sit at the tables where they will take the surveys. When they are comfortable, lead them in the following prayer: "Dear God, thank you for the beautiful diversity of your young people who are represented in this group. Thank you for loving and accepting us as we are. Help us now as we express ourselves through these surveys. May we be honest and open so that what we say can become a useful tool in your service. In Christ's name, Amen."

■ **Conducting the youth survey.** As administration leader, you have two important functions during the survey. One is to handle the specifics of detail: distributing the survey efficiently, guiding people in filling it out completely, collecting the survey booklets and answer sheets from the group.

The second function is equally important: setting the tone of the group so people will take the task seriously. When appearing before groups, many people handle their discomfort by making light of the activity. The survey administrator should resist any impulse to joke about or trivialize the youth survey. Though taking the survey may seem like "test time at school," important decisions will be based on the results. So urge the teenagers to undertake the work seriously.

Distribute the surveys, and ask the young people not to begin until you have gone over the instructions and have answered any questions. If your group has more than 20 or 30 members, enlist one or two helpers to speed up distribution.

Be sure everyone receives a survey, an answer sheet and a pencil. We suggest that everyone use a pencil for two reasons. First, the young people can erase pencil marks if they change their mind on particular questions. Second, pencil marks are more anonymous than pen or felt-tip marks.

Tell group members why you are administering the youth survey and what you hope to learn from it. Say: "We are glad you are here to help us learn what you are thinking. We arranged for you to take this survey because we want to know more about you, about your experience in this church and about your interests. This survey will help us plan our work better as we try to meet your needs."

Thank them for agreeing to take the survey, and reassure them that their responses are completely anonymous. Remind them not to write on the survey booklet or to put their names on the answer sheets.

Then read through the instructions together, adding any special instructions or emphasizing important points. If you are asking the group only to take certain portions of the test, explain exactly what you want. Answer any questions participants might have. Ask them to stay seated when finished so as not to disturb others.

After everyone is finished, have the teenagers fold their answer sheets to hide their responses. Then collect the sheets in large envelopes. Thank the teenagers for participating in the survey, and tell them when you expect to be able to report the results to them.

Whenever the completed answer sheets are not being used, keep them in a secure place—locked in a church vault or cabinet, or stored in an adult leader's home. Otherwise, young people's curiosity and inventiveness could lead to unauthorized study of unprotected answer sheets.

■ **Activity and food.** After spending an hour taking a survey, the young people will definitely be hungry. So plan a pizza-building party that will highlight the meeting's theme—that everyone makes an important contribution to your group. With the church supplying the dough, sauce and cheese, ask the teenagers to bring their favorite pizza topping.

While the group members are completing the survey, ask adult volunteers to prepare the pizza dough and sauce, placing the incomplete pizzas on large tables. Then when everyone has finished the survey, have the teenagers add their toppings to the pizzas.

While the pizzas are cooking, the kids can build "body sculptures." Have them divide into teams of six or eight people to build human pyramids or other "sculptures." They may want to be a car, fish, skyscraper or just about anything. Everyone on the team should be a part of the effort. The team that can hold its structure the longest wins.

One word of caution: Don't let the teams do anything risky or dangerous. A few bruises can be expected when pyramids collapse amid groans, cheers and laughter, but a broken arm can ruin the meeting.

If you are still waiting for the pizzas after all the teams are finished, try to form one big pyramid. Then tell someone on the bottom row to leave. You can then remind the kids how the pyramid crumbled when you discuss the importance of each person in the group.

When the pizzas are ready, dig in! The kids won't need any instructions.

■ **Discussion.** Answering a series of thought-provoking questions can be excellent preparation for a discussion. Such a discussion can fix the event more firmly in the participants' minds, making them more eager to know what their group as a whole is like. It also offers the benefit of immediate group input on questions each person had to answer individually on the survey.

After group members have finished the pizza, invite them to sit in a circle for a discussion time. Begin by asking participants which survey questions caused them to examine something they hadn't thought of before. What questions are they still debating? What questions about their future would they like to discuss as a group? What questions made them the most uncomfortable? Why?

Once the teenagers have expressed their thoughts about the youth survey, you can guide the meeting in several directions. Here are some ideas:

Right and Wrong (Questions 115 through 120). As reported in *The Quicksilver Years*, (by Peter Benson, Dorothy Williams and Arthur Johnson), the question of right and wrong is something young people would like to discuss more with

their parents—particularly when the discussion is not attached to a specific incident. What makes certain things right or wrong? Are some things right or wrong regardless of whether another person is involved? What does scripture say?

A good, non-threatening way to deal with questions of right and wrong is to role play by asking teenagers to assume the perspectives of a variety of people. (This exercise also reveals how teenagers perceive different people and professions.) If you are discussing the issue of sex, for example, the group members could be doctors, teachers, politicians, parents, pastors or "typical" high school students.

Smaller youth groups can hold a panel discussion in which these "experts" answer questions from the "audience." Larger youth groups might want to divide into small groups of "experts" to debate the questions individually.

Group members can be as creative as they want. Some "hams" may try to imitate the voice, language and gestures of their person. Or some may be able to make a hat or a prop out of paper to represent their "profession." In the midst of the creative involvement, the teenagers can express themselves more freely than in a general discussion.

What I Want in Life (Questions 3 through 26). Age sometimes influences values. Adults embrace different values than teenagers. And seventh-graders have different values from seniors.

With this idea in mind, divide the group into teams according to grade. Then ask the members in each group to choose one thing that represents what they think their "typical" classmates value the most in life. For instance, they might choose a dollar bill to represent wealth, a mirror to represent good looks or a snapshot to represent friends or family. Bring the teams back together to explain and discuss their choices. Ask questions like the following:

1. Do you agree with your classmates' values? Why or why not?

2. Why do you think different ages have different values?

3. If you could change your classmates' values, what would you substitute for the item you selected?

The same procedure can be used to discuss their parents' values, the church's values, society's values or the youth group's values. Try as many different angles as seem appropriate for your group.

My Feelings About My Church (Questions 133 through 138). Since teenagers may be reluctant to express directly their feelings about the church, try this exercise:

Tell the group members to imagine that they have just moved to a new city without any churches, so they have to start a church for themselves. What would it be like? Ask them to brainstorm ideas. Do not argue with them or tell them that something is impractical or impossible. Instead, listen to their dreams and try to read what they are saying between the lines about your church.

If they are having trouble getting started, prompt them with questions like these:

1. Would you want it to be a small church or a large one?

2. What kind of pastor would you want?

3. What would your building be like?

4. What activities would you have? Sunday worship? Picnics? Sunday school? Youth group fellowships? Bible studies?

After they have run out of ideas and suggestions, challenge them to try to give life to some of their ideas in your church through their own involvement.

■ **Closing.** Read 1 Corinthians 12:12-26, where Paul talks about the many different parts of the body of Christ.

Then say: "Let's pretend that you're the little toe of the church. Now, you may think a toe is not very important. But have you ever broken your little toe? It's almost impossible to walk, isn't it? Our bodies need every single part that God has given us.

"The church is the same way. You may not think that you have much to offer the church, but God has a purpose for you as a part of Christ's body.

"Today you have answered many questions about who you are, what you believe and what you want. I'd like to challenge you in the next week to think about what part you can play in the body of Christ. Will you be the church's hands, serving the people around you? Will you be its arms, offering loving hugs to those who are hurting? Or will you be its voice, sharing with your friends the good news that God loves us and accepts us just as we are?"

After a few moments of silence, close with prayer.

Tabulating and summarizing

Once the youth survey has been administered, the tally leader must correlate all the data from individual answer sheets to form a composite profile of your youth group. This process involves three steps:

1. Preparing the answer sheets.

2. Transferring the raw data to the tally sheet.

3. Completing the summary sheet.

■ **Preparing the answer sheets.** Before tallying the scores, organize the answer sheets. First look for any sheets with many missing answers or surveys that weren't finished. If your youth group has more than 50 members, an occasional missed question is inconsequential. But if several respondents skipped whole blocks of questions, you will need to adjust your calculations of some questions to assure accurate percentages.

Decorator sheets. Occasionally—for reasons unconnected with the youth survey—someone feels the need symbolically to defy authority. Instead of marking the answers that reflect his or her feelings, the young person will arbitrarily circle responses to form a geometrical pattern. Such a ''decorator'' sheet can be easily identified. The teenager may answer every question with the middle response, or he or she may prefer diamond designs or zig-zags. Whatever the pattern, discard the decorated sheet before you begin the tally process.

If any participant marked his or her answer sheet so that it is identifiable, erase or cover up the marks.

Subgroups. If you want to compare different segments of your youth group to each other, divide the answer sheets into subgroups before tabulating the results. If you are giving the survey only to seventh-through ninth-graders, you might want to know how the grades differ. If you are surveying seventh- through twelfth-graders, you could record seventh- and eighth-graders' answers in one category, ninth- and tenth-graders' in another, and eleventh- and twelfth-graders' in the third. Or you may want to analyze differences between the girls and boys in your group.

To compare subgroups, divide the collected answer sheets into stacks according to subgroups. Number the first pile sequentially, then the next pile straight through and then the third. Record the breaks between subgroups (for example, numbers 1 through 42 are seventh- and eighth-graders; 43 through 81 are ninth- and tenth-graders; and 82 through 99 are eleventh- and twelfth-graders).

If you are not calculating the responses of any subgroups, simply number all the stacks sequentially. This identifying number is important since the young people did not write their names on the answer sheets.

One word of caution: Calculating subgroup totals along with the results of the group as a whole can quickly become overwhelming. If you think subgroup scores would be useful, separate and tally the answer sheets as in subgroups, but summarize the whole group's answers before calculating the subgroup percentages. Use this general information to complete your basic reports. Then you'll have a better idea of the time involved in each calculation and the usefulness of the information. You can then decide whether to prepare subgroup data on all questions or on only one or two sections.

■ **Transferring the data to the tally sheet.** The tabulation process is not difficult, but it does take time. The job goes more quickly and more accurately if people work in tally teams of two.

Photocopy enough tally sheets for each tally team. Each team will also need pencils with erasers, a simple calculator and a straightedge ruler. Ask teams to bring their own, but also have several on hand for those who forget.

Distribute the answer sheets to two-person tally teams. Give each team surveys from only one subgroup, and be sure that each subgroup's answers are recorded on a separate tally sheet. Keep track of each team's stack by noting which team has which number sequence, and remind the teams to write their sequence on the top of their tally sheet.

Here is the basic tally process: One person reads the answers (for example, ''1—M; 2—G; 3—V; 4—S; 5—N''), while the other person records the responses in the column marked ''Tally answers'' using the ''score'' method ($\cancel{IIII}$ $\cancel{IIII}$ III). See Diagram 3 for an example.

Stress to the teams the importance of

Diagram 3

TALLYING THE SCORES (SAMPLE)

First person's answers

75. A Ⓑ C D

76. A B Ⓒ D E

77. A B C Ⓓ E

Second person's answers

75. A B Ⓒ D

76. A B C Ⓓ E

77. Ⓐ B C D E

Third person's answers

75. A B C Ⓓ

76. A B C D Ⓔ

77. A Ⓑ C D E

Fourth person's answers

75. A Ⓑ C D

76. A B C Ⓓ E

77. A Ⓑ C D E

Fifth person's answers

75. Ⓐ B C D

76. A Ⓑ C D E

77. A B C D Ⓔ

Tally sheet

Question	Response	Tally answers	Total
75. Often lonely	A	I	1
	B	II	2
	C	I	1
	D	I	1
76. Do wrong	A		O
	B	I	1
	C	I	1
	D	II	2
	E	I	1
77. Parents like my friends	A	I	1
	B	II	2
	C		O
	D	I	1
	E	I	1

Summary sheet

Question	Total responses	$\frac{\text{Total responses}}{\text{total group size}} \times 100$	Percent
75. Often lonely	A+B 3	$\frac{3}{5} \times 100$	60% say, "I feel lonely quite often or every day."
	C 1		
	D 1		
76. Do wrong	A+B 1	$\frac{1}{5} \times 100$	20% say, "My friends often or very often try to make me do things I know are wrong."
	C 1		
	D 2		
	E 1		
77. Parents like my friends	A 1	$\frac{1}{5} \times 100$	20% say, "My parents like all of my friends."
	B 2		
	C O		
	D 1		
	E 1	$\frac{1}{5} \times 100$	20% say, "My parents don't like any of my friends."

transferring *all* of the answers accurately from the answer sheets to the tally sheet. Allow the tally teams regular breaks to avoid carelessness when they become tired.

If, by chance, one of the tally teams connects an answer sheet with a particular young person, insist that the team keeps all information strictly confidential. The young people have put their trust in the process, and the tally team could seriously damage someone's trust and self-image by revealing his or her answers to particular questions.

■ **Completing the summary sheet.** When the teams have finished recording the answers, add the totals from the different sheets and transfer that information to the summary sheet (see Diagram 3). In some cases the summary sheet says to add the totals of two or more responses (see, for example, question 65). Do this as you transfer the data from the tally sheet to the summary sheet.

Then calculate the percentage of teenagers who gave the specified answer to the question by dividing the number of responses by the total number of kids and multiplying by 100. Fill in that percentage in the appropriate column. Continue this process for the entire youth survey.

The summary sheet is not designed to calculate all of the variables and details for each question. Rather, it helps pull out and summarize the most useful information for most youth groups. [For example, instead of separately calculating how many participants say religion is "very important" and those who say it is "somewhat important" (question 84), the summary sheet records only those who answered "very important."] If other responses are of particular interest to your group, calculate those responses in the shaded areas.

Most groups studying the survey results will not need—or want—to know all the details on the summary sheet. But these detailed figures will serve as the basic source of information for the shorter reports you make to various groups. They will also be a detailed resource for any questions that arise during a meeting.

You now have useful data about your youth group. The next step will be to interpret that information to others and to use it as a tool in the church's ministry.

CHAPTER TWO

INTERPRETING THE RESULTS

When they're honest, most adults will admit that they wouldn't want to repeat their teenage years. Despite glamorous stereotypes of care-free teenagers, adolescence has always been a difficult time of confusing and awkward changes—new body, new thinking ability, new freedoms, new challenges, new frustrations.

First come the physical changes as bodies grow, body parts change in proportion to one another, and some parts even begin to function differently. These changes often leave teenagers feeling awkward, confused and embarrassed.

The size of teenagers' worlds also grows as parents allow more and more unsupervised activity. While this newfound freedom is usually enthusiastically welcomed, teenagers also face new and puzzling expectations and challenges.

Then teenagers discover that their childhood social skills are no longer adequate. Learning how to converse at an adult level, knowing when to stop kidding, and reacting sensitively to another person's feelings are all new skills to learn by trial and error—often painful error.

Because teenagers develop new analytic and speculative skills, suddenly everything is open to question. "Why do we have such dumb furniture?" "Why do I have to go to school?" "Why not paint my bedroom black?" In short, they emerge from a relatively restricted, understandable world into a universe of seemingly endless possibilities. The change is sometimes a wonderful gift. Sometimes it's a heavy burden.

As if such changes weren't enough, today's fast-paced world forces junior highers (even upper elementary kids!) to face tough questions and choices that their parents didn't face until after graduation. Adolescents face increasing pressure to look and act grown-up at ever earlier ages. Wearing makeup is no longer uncommon for junior highers. The sports world imposes the pressures of adult life on very young children, organizing, training and outfitting them as if they were professionals. And television and other media introduce youngsters to vivid sexual encounters and violence long before they can handle the images responsibly.

Because adolescents are rushed into adulthood, they develop a superficial gloss of sophistication that makes them appear much older and more mature. As a result, many adults wrongly assume that teenagers have the wisdom, knowledge and values to match the image.

Yet they rarely do. For example, Search Institute's research has shown that, despite up-to-date fashions and carefully applied makeup, one-third of teenage girls don't feel good about their bodies. Many young people say life has no purpose for them. And many of them don't think they have many friends at church. These young people need love, guidance and acceptance from parents and other adults. They need adults who care enough to listen closely to the needs and worries behind the "I've got it all together" image.

Despite the increased pressure on them, today's young people are still just as inhibited as teenagers of previous generations about asking for adult advice. Adolescents want to know what adults think, how their parents handled difficult situations as teenagers and how to make moral decisions; but few adolescents will ask. Search Institute's national survey revealed a high percentage of young people who did not seek help from anyone when they had problems.

One important function of this youth survey is to open up some of the young people's questions for discussion without them having to feel stupid for asking. For example, a group member may wonder if he or she is the only teenager who feels lonely and has trouble making friends. But he or she would never ask anyone. Or someone struggling with his or her own values may not know whether to believe peers who say: "Go ahead and try a joint. Everybody's doing it." Your survey results should help you identify some of those questions and answer them without anyone having to ask.

As you interpret the survey data, keep the teenagers' turbulent world in mind. Celebrate and affirm the good news you find. Relish the pleasant surprises. And when you find disturbing or bad news, avoid judging the teenagers harshly. Instead, empathize with their problems and try to discover ways to help them work toward positive change.

The perils of interpretation

When you use a power tool, you need to understand not only its benefits but also its dangers. If you fail to note the precautions, the tool's usefulness could be tragically overshadowed by irreparable injuries.

In a sense, this survey is a "power tool" that retrieves information that wouldn't otherwise be available. And like other power tools, the survey can be dangerous if misused.

The greatest danger in administering the survey is to misinterpret the results. Interpretation can go wrong in at least two ways:

■ **Under-interpretation.** To under-interpret the survey results is to explain away as inconsequential a difference, surprise or piece of bad news that actually calls for careful analysis and action. The under-interpreter might dismiss a statistic by saying, "That score is low because of Whatsisname's awful program last year." Or: "Well, how do you expect our kids to know each other? They go to five different high schools." Or, "That's nothing to worry about; kids are just that way nowadays."

If you begin rationalizing all the problems that are brought to light by the survey, then conducting the survey has only wasted your time and energy. Statistics from your group *do* mean something. When percentages are high, a whole lot of kids—each without knowing what the others wrote—are telling you something significant. If you hear a loud chorus on any question, pay attention.

■ **Over-interpretation.** Over-interpreters exaggerate negative information, thinking the situation is much worse than it really is. And because the news isn't entirely good, all past work is seen as failure.

For example, over-interpreters would see as overly significant the fact that your group scored low on a single question in describing the importance of church life. Of course, the low rating may be significant. But it's premature to base major decisions on a single question. Instead, look for matching, reinforcing or contradictory data before jumping to conclusions.

One of your best guides in interpretation is your group's history, memory and experience. If the survey results fit your group's background, then you can use those results to undergird your own understanding of your ministry. But if they don't match your own knowledge, then you should look for other signs that corroborate or oppose the new data before coming to a final conclusion.

Listening to the data

The purpose of conducting this survey has been to learn what your group members think and feel about themselves, their church and their world. Let the information speak for itself, thus focusing your attention on who your kids really are and on what they need. Here are several suggestions for listening to what the teenagers are saying through the survey results:

■ **Compare the results with your presuppositions.** Before administering the survey, read through all the questions to get a feel for what the survey covers. Then have members of the steering committee predict how the young people will respond by filling in the percentages on blank copies of the summary sheet (page 65). They need not answer every question. Rather, someone might fill out the section on right and wrong (section K), for example, while someone else completes sections M and N on teenagers' impressions of the church.

This preparation will help you compare what teenagers actually think and feel with what you thought you already knew about them. As committee members compare the actual results with their guesses, ask: Which responses did we predict accurately? What data conflicts with our knowledge of the youth group? In what areas do we know the kids well? Where do we not know them well at all? What were the surprises?

■ **Compare data within a section.** Look for responses that differ from the overall pattern for a given topic. Suppose, for instance, the teenagers are generally positive about your congregation, but only a very small percentage of them say that some of their best friends belong to the church. That sudden low in an area of highs signals something worth investigating.

■ **Compare the results with your goals for your ministry.** Your own hopes, expectations and goals for the teenagers and the youth group are the most useful reference points for your own ministry. For instance, ask yourself: Is it okay with us that a third of our group members have cheated on tests? Are we content with 20 percent of our kids saying they don't have many good friends at church? Can this church deal with the fact that 15 percent of youth group members have engaged in premarital sex? Such questions will highlight areas where the youth ministry may be falling short of its goals, or where new goals are needed to address unmet needs.

■ **Look for explicit suggestions.** You don't need fancy comparison figures to learn from What I Want From My Church and How Well My Church Is Doing (sections O and P). The young people are telling you where their own interests lie and how well they think those interests are being served. There could scarcely be a clearer directive on what kinds of programs would be their favorites. Simply match the similar questions in the two sections (for example, questions 139 and 151 both concern learning about the Bible) to see what is important to the teenagers and whether they believe the church meets those needs.

■ **Ask interested people to interpret the information.** Several individuals who know the youth program but who are not presently involved in its leadership should look through the summary sheet, noting percentages on individual items, groups of items or entire sections that seem particularly interesting. Then these people can get together to pool their thoughts and share them with the steering committee. Their ''outsider'' perspective can provide fresh insights that might not surface otherwise.

■ **Answer any specific questions you have.** By the time you are ready to interpret data, you and your youth committee should already have several questions that you hope to answer with the data. Look for the questions in the survey that would yield those answers, and discuss what you find with the committee. If, for example, you have questions about the teenagers' values, you would examine sections I and K (What I Do and Right and Wrong).

What you learn

While all the tedious work of tallying and summarizing scores may be time-consuming, interpreting the survey is really the most demanding part of the process. Not only do you spend a great deal of time analyzing statistics, but the data may threaten your presuppositions and goals for your ministry. That can be emotionally and physically draining for leaders who have invested many hundreds of hours—and some, their lives—in youth ministry.

At the same time, discussing the implications of the survey can reinvigorate leaders who have felt trapped in old programs,

emphases and assumptions. As they work with the data, they can begin to see new approaches to old problems and new problems that require creative responses. The fog lifts and you begin to see the youth ministry landscape more clearly.

As you work with the data, pieces will begin falling into place. You finally understand why some group members always seemed reluctant to invite their parents to meetings: They feel like they cannot communicate well with their parents. Or you discover why meetings on hot topics always go over so well: The kids long for more feedback on the tough questions that bombard them.

Now it's time to begin using what you've learned.

CHAPTER THREE

REPORTING THE RESULTS

As news of the youth survey spreads through the church, members will begin to wonder what you learned. This interest creates an ideal climate for sharing the needs, strengths and ambitions of your group members, and for explaining your vision for your ministry.

People will want to know about the survey—but they won't want to drown in an ocean of raw data. If you try to present too much information at once, eyes begin to glaze over and minds wander. It is better to present a short report and let the listeners ask for more information. Your completed summary sheet will keep at your finger tips information not included in the presentation.

Few groups will want to wade through all the statistics. Select highlights from various sections of the survey that will be of specific interest to a particular group, and present that information concisely and creatively.

Several elements should be included in every report: the total number of youth surveyed; the number of boys and girls; and, if applicable, the size of your subgroups. Then report four to six positive statistics. Also share any information that surprised you and anything that points toward programming changes.

Include some negative statistics in your reports. Be aware, though, that people who feed on bad news may try to disrupt the direction and tone of your meeting by rehearsing mistakes of recent history, placing blame, using the past to excuse or explain the current situation, or pining for the good ol' days.

The only benefit of reciting past experience is to help avoid repeating mistakes. If someone tries to twist the report to focus on the past, suggest that you can't change the past, but you can influence the future. Therefore, a more constructive response to the bad news is to think of ways to confront the problems, transforming them into opportunities for more focused, effective ministry.

Short reports

Lots of people will want to know what you have learned through the youth survey. Present short reports to various groups soon after you have compiled the data. Use the meetings to introduce people to the survey findings and to answer any questions they have. Since some of the groups may not know much about the youth ministry, the overview gives you an opportunity to educate them about your program. The following groups may want reports:

■ **The teenagers themselves.** You'll have difficulty containing the young people's curiosity. They may be slightly nervous about what you'll discover, and they may be uncomfortable knowing that many people will see the results. So report to them first, highlighting key sections of the survey. Try to balance positive and negative statistics.

Once the kids have had time to look over the results, give them time to ask questions, express disbelief or argue with the findings. They need the opportunity to talk about their feelings. Assure them that the results will not be used to "preach at" them, but only to help them. Listen carefully to their concerns; they may be pointing to specific problems. Explain again that the results will help you as you find ways to meet some of their needs.

■ **Parents.** After the young people themselves, parents are probably the group most eager to hear the results. You can share your discoveries either in print or in a parents meeting. The group session generates much more support and enthusiasm, but print usually reaches more people. A combination of the two is probably best.

Even if there are some unpleasant surprises in the data, there will almost certainly be some encouraging news, too. Parents will be happy to hear those good words. In the junior and senior high years, few young people take the initiative to tell their parents how much they trust and appreciate them. The survey results can help the kids express their feelings.

The following sections will likely contain interesting information for parents:

1. Where I'd Go for Help (section G). Report on one or more items that show particularly high percentages of young people saying they would go to their parents for help. Also mention any topics on which teenagers said they would not seek help from anyone, thus showing parents areas in which improved communication is needed.

2. What I Want From My Church (section O). Do the teenagers show a particularly strong interest in any program topics? Parents could use that information as they help their children schedule activities. Parents might also discover some needs that could be met in the home.

■ **The youth ministry steering committee.** The steering committee will spend a great deal of time with the survey results, rethinking aspects of the ministry and planning new programming (see the leaders planning meeting, page 29). However, before moving into these detailed discussions, meet to discuss the survey as a whole, answering particular questions and discussing general concerns. This introductory meeting may also point out specific concerns and issues that will help you as you plan future planning sessions.

■ **The church board.** We have suggested a special meeting for church leaders to focus on the teenagers' view of the church (see page 33). In addition, the church board will likely want to get an idea of the bigger picture. Spend 15 minutes or so at a regular board meeting presenting highlights from the survey and answering questions. Not only will the presentation remind board members of the importance of your ministry, but it will arouse their interest in the in-depth meeting. Be sure to invite board members to this meeting.

■ **The congregation.** Sharing the results with the congregation demands the most creativity, since the group is large and diverse. Try several different approaches. Here are some ideas:

1. Write a series of articles for the church newsletter.

2. Ask an artistic youth group member to draw posters or charts based on the statistics, then place them in strategic places around the church.

3. During regular Sunday morning announcement time, have group members share some of the findings. They might even want to build on the "puzzling" theme of the pre-survey publicity by telling the congregation how some of the pieces fit together.

■ **The budget committee.** This important group will likely want at least a brief report. A longer report may be necessary later if the steering committee recommends program changes involving additional expenditures.

Planning for the future

As interesting as the reports and analysis may be to the church, it is important to move on to the next step: planning.

A common problem in church planning is that issues are obscured by debates over different people's understanding of the needs. As a result, most of the group's energy is wasted in arguing about what different people *think* the teenagers want or need or believe or do.

One of the major benefits of taking a youth survey is that you don't have to guess any more; instead, the young people have *told* you about themselves—what is important to them, what they do, what they believe. Your task is to transform that information into concrete plans for ministry.

The goal of your planning meetings should always be to use the survey information as a foundation for building your youth ministry program. As you work with each piece of the puzzle, keep in mind your overall goals. Otherwise, trying to combat too many issues on too many fronts will fragment your ministry and dilute its power.

Based on section I in the survey (What I Do), the following meeting plan is designed as a model for dealing with the various data as you seek to revise and fine-tune your youth ministry. You can use a similar approach to address any of the other sections as well. This meeting—which deals almost entirely with kids' negative behaviors—should help you discuss this potentially disturbing information in a positive, action-producing atmosphere.

The meeting is designed for your youth group's adult and teenage leaders. The young people can provide their personal insights into various problems and can correct any misperceptions that arise.

■ **Preparation.** Make a handout or transparency of the results in section I (What I Do). Include the size of the group surveyed and the survey results. If the figures are very disturbing, prepare another handout or transparency of some positive results from other parts of the survey.

For the opening time, clip five or six current newspaper or magazine stories that relate to various teenage problems (suicide, drug abuse, pregnancy, etc.). Gather newsprint and markers for the discussions. And photocopy the worksheets (Diagram 4, page 31) for the small group brainstorming.

■ **Opening.** Begin by asking everyone to close his or her eyes. Then read a key paragraph or two from each news article, pausing between each one. When you are finished and have given people enough time to let the array of problems sink in, voice this prayer:

Lord, our young people live in a troubled world.
Give us . . .
    your *openness*, that we may understand their struggles;
    your *compassion*, that we may love them as they are;
    your *wisdom*, that we may guide their journeys; and
    your *vision*, that we may see beyond the problems of today to the

promise of tomorrow.
Amen.

■ **Share the data.** Introduce the meeting by saying: "Most of the topics we will discuss today are ones that worry all adults who care about kids: drinking, drug abuse, shoplifting, cheating, fighting and so on. Our youth group members were asked to tell us whether—or how much—they were involved in these negative behaviors.

"We do not share this information with you to condemn our young people or to denounce past ministry efforts. Rather, we want you to understand the young people so that our future planning will meet their specific needs and address appropriate concerns.

"Let's now look at what our kids told us about themselves."

Distribute the handouts or display the transparency of section I. If you prepared a second "good news" page, distribute or display it as well. After giving people time to read through the list, ask them to note the three most disturbing statistics they see and the three most reassuring ones.

■ **Celebration.** Post three sheets of newsprint on the wall. Write "What to Celebrate" on the first, "With Whom" on the second and "How" on the third. Ask each participant to point out some good news from the data. List their comments on the first sheet. Then ask for ideas about who should hear this news (the teenagers, church, parents, etc.) and how to celebrate it. Note these ideas on the second and third sheets.

■ **Challenge.** Now ask each person to name the three most disturbing statistics. List these items on a new sheet of newsprint. If many people point to the same problem, simply add tallies to the original entry. The repetition underscores the concern.

Once you have completed the list, work with the group to arrange the con-
cerns around particular themes or problems as much as possible. Then narrow the list to the two or three greatest concerns.

■ **Small groups.** When the group is satisfied that it has isolated the two or three greatest concerns, divide the participants into two or three small groups, depending on the number of concerns you identified. Assign one concern to each group to brainstorm, using the Leaders Brainstorming Worksheet (Diagram 4, page 31) as a guide. The participants can suggest study material, program ideas, staffing changes, congregational support, training programs, special events—anything they think might help. Insist that no ideas should be criticized or defended at this time; nothing is off limits.

When they begin to run out of ideas, ask them to choose the four ideas that seem most feasible and to list these on the worksheets. Then have them think about the pros and cons of each idea, noting them on the worksheet. After the small groups have brainstormed for about 15 minutes, ask them to list their ideas on a sheet of newsprint to present to the whole group.

■ **Plan action.** When the groups have finished their lists, bring them together to talk about their ideas. Label sheets of newsprint "Short-Term Goals" and "Long-Range Planning." Have the group agree on the most effective ideas for meeting the various needs. Then have the participants decide which ones should be short-term and long-term goals. If, for example, one of the major issues is substance abuse, the group could decide that an educational program from the police department's drug enforcement division is a good short-term project. A long-term goal might be to begin a support group for parents who are particularly concerned about substance abuse. Note the ideas on the newsprint as they are mentioned.

Diagram 4

LEADERS BRAINSTORMING WORKSHEET

Problem: _____

Here are several ways to deal with problems in the youth group: educational programs, individual counseling, parent education and support, social/political action, additional staff, new volunteers, new programming, special leadership training, seminars, retreats and so forth. Which of these (or other) ways would be most effective in addressing your particular issue? Brainstorm as many specific ideas as you can. List them in this space. Do not evaluate or criticize any of the ideas at this time.

_____	_____
_____	_____
_____	_____
_____	_____
_____	_____

When you have run out of ideas, pick the four that seem most feasible and discuss the pros and cons of each.

Idea: _____

Pros	Cons

Idea: _____

Pros	Cons

Idea: _____

Pros	Cons

Idea: _____

Pros	Cons

Set up a schedule for implementing the short-term goals, and assign responsibilities. Make notes on the long-range planning ideas for future meetings. If you'd like, publish the plans and ideas in the church newsletter so people will know the youth survey is being used.

■ **Closing.** After dwelling on these tough problems for an hour or so, the leaders may feel overwhelmed. There seems so much to do with so little time and so few resources. It might be tempting to despair. Thus a word of hope and encouragement is an appropriate conclusion to the meeting.

Read Colossians 2:1-6. Tell the group that Paul knew how discouraging things could get sometimes, so he wrote to the churches hoping to renew their vision. He reminded them that none of them had to manage their problems alone; they had one another. He also reminded them that they themselves were not the only resource; rather, they were building on a foundation laid by Christ. Finally, he told them that he hoped they would continue to live rooted in Christ's love and overflowing with thankfulness.

Then say: "We need to hear Paul's words of encouragement today in the midst of the challenges we face. Paul reminds us that God has called us to his mission, and he will give us the power and love we need to accomplish our task. Therefore, let us move forward, sure of God's presence in our world and confident in his ultimate victory."

Close with a group prayer, asking the leaders to recommit themselves to the work to which they have been called.

How teenagers experience your church

Too often, youth ministries are seen as separate from the rest of the church's program. The congregation makes plans without thinking of those plans' impact on the youth ministry program, and vise versa. As a result, in some churches the two groups interact only during budget meetings when they are competing for limited funds. Working together with a common vision would not only use less competitive energy, but it might also result in more effective ministry.

This meeting is designed to foster constructive dialogue between the youth program and the total church ministry. The discussion should help the groups discover ways to work together for mutually satisfying goals. It should also underscore the importance of the church's ministry to young people.

■ **Publicity.** Send letters to all the church board members, inviting them to the meeting. Explain that you will be analyzing and interpreting important information about the church's youth ministry.

■ **Preparation.** Make enough copies of sections M and N from the survey (My Church and My Feelings About My Church) so each member of the leaders' group can answer the questions himself or herself. Prepare handouts or transparencies of summary sheet of these same two sections.

Fill in Diagram 5 (page 34) by transferring the summary information from sections O and P to the chart. (See Diagram 6 for an example.) First write the averages from questions 139 to 150 in the column labeled "What's important." Then enter the data from questions 151 to 162 under "How well we do." Plot the averages from the "What's important" column in the grid. Connect the points with a solid line. Then plot the averages from the "How well we do" column, and connect the points with a dotted line. Duplicate this chart or make a transparency.

Bring newsprint and several markers. Also, a pocket calculator will be useful to figure the church's "grade-point average" during the discussion.

■ **Opening.** Begin the meeting by leading in prayer. Ask God to open the participants' hearts and minds to what they will learn. Pray for clear vision as the church seeks to minister to young people.

■ **Your own church experience.** After the prayer, ask participants to relax and close their eyes again. Tell them to let their minds carry them back to their own teenage years in the church. If they weren't involved in a church at that time, suggest that they recall their impressions of church life from their churchgoing friends.

Once you have given them time to "become teenagers" in their minds, guide their thoughts with questions like the following, pausing between each one:

1. What is the church building like to

Diagram 5

WHAT'S IMPORTANT / HOW WELL WE DO

Question	Average scores						What's* important	How well we do**
	5	4	3	2	1			
Learn about the Bible (139, 151).								
Learn what it means to be a Christian (140, 152).								
Learn what is special about me (141, 153).								
Help my religious faith grow (142, 154).								
Help make good friends (143, 155).								
Get to know adults who care about me (144, 156).								
Have opportunities to help other people (145, 157).								
Learn how to make decisions about right and wrong (146, 158).								
Learn about sex and sexual values (147, 159).								
Learn values about alcohol and drugs (148, 160).								
Have lots of fun and good times (149, 161).								
Learn what Christians should do about big issues (150, 162).								

Legend
*What's important: _____
**How well we do: -----------------------------

Diagram 6

WHAT'S IMPORTANT / HOW WELL WE DO (SAMPLE)

Question	Average scores					What's* important	How well we do**
	5	4	3	2	1		
Learn about the Bible (139, 151).						4.6	2.8
Learn what it means to be a Christian (140, 152).						4.2	3.0
Learn what is special about me (141, 153).						3.1	2.7
Help my religious faith grow (142, 154).						4.5	3.5
Help make good friends (143, 155).						3.4	3.1
Get to know adults who care about me (144, 156).						2.8	2.7
Have opportunities to help other people (145, 157).						4.1	2.0
Learn how to make decisions about right and wrong (146, 158).						4.6	3.3
Learn about sex and sexual values (147, 159).						4.2	3.5
Learn values about alcohol and drugs (148, 160).						3.8	2.9
Have lots of fun and good times (149, 161).						2.1	2.1
Learn what Christians should do about big issues (150, 162).						3.9	1.5

Legend
*What's important: _____
**How well we do: -----------------------------

you as a teenager? How does it look from the outside? What does the sanctuary smell like? Is it brightly lit? dim? What colors do you see?

2. When the building is filled with people, how do you feel? warm and comfortable? restricted? lonely? happy?

3. What faces come to mind? Are there any adults? Who are they? Do you know them well? Do you think they know you and love you? Or do they seem to disapprove of what you do?

4. As a teenager, do you enjoy church? If your parents wouldn't come, would you? What is the best part about church? the worst?

After letting the images develop for three or four minutes, ask the adults to open their eyes. Distribute copies of the questions in sections M and N from the youth survey and have everyone answer them as they would have as teenagers in the church they attended. When they finish, suggest they describe some of their own memories about church life as teenagers. Were their experiences basically positive or negative? What were the most significant elements in their teenage church life? Note their impressions on newsprint.

■ **Thinking about your church.**
Now ask the leaders to imagine they are teenagers in your church today. This exercise will help them articulate their own preconceptions before they examine the survey answers. What do they as teenagers like about this church today? What do they dislike? Write their impressions on a second sheet of newsprint.

Next, project or distribute copies of the summary of sections M and N—My Church and My Feelings About My Church. Explain that this summary represents how teenagers feel about the church. The results highlight their level of comfort and trust in the congregation.

Give the leaders time to look over the

sheets, asking them to note surprises, discrepancies and questions. Briefly discuss whatever caught the leaders' eyes. What pleasant surprises do they see? What responses seem odd? Which items cause the greatest concern?

Write the following grade scale on newsprint:

A—Excellent
B—Good
C—Mediocre
D—In trouble
F—Crisis in progress

Ask: "If the church were getting a report card based on the teenagers' responses, how well would we do?" Have each leader vote on the church's grade by raising his or her hand as you call out grades. Record the number of responses beside each letter. Then figure the grade-point average by multiplying the number of A's by four, B's by three, C's by two and D's by one. Total the products and divide by the number of people in the room.

For example, if four people say A, eight say B, five say C, two say D and one says F, calculate the g.p.a. like this:

$$4 \times 4 = 16$$
$$8 \times 3 = 24$$
$$5 \times 2 = 10$$
$$2 \times 1 = 2$$
$$1 \times 0 = \underline{0}$$
$$52 \div 20 \text{ people} = 2.6 \text{ g.p.a.}$$
(C)

Discuss your group's score. Do you think it's generally accurate? Does it trouble you or please you? What have you seen or experienced in the church that confirms or refutes this grade?

■ **What's important to the teenagers.** Although survey sections O and P have similarities with sections M and N, they go a step further in showing how satisfied your young people are with their church life.

Distribute copies of Diagram 5, which compares what is important to the teenagers with how well the church handles that topic. Have the group isolate the four or five most important topics to the teenagers. List them on newsprint. What do these ratings say about the kids' needs? On the grid find the topics that have the greatest distance between what is important and how the church is doing. This space indicates how the young people evaluate their church experience. The smaller the gap, the greater the satisfaction. Discuss the discrepancies. Are they large? Do they concern you? Are there any patterns that point to more general problems in the ministry?

When the adults seem to have a good feel for the teenagers' concerns, ask participants to pretend once again that they are teenagers. But there's one difference this time: Now they are responsible for the church's ministry. In other words, how would they run the church if they were the teenagers who took the survey?

First ask them what they would keep the same. What elements of church life already meet teenagers' needs? Note the ideas on newsprint. Then find out what they would change. How would church life be different if teenagers ran things? List these ideas as well.

When they run out of ideas, ask participants to examine the two lists they just made. Are some of the ideas for change practical? If so, who should begin working on them? Would they involve the whole church or just the youth program? What areas of the current programming should be emphasized and affirmed more? Keep notes on the ideas to bring up at future planning meetings.

■ **Closing.** Ask the leaders to share one thing they've learned about the teenagers from the discussions. They can mention good news, bad news or challenges.

Then have a prayer time in which the leaders voice prayers for the youth ministry and dedicate themselves to supporting and affirming teenagers' place in the church. Conclude by voicing a short prayer of thanks for these dedicated church leaders. Ask God to guide the church as it seeks to continue to minister to young people.

Your influence on your teenager

Sometimes a child's adolescence is as difficult for parents as it is for the child. Parents wonder whether they're parenting adequately; they worry about their child's future and happiness; they fret over his or her school performance; and they agonize over the possibility of their child becoming involved in substance abuse.

Adding to the stress, parents often feel cut off from their teenagers as the young people begin testing their wings and leaving the nest. And in the face of strong peer and media pressure on teenagers, parents often wonder whether they have any influence over their own teenagers.

However, if your teenagers are similar to those who have participated in national surveys, your survey results should affirm that parents *do* have influence over their kids. This meeting is designed to reassure the parents and to encourage better communication in families.

■ **Publicity.** Send letters to the parents of all youth group members, inviting them to attend this special follow-up meeting about the survey. Explain that they will have opportunities to learn more about their teenagers and to talk with other parents about parenting. Also make announcements in church and through the church newsletter.

■ **Preparation.** Photocopy the following material to distribute to the parents: section C from the summary sheet and the Parents Survey (Diagram 7, page 39). Draw or make a transparency of Diagram 8 (Where I'd Go for Help, page 43) on newsprint, but do not fill in any of the information until the discussion on parental influence.

Make name tags for parents that say the following:

I'm _____,
parent of _____ _____.
Being a teenager's parent is,
in a word, _____.

■ **Crowdbreaker.** Since some of the parents may not know each other well, spend some time getting acquainted. As people arrive, ask them to fill out a name tag. Then have them mingle with other parents, asking for explanations of the other parents' one word. After 10 minutes or so, gather together and have each parent make one statement telling what they enjoy the most about being a teenager's parent.

■ **Opening.** After leading the parents in prayer, distribute the Parents Survey (Diagram 7, page 39) and give everyone time to answer the questions. Tell them the surveys are designed to help them think about their teenagers' needs, not to reveal personal information to others.

■ **Teenagers' wish list.** When the parents complete their surveys, distribute copies of the summary of section C. Ask parents to look over the responses and to compare questions 47 through 54 with

Diagram 7
PARENTS SURVEY

Circle the number below that best represents your own perception of the degree to which you do each of these things. No one will see your answers; this survey is for your personal reflection only.

	Consistently					**Never**
1. I give my teenager complete freedom.	5	4	3	2	1	0
2. I spend a lot of time with my teenager.	5	4	3	2	1	0
3. I regularly yell at my teenager.	5	4	3	2	1	0
4. I regularly tell my teenager how I feel about such things as teenage sex and drug use.	5	4	3	2	1	0
5. I express a lot of interest in the things my teenager cares about.	5	4	3	2	1	0
6. I give my teenager a lot of responsibility.	5	4	3	2	1	0
7. I regularly tell my teenager I love him or her.	5	4	3	2	1	0
8. I believe I can trust my teenager completely.	5	4	3	2	1	0

their own responses on the Parents Survey. What surprises do they see? What is the good news? Affirm the parents in the areas where teenagers seem most satisfied.

Highlight the top two or three percentages in questions 47 to 54. Tell the parents to think of these responses as requests. Ask: Which requests are reasonable? Which ones would parents most like to grant?

Divide the parents into groups of four to six. Have them discuss ways they've each met some of these requests. For most parents, which requests are easier to meet? Which are most difficult? What successes have they had on the difficult ones?

After 15 to 20 minutes, bring the groups back together to share their best ideas. List them on newsprint. (You might even want to include them in the church newsletter as advice from parents to other parents.)

The parents have discussed ways to meet their teenagers' needs within their families. Now ask them to think of ways in which parents could work together to meet some of the teenagers' requests in responsible and acceptable ways. Would the parents like to meet as a group with their kids to explore their feelings about some of these topics? What other options are feasible?

■ **Family communication.** Our research at Search Institute has shown that communication about religion in the home greatly influences certain attitudes and behaviors among children. For example, children who report conversation about religion at home are more likely to say religion and the church are important in their own lives. They are also more likely to be involved in helping others.

In contrast, they are less likely to place a high value on having money, fun and the freedom to do whatever they want. Moreover, they are not as susceptible to nega-

tive peer pressure.

Focus the parents' attention on questions 55 to 59 on the summary sheet. What are their reactions? Keep notes on their comments for future planning. Ask them questions like the following:

1. What is more difficult: doing service projects with the family, or talking about your faith with your teenagers? What makes each difficult? How have some families managed to do these things?

2. Would you like the church to prepare or organize some resources for family discussions about religious faith for you and your teenagers? What resources would be most helpful?

3. Would you like to do joint service projects with your kids if you had help? What kinds of service could most families offer?

■ **Parental influence.** Parents often sense that their influence over their kids is rapidly slipping away. However, the percentages in section G may reveal that parents' influence is greater than they think. National research has shown that teenagers are most likely to consult their parents when really important issues are at stake.

Read each or some of the following case studies, depending on your time limitations. After each case, ask the parents to raise their hands to indicate which of the following people the teenager will go to for advice:

1. A parent or guardian
2. A peer
3. An adult friend or relative
4. A minister or youth worker
5. Nobody

In the appropriate column on the newsprint (Diagram 8), record the number of parents who voted for each response in the row labeled "Our guess" (see the example in Diagram 9).

1. Judy is a freshman at Central High. She has always done well in school—A's have been common on her report cards. But no matter how hard she tries this year, she does poorly. Her teacher talked with her several times, but even the coaching doesn't help.

Judy knows she should talk with someone about her problem. She wonders who would listen without getting mad at her or laughing. Whom do you think she will choose to talk with?

2. Last night's basketball game was terrible. Jerry was ejected from the game for picking three fights. It was humiliating, particularly since his youth group had planned a pizza party after the game.

Jerry just doesn't know what has gotten into him lately. All the guys think it's great when he beats up someone, but he knows his temper is out of control. He doesn't know whom to go to for help. Whom do you think he will choose to talk with?

3. Christy hasn't been able to concentrate during church ever since summer camp. Every time she sits with her friends in the second pew on the right, she gets a lump in her throat.

It happened on the first night of camp. Right after their sponsor checked on their cabin, Christy and her two best friends had sneaked out for what she thought would be innocent mischief. Instead, when they got to the edge of the woods, her friends sat down and started rolling a marijuana joint. They thought it was hilarious to smoke joints on a church retreat, and they pushed Christy to join them. She refused, saying she needed to go back to the cabin. They made her promise not to tell anyone.

The incident haunts Christy. She knows she has to tell someone. Whom do you think she will choose to talk with?

4. Manuel and Sarah have dated for three years—ever since they were fresh-

men. They met at a youth group lock-in, and they've been leaders in the group ever since.

Everyone thinks they should get married. But their parents want them to wait until after college. In fact, Sarah's parents have said that she's on her own with tuition if she gets married.

At the same time, though, Sarah and Manuel can't imagine just holding hands and hugging for five more years. Manuel decides he needs another opinion on the matter—someone who will take his dilemma seriously; someone who will give him loving, Christian advice. Whom do you think Manuel will choose to talk with?

5. It shouldn't be a big deal. All Annette did was borrow her sister's pearl necklace for her date last weekend. It matched her new dress perfectly, and she returned it in perfect condition.

But Annette knew the family's rule: Never borrow anything without asking for permission. For a week now, Annette hasn't been able to face her sister. She is afraid to say anything, fearing her sister's hot temper. Maybe she should talk with someone else, she thinks to herself. Whom do you think she will choose?

6. For years Tony has planned to become a chemical engineer. All his friends jokingly call him "Dr. Einstein," and his favorite uncle keeps asking if Tony will hire him someday. Even the pastor talked about Tony recently in a sermon on the importance of sticking with goals in life.

But during the youth Bible study this fall, Tony began wondering whether God wants him to be a missionary. Tony really feels at home helping people, and an agricultural missionary recently told the youth group that scientifically trained missionaries have a tremendous impact in hunger relief efforts. Tony feels torn between his plans and his heart. He needs someone to help him sort out his thinking. Whom do you think Tony will go to for advice?

After you have read all the case studies and the parents have voted on the responses, go back and complete the chart with your survey data (see Diagram 9 for an example). Pause between columns to discuss the data. Which statistics surprise the parents? encourage them? concern them?

For instance, you may find that very few young people go to a member of the clergy when faced with tough questions. Does this fact surprise or worry parents? If parents would like their children to see a pastor more often when dealing with major questions, what might they do to change this tendency?

When you have looked at each of the topics, ask the parents to focus on the data on parents. How do the responses make them feel about their own influence over their teenagers? Is their influence greater or less than they thought?

Have them look at the situations in which the lowest percentages consult parents. Why do parents think a particular score is low? Is it important to change it? If so, how? As a group, brainstorm ways to build communication on particular topics. Parents who feel that their communication is good may want to tell the others some of their methods. Note the ideas on newsprint, and listen for any clues to particular areas that need work.

■ **Closing.** Point out to the parents that though there may be challenges to overcome, the survey shows teenagers really do trust and love their parents. Remind them that they are not alone as parents; their heavenly Father watches and guides each of them just as they seek to watch and guide their own children. Ask parents to form a circle and join hands for a prayer of dedication. Close with the following prayer:

Our Heavenly Father,
    We thank you for the opportunities to give life and to guide our children as they grow and mature in Christ's image. Thank you for . . .
    the memories they brought to our past;
    the joy they bring to our present; and
    the hope they give to the future.

Help us as we seek to nurture our children through their teenage years. Give us . . .
    patience when they disappoint us;
    generous spirits when they fail; and
    peace in the knowledge that you will be with them wherever they go— to the mountaintops of joy or into the valley of the shadow.
    In the name of your beloved Son, Jesus Christ, Amen.

Diagram 8
WHERE I'D GO FOR HELP

	School	Feelings	Drugs	Sex	Guilt	Future	
Parents							Our guess
							Survey
Peers							Our guess
							Survey
Adult friend or relative							Our guess
							Survey
Minister or youth worker							Our guess
							Survey
Nobody							Our guess
							Survey

Diagram 9
WHERE I'D GO FOR HELP (SAMPLE)

	School	Feelings	Drugs	Sex	Guilt	Future	
Parents	10	8	4	7	11	6	Our guess
	45%	38%	40%	50%	38%	65%	Survey
Peers	14	10	12	6	8	10	Our guess
	22%	30%	22%	14%	30%	4%	Survey
Adult friend or relative	6	7	2	8	10	8	Our guess
	10%	12%	15%	20%	15%	15%	Survey
Minister or youth worker	7	10	14	8	3	10	Our guess
	6%	5%	4%	2%	10%	6%	Survey
Nobody	2	3	7	10	7	5	Our guess
	17%	15%	19%	14%	7%	10%	Survey

CHAPTER FOUR

APPLYING THE RESULTS IN PRACTICAL PROGRAMMING

Each section of the survey points to specific programming ideas for youth group meetings. By taking the survey results into account in planning, you can be sure that you are addressing the teenagers' real needs. You also let them know that you take their concerns and needs seriously. As the young people see you responding sensitively to their responses on the surveys, you may begin to find them becoming more open with you about parts of their personal lives beyond the scope of the survey.

The five meetings in this chapter are designed around specific sections of the survey, incorporating the survey results into a variety of activities and discussions. Use these meetings as models in planning additional meetings.

You may decide that other sections of the survey would be particularly appropriate for meetings for your group. If so, rely on the following guidelines in your planning:

1. Based on the survey findings, decide what section is most urgent for your group.

2. Define the meeting's purpose. What do you hope to accomplish with the meeting?

3. Throughout the meeting, be sure to maintain the anonymity you promised on the survey. Never ask questions like: "What did you say about this in the survey?" Your goal is to discuss the needs revealed by the survey, not to discover what the kids said.

4. Include the following elements in your meeting:

■ **Opening:** This gets the kids thinking about the meeting topic in creative ways. It also sets the tone for the session. Use community-building activities, games, simulations or music that relates to the theme to introduce the meeting.

■ **Learning:** Use discussion, small groups, role playing or other teaching methods to deal with the substance of your meetings. Prepare handouts, charts or diagrams where appropriate.

■ **Response:** Allow the kids time to respond to the meeting's substance. Teenagers learn best when they are actively involved.

■ **Closing:** Wrap up the meeting with an affirmation, devotion, song or prayer.

5. For additional guidelines for planning and leading meetings, see *The Youth Group Meeting Guide* (Group Books).

What I want in life

Based on section A of the survey (What I Want in Life), this meeting is designed to help young people think about their future and what is important to them.

■ **Preparation.** Decorate the meeting room to look like the year A.D. 2020. For example, put pictures of spaceships on the walls and find flashing or ultraviolet lights. Find recordings of futuristic electronic music to create atmosphere. (Sound tracks of science fiction movies would be appropriate.) Purchase light snacks that would be appropriate for a reunion—crackers, cheese, punch, etc.

Have construction paper, scissors, tape and markers available for the kids to use to make costumes to represent who they are before they enter the room.

Make enough copies of Diagram 10 (Youth Group Reunion, A.D. 2020) for each young person.

On newsprint, write the five qualities with the highest percentages from the summary section A to post during the first discussion time. Also bring enough pencils and sheets of paper for each group member.

■ **Opening.** As the young people arrive at the meeting, stop them outside the room and give them copies of Diagram 10, which tells them what to do. Have futuristic music playing softly in the room as the kids mingle and learn about each other's dreams for the future. Provide snacks to add to the reunion feeling.

Ask several adult volunteers to come. They can play the role of retired patriarchs and matriarchs. They can also ensure that the young people follow the directions.

After 15 or 20 minutes of mingling, turn off the music and say:

"It's been a long time since we've all been together. It's hard to imagine that we were all once young. When I look out at the group, I get tingles down my spine thinking that you folks could turn out so well and achieve so much.

"I'm sure that you each didn't get a chance to get reacquainted in this short time, so I think it would be interesting for us all to pair up with someone we haven't talked with to learn about what our partner has been doing all these years, and then tell the group what we've learned."

Have the kids pair up, learn about each other and then tell the group what they find out about their partner. After you've heard from the teenagers, have them close their eyes. Turn on the music softly at first and gradually increase the volume to quite loud. Then suddenly turn it and all the lights off. After 30 seconds or so, tell the group members that the time machine must have returned them back to their original age, and it's time for a youth group meeting.

■ **Discussion.** Post the sheet of newsprint that lists the five most important qualities from the summary of section A. Ask: "Do these priorities accurately reflect your own personal values? Why or why not? Does the person you created for the year 2020 reflect these qualities? If not, what qualities does the created person show?"

Divide the teenagers into five small groups, and assign one of the top five values to each group to discuss. Here are some ideas of questions they should discuss, which you may want to list on newsprint:

1. Is this value in the right place in the list? Would you yourself place it higher or lower?

2. Why is this value so important?

3. Should it be important to Christians?

4. Can you think of other values that should be higher on the list for Christians?

5. If this value seems too high on the list, how would you go about making it less important?

6. If another value should be on the list but isn't, how would you move it up on the list?

After about 10 minutes, bring the groups back together and have them report on what they discussed.

■ **Epitaphs.** Distribute a pencil and sheet of paper to each person. Explain that most people would include two kinds of values when they talk about what is important. Those values could be labeled "What I do" and "Who I am." The first category

---

Diagram 10

YOUTH GROUP REUNION, A.D. 2020

STOP!
ENTER AT YOUR OWN RISK

The room you are about to enter has been turned into a time machine by alien forces from the planet Neptune. If you enter the room, you will no longer be a teenager, but will be transported into the future to a reunion of your youth group in the year 2020.

So before you enter (if you're brave enough to enter), think about who and what you want to be in about 30 years. Using the materials provided, make props to represent who you are as an adult.

Then go into the room and reintroduce yourself to all your old high school friends—you've changed a lot since they knew you. Find out what they're doing as middle-aged adults. What kind of work do they do? Are they single or married? Do they have children? Are they famous?

Remember, you can't talk about being a teenager or about anything that's going on in your life right now.

includes all the outward things you see—professions, talents, skills, possessions. The second one is sometimes less obvious to the eye—personality, character, faith. Most people probably focused on the first category during the Youth Group Reunion. But the second set of values also influences who you will become and how you will be remembered.

Explain to the young people that they can learn a lot about a person by reading the epitaph on his or her tombstone, since people try to capture a person's essence in the inscription. Sometimes the epitaph will be simple, saying something like . . .

Here lies
ANDREW M. SMITH,
a child of God.

Other times it will be more elaborate. For example,

Here lies
MARY J. WILCOTT
A sensitive poet,
A dedicated Christian,
A loving mother.

Sometimes epitaphs are poems, Bible verses or famous quotations.

Once the young people understand epitaphs, ask: "How would you like to be remembered when you die? What would you want your epitaph to say about you?" Give everyone several minutes to write his or her epitaph on the sheet of paper. Then go around the room and let each person who so wishes read what he or she wrote.

■ **Closing.** Ask the young people to join hands in a circle to dedicate the future to God. Pray that God will open their lives to the possibilities of the future. And ask God to shape each young person into the kind of person he or she is created to be.

Faith—what difference does it make?

What dimensions of faith are important to teenagers? How does their faith affect their lives? Based on section H of the youth survey (My Christian Faith), this meeting helps teenagers think about the connection between beliefs and behaviors.

■ **Preparation.** Gather paper and pencils for each young person; newsprint and markers to use during discussion times; and masking tape to make a cross on the floor.

■ **Opening.** Play the following game, called I Remember. Distribute pencils and sheets of paper to all the kids. Then divide them into pairs and have them interview each other about their past. Ask questions like the following:

1. Where were you born?
2. How many times have you moved?
3. When did you start coming to church?
4. What is the best thing you've ever done?
5. Which single person has affected your life the most?
6. Which single event has had the most impact on your life?

After the pairs have finished their interviews, have the kids sit in a large circle and give a synopsis of what they learned in their interviews.

■ **Faith's influence.** Explain to the group members that many events, places and people influence who we are and what we do. Another factor that shapes what we do is our faith.

List the following areas of life on newsprint: family, school, church, friendships, dating and recreation. Have the young people think about how much impact faith has on each of these areas. Then have the group come to a consensus and rank which areas are influenced the most and the least by their faith. Number the areas in the order the group chooses.

Tell the young people the percentage of the survey participants who said their religious beliefs greatly influence how they act at school and with friends (question 89). Ask: "Does this percentage accurately reflect the attitude of the group? In what ways does your faith affect what you do at school and with your friends? When you're with your friends, can they tell that you're a Christian? Why or why not? What is it about your faith that they can see?"

Divide the teenagers into groups of four or five. Ask them to tell each other about experiences they've had when it has been tough to be a Christian. Perhaps their friends were trying to make them do things they knew were wrong. Or maybe they saw something dishonest or unfair being done and wanted to speak up—but were afraid to. When everyone has participated, have the group members talk about ways they have coped with these pressures.

Bring the whole group together to report on the different discussions.

■ **Faith's dimensions.** The survey (questions 91 to 96) asked the young people to indicate whether they consider the following activities to be important parts of what God wants them to do:

1. To pray;
2. To worship;
3. To read the Bible;
4. To help get rid of hunger, poverty and war;
5. To tell people about Jesus; and
6. To spend time helping other people.

The first three activities represent the "vertical" dimension of faith, while the last three represent the "horizontal" dimension. The vertical dimension focuses on an individual's relationship with God. The horizontal dimension emphasizes how faith impels people to serve others. Comparing the first three statistics to the last three reveals which dimension of faith is more important to the group members.

Divide a sheet of newsprint into two columns. Label one "vertical" and the other "horizontal." Ask the group members to name all the things the group has done in the past six months—Bible studies, outreach, retreats, service projects, etc. Include ways the young people have participated in the total church programs, through music, worship and so forth.

As each young person mentions an activity, have him or her decide whether that activity is part of the "vertical" or "horizontal" dimension of the Christian life. List the activities in the appropriate column. If some of the activities incorporate both dimensions, write them in both columns.

When the lists are complete, write the percentage scores from survey questions 91 through 96 in the appropriate column (questions 91 to 93 as vertical; questions 94 to 96 as horizontal). In this way you can show which dimension the teenagers themselves consider to be more important.

Ask: "Do the activities and scores make up an accurate picture of our group? Are we comfortable with that picture? If we emphasize one dimension over the other, do we want to do more of the other? How could we get a better balance?"

Give each person a sheet of paper and a pencil. Say: "As you think about the vertical and horizontal dimensions of faith, draw a picture of a balanced Christian, using various objects as symbols of various activities. For instance, someone might give his or her balanced Christian a Bible to represent the vertical dimension and a towel to represent the horizontal part. When they have finished drawing, have them explain their pictures.

■ **Closing.** Make a large cross on the floor using masking tape. Have the young people each say one thing they would like to do to bring more balance to their Christian life. Then ask them to form a human cross. If they feel the need to work on an upward-reaching activity, have them stand along the vertical beam of the cross. If it is an outward-reaching activity, have them stand on the horizontal beam. When the whole group has joined the cross, ask the kids to join hands and sing one verse each of "Father, We Adore You" and "Pass It On" to represent faith's two dimensions. Close by leading the group in the Lord's Prayer.

Making moral decisions

Teenagers constantly face moral choices. Section K of the youth survey (Right and Wrong) asked group members their views on several moral issues. This meeting is designed to discuss the importance of moral standards and to help teenagers think about who influences their values.

■ **Preparation.** Gather the materials you will need for the opening relays. Be sure to include simple prizes for the "winning" team.

Complete Diagram 11 (page 52) by adding the percentages from the summary of section K. Make enough copies for all the young people. Bring markers and several sheets of newsprint.

Find construction paper, several pairs of scissors, lots of colored markers, glue, tape and envelopes for making thank-you notes.

■ **Opening.** Divide the young people into two teams to play relays (three-legged races, carrying eggs in spoons, obstacle courses, etc.). While the teams are organizing, whisper to one team that it should try to win at all costs. You won't penalize the team for cheating.

Play two or three relays. When the team wins, tell the members how great they are and reward them with tokens— bubble gum, candy bars, etc. When the other team protests, pay no attention. And if the other team also starts cheating, make it start the relay again. Be *very* strict!

After the relays, discuss the experience. How did the members of the "losing" team feel when they could see the other team blatantly cheating? Was the losing team tempted to cheat? What about members of the "winning" team? Was the thrill of victory tainted because they knew they had cheated?

■ **Who and what guide your decisions?** Distribute copies of Diagram 11, which consists of discussion questions and the summary from section K. Divide the young people into six small groups, and assign each group one of the issues raised in section K. Tell them to use the questions on the handout to guide their discussions. After 15 to 20 minutes, bring all the group members back together to share what they have learned. Whom do they rely on the most for guidance? Whose standards do they rely on most heavily?

Draw two columns on three different sheets of newsprint. Label each column with one of the following areas of life: faith, career, recreation, clothing, music and friends. Ask the kids who influences them in each area of life. For instance, they might say parents influence careers and rock stars influence how they dress. Note their comments on the newsprint.

Now ask the young people to think of someone who has helped them more than anyone else when they've had to make a tough decision. It could be a parent who has guided them through a tough time at school or with a broken friendship. Or a girlfriend or boyfriend who has helped them withstand peer pressure. If some of the kids want to describe their person, give

Diagram 11

DISCUSSION HANDOUT FOR RIGHT AND WRONG

Survey results

_____ % of you disapprove of sexual intercourse for two unmarried 16-year-olds who love each other (question 115).

_____ % of you disapprove of racial discrimination shown by trying to keep a minority family from moving into a neighborhood (question 116).

_____ % of you disapprove of cheating on a school test (question 117).

_____ % of you disapprove of lying to your parents (question 118).

_____ % of you disapprove of 16-year-olds drinking a couple of beers at a party (question 119).

_____ % of you disapprove of stealing a shirt from a store (question 120).

Discussion questions

1. If at least three-quarters of the group disapproved when answering your question, why do you think everyone basically agrees on this question? If the percentage is lower, why is there disagreement?

_____

_____

2. What drives some people to do this? What are the possible consequences of their actions? _____

_____

_____

3. Is it okay for each person to make up his or her mind individually on this issue? Or are there objective standards that should be followed by everyone? _____

_____

_____

4. Rank the following influences in terms of their importance in helping you as an individual decide whether this action is right or wrong.

_____ My feelings   _____ What I've learned in church

_____ My needs   _____ What my parents think

_____ Laws   _____ What my teachers say

_____ Scripture   _____ What my pastor says

_____ Past experience   _____ What celebrities say and do

_____ Other: _____

them time to do so.

Distribute materials for making thank-you notes—construction paper, pens, scissors, tape and so on. Explain that too often other people help us and we never think to thank them. Tell the young people that you are giving them the opportunity to make a thank-you note to send to the person who has helped them with their tough decision. Give each person an envelope to address to the person. (If people don't know the address, tell them that they can add it later.)

■ **Closing.** When the kids have finished making their thank-you notes, tell them that the apostle Paul often included messages of thanks in his letters to people and churches. Read Philemon verses 4-7 as an example. Say that the letters of thanks the group members have just written are also letters of thanks to God for giving them people to support them and help them through life.

Have the group members sit in a circle and sing a favorite praise song. As they sing, ask them to put their letters of thanks in a stack in the middle of the room as an offering to God. After the song, lead the kids in the following closing prayer:

Dear God,

Thank you for giving us friends and families who love us, support us and teach us as we seek to grow in your image. Thank you for their patience and kindness.

Help us to follow your way as we make choices in this world. Forgive us when we fail, and give us the strength to keep trying.

In the name of your Son who came to show us the way,

Amen.

■ **Mail letters.** After the meeting, have the church mail the letters for the teenagers. If some people didn't know the full address of their person, ask them to add it as soon as possible.

Being a better friend

Having friends is very important to teenagers. Yet they often lack the necessary skills for making or being friends. The youth survey results likely showed that your teenagers are particularly interested in learning how to be better friends. Based on section F of the survey (My Friends), this meeting is designed to help them see the qualities of good friendships and see how to be better friends.

■ **Preparation.** Locate a recording of Michael W. Smith's "Friends" (from his *Project* album) for use in the opening. Be sure a good record or tape player is available.

Gather enough paper and pencils for everyone in the group, and bring plenty of newsprint. Prepare a handout (or write on newsprint) the survey results from section F to share with the group.

Prepare "situation cards" for the role-playing exercise. Write the following situations (or others you think of) on index cards to distribute to the teenagers who will pair up as partners to role play. You will need enough cards for half the group. Duplicate the situations on several cards if necessary. Here are some ideas:

1. You've just been chosen as the captain of the basketball team—and you're only a sophomore. You're *really* excited. You can't wait to tell your partner—your best friend—who goes to another school and hasn't heard your good news. How does he or she react to your good news? Is he or she also excited? Or does your partner dismiss your honor as trivial? How

does that reaction make you feel?

2. It's the end of the school year, and you just found out you failed algebra. If you want to graduate with your class, you have to go to summer school. But your family has been planning a trip to Europe this summer. Your parents will kill you when they find out that you're wrecking their long-awaited vacation trip. You want to tell your partner about your dilemma, hoping he or she will be understanding. How does your partner react?

3. You and your partner have been friends for a long time. But your friend has been getting on your nerves lately. He or she won't let you do anything by yourself. Whenever you try to study or read, your friend calls and wants to come over. And now he or she won't even let you do things with other people. You've decided that you don't want to be friends anymore. Tell your partner that you don't want to see him or her again, and say why. What is his or her reaction?

4. You've fallen in love with the junior who moved to town last summer. You've dated a couple of times, and you've never had so much fun. But you haven't been able to bring yourself to tell your friends, because this person is really smart, quiet and shy. You've heard people call him or her a nerd. But your excitement is bursting at the seams, and you have to tell your partner. How would you do it? Does his or her response make you want to tell others or to keep your excitement to yourself?

5. You're steamed. Your partner didn't

keep a promise to cover for you last Saturday night. You had asked your partner to tell everyone that you spent the evening with him or her. But when your parents called to ask a question, your friend has said where you really were. You thought you could trust your partner; now you're not sure. Explain to your partner what he or she did to you, and say you won't speak to him or her again. Then turn your back and refuse to respond to anything he or she says or does. How does your partner react to your stubborn silence?

■ **Opening.** After all the kids arrive, play Michael W. Smith's song titled "Friends." Ask everyone to close his or her eyes and concentrate on the lyrics. Then discuss briefly the connections between friendships and faith that are suggested in the song.

Share the results from section F of the survey about the importance of friendships. Answer any questions the teenagers have.

■ **Confiding in friends.** Divide the teenagers into pairs to be partners for the role-playing exercises. Tell the pairs that the exercises are designed to help them see how well they communicate with their friends. Ask everyone to try to adopt his or her role as if it were real.

Distribute one situation card to one person (the confider) in each pair. The other person (the confidant) should not know the content of the card. The confider will then share his or her news as he or she would in real life. The other person should react as he or she normally would. After 5 or 10 minutes, have the pairs switch cards with another group and reverse roles to repeat the process.

When both people have tried both roles, have the pairs get together with two or three other pairs to discuss the experience. Have them discuss questions such as the following, which you may want to post on newsprint:

1. How did you feel in each role?
2. Is it easier to share your feelings or to listen to someone else's?
3. What kinds of situations are the easiest to talk about? the most difficult?
4. Can you be a friend to someone who doesn't want you for a friend? Why or why not?
5. What did you learn about friendship from this exercise?

Give the groups 10 minutes then bring everyone together. Ask the kids to suggest the qualities of true friendship based on their discussion. List their ideas on newsprint.

■ **Christian friendship.** Read Luke 6:32-36 in which Jesus teaches about loving those who hate us. Ask: "According to this passage, is friendship among Christians different from other kinds of friendships? What kind of friend does God want us to be? What's most difficult about Jesus' type of friendship? How can we work at being better Christian friends?"

■ **Closing.** Give everyone a sheet of paper and a pencil. Ask them each to write one thing they can do in the next week to be a better friend. Then have them fold up their paper and put their name on the outside. Collect the papers, assuring the kids that no one will see what they wrote. Give the sheets back the next week to let each person assess his or her own progress.

Conclude the meeting by asking group members to join hands in a circle and sing "Blest Be the Tie That Binds," from *Songs* (Songs and Creations). Dismiss the group with prayer.

Faith and worries

Since today's teenagers are exposed to so much at such early ages, it is not surprising that their worries are often deeper and more varied than in the past. Based on section B of the youth survey (What I Worry About), this meeting helps group members think about their worries and discover ways to share the burden of those concerns with others.

■ **Preparation.** Gather magazines and newspapers with a selection of pictures and articles on world and personal problems to tear out for the opening activity. Have plenty of pins to make the articles and pictures into a collage on the bulletin board.

Arrange the responses in section B in the order of percentages so that the greatest concern is first, the next greatest is second and so forth. Type a handout based on this information, or list the worries in order on newsprint. Copy the Worries Worksheet (Diagram 12, page 57) to distribute to each group member. On newsprint, write the following discussion question about the kids' greatest worries:

1. Why do people worry?

2. How does worrying affect them over the short term and the long term?

3. What good things does worrying prevent them from doing?

4. Does worrying have any positive effects? If so, what are they?

5. Are there different levels of worries (i.e., the difference between worrying about a terminally ill relative and worrying about a test)? If so, what are they?

6. Is it ever good to worry? Why or why not? When?

Bring a special effects record, candles and matches for the crisis simulation. Supply small pieces of construction paper (3×5) and tape or glue for the closing exercise. Also bring a recording of meditative music (such as that of John Michael Talbot) to play during the closing exercise.

■ **Opening.** As the young people arrive, have them find and tear out pictures and articles in the magazines and newspapers that represent the things they worry about and pin them in a collage on the bulletin board.

For instance, an article on nuclear weapons could represent concern about nuclear war; a picture of a couple could symbolize concern about friendships; a photograph of workers could stand for worries about getting a job; a picture of students could represent concern about grades; or an obituary could symbolize fear of death.

■ **Greatest worries.** After 10 minutes, have the kids look at the collage and isolate what they think are the three or four greatest worries. Then distribute (or show on newsprint) the results from survey section B, in order from greatest to least concern. Point out the five top worries and the five lowest worries. Do the young people have trouble believing the placement of either group? How should the order be rearranged? Why?

Divide the kids into five small groups to discuss worries. Ask them to focus on the discussion questions you wrote on

Diagram 12

WORRIES WORKSHEET

Worry: _____

1. Why do we worry about this? _____

_____

_____

_____

2. What is the worst thing this worry could bring to pass? _____

_____

_____

_____

3. What is the best possible outcome in terms of this worry? _____

_____

_____

_____

4. What things can we do to help overcome this worry (action, prayer, change of attitude, etc.)? _____

_____

_____

_____

newsprint.

When the groups have had time to answer these questions, distribute the Worries Worksheet (Diagram 12) to each person, plus ones to use as master worksheets for each group. Assign each small group one of the five top worries from the survey, and have the members fill out the worksheet for that worry. Have each group compile a master worksheet to present to the whole group.

■ **Crisis simulation.** Arrange for someone suddenly to turn off all the lights in the room toward the end of the discussion so that the kids are taken by surprise. Then start playing the sound effects record that simulates a crisis—a tornado, an invasion, etc. Have someone else run in the room to announce what has happened.

For instance, if you are simulating a tornado, the person might frantically say: "Everybody get under a table or something! A tornado was just sighted less than a mile away. All the warning sirens are going off. Try to remain calm, but it looks like it's headed our way."

Allow for a little initial laughter, but then ask the teenagers to imagine what it would be like if they really were in a crisis. What would they feel like? What would they be thinking?

After several minutes, turn the lights back on and ask group members to describe how they would feel in the middle of a crisis. Would they have "butterflies"? Would they be able to think about anything else? Could they do anything else—homework, reading or talking on the phone—during the crisis? What things do fear or worry prevent us from doing?

■ **Learning from our faith.** Does faith affect the way Christians worry and what they worry about? Divide the group members into four groups to consider how faith can help them with their worries. Assign one of the following scripture passages

to each group to read and discuss:

Matthew 6:25-34

Philippians 4:4-7

Luke 10:38-42

Psalm 20

Then have each group answer the following questions, which you may want to write on newsprint:

1. Does your faith help you with the day-to-day worries? with the long-term worries?

2. What does this passage teach us about worrying?

3. What promises does it make to us in terms of what we worry about?

After 10 minutes, bring the whole group together to report on each small group's insights from the scripture passages.

■ **Closing.** As several of the passages say, one way that faith can help Christians deal with worries is by sharing those worries with God.

Turn on the meditative music you selected. Then distribute the small pieces of construction paper to the kids. On one side have them each write a worry they want to turn over to God. On the other side have them each write their name. Assure them that no one will read what they write. As they finish, ask group members to paste or tape their worries (with only the names showing) on the newsprint in the shape of a cross. The result should look like Diagram 13 (page 59).

When everyone has added his or her worry to the cross, lead the group in a closing prayer of dedication, asking God to give each person peace in the midst of worries.

Before group members leave the room, take down the cross of cares and fold it up. Dispose of it so that no one will find it and read the worries.

Diagram 13

CROSS OF CARES

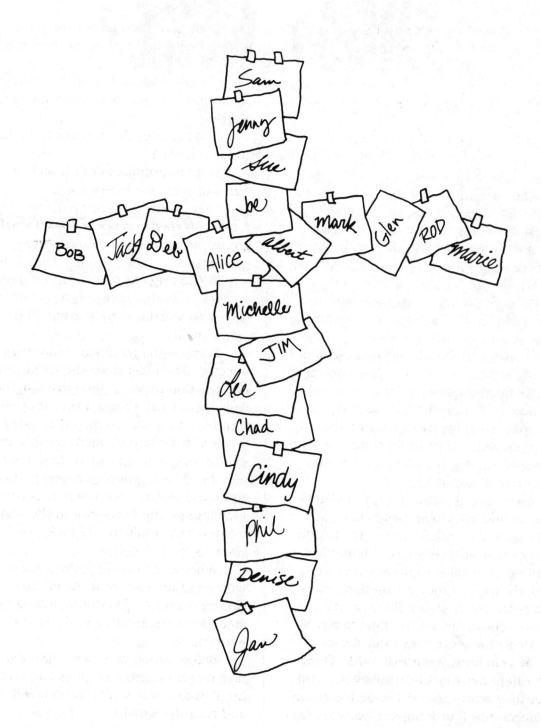

WHERE DO WE GO FROM HERE?

The goal of this exercise—with all its administrative detail, time, and study—has been knowledge. If you, your adult leaders and the young people now have a more detailed and more accurate understanding of your youth ministry, then the process has been successful.

Though this knowledge may be interesting in itself, it will be useful only if it becomes a bridge to a more accurately focused youth ministry. In the process, it should help create a more compassionate and caring atmosphere for that ministry by renewing and strengthening relationships among the teenagers themselves, between group members and adult leaders, between teenagers and their parents, and between young people and God.

Many people enjoy working with the numbers and mathematical relationships that emerge from surveys. But the numbers should never be seen as ends in themselves. Neither should they become masters of your vision for the congregation's young people. Rather, the numbers are only tools to use in building your youth ministry.

At the same time, though, the information *is* an important tool, and it deserves your careful attention. By stacking up what one young person after another perceives, hopes and fears, you begin to see the strengths and the needs of your particular group—needs that have previously been hidden in one-to-one daily interaction.

The impact of research

In the early 1980s when a Search Institute national survey ("Young Adolescents and Their Parents") uncovered a number of surprises, many national youth-serving organizations responded by making major organizational changes. For example:

■ Church groups had assumed that a good spiritual education would shield most kids from experimenting with alcohol and other drugs. Strictly speaking, the assumption was accurate; the study showed that "most kids" were *not* involved in such experimentation. However, the number who *were* involved came as a shock, prodding the organizations to take more seriously their responsibility for anti-drug work.

■ The study also found that peer pressure to behave illegally or immorally started at an earlier age than most adults had assumed. National leaders learned that the time to begin educating against that pressure was not high school, but the upper elementary grades.

■ The survey compared fifth- and sixth-graders' beliefs, concerns and understanding with those of eighth- and ninth-graders. It discovered that the needs of the two groups were quite different. As a result, some youth-serving organizations restructured their national programming to emphasize more the needs of younger adolescents—without, of course, abandoning the older teenagers.

Building on your research

As these examples show, research *can* change things. And it can do so as surely for individual, local congregations as for national organizations.

Your research may have resulted in a number of outcomes. First, much of the data probably confirmed your hunches about your teenagers. Good. That's one of the purposes of research—to verify what you have sensed and to give you confidence in your planning.

Another possibility is that the data contained some bad news. The survey may have shown that your young people think or want or do things that shock or trouble the adults. That's good, too. Sometimes it takes a jolt to galvanize you into concerted action on something that you've been meaning to do for years but haven't—and probably wouldn't. The bad news may be the perfect impetus you need, and your youth group will ultimately benefit.

A third possible outcome is also valuable: pleasant surprises. We hope you discover an untapped reservoir of concern for others, or an increasing interest in serious Bible study, or unvoiced respect and love for parents. Such surprises can open important doors for ministry.

A beginning

With the survey completed and analyzed, you have established a solid foundation of knowledge about your youth group. Certainties have replaced guesses. Hazy glimpses of private lives have become detailed portraits.

Yet the loneliness the teenagers revealed is unchanged. The problems with alcohol abuse, unhappy family relationships or premature sexual experience still linger. And the teenage struggles for intimacy, freedom, affirmation and support are as difficult as ever.

So what *has* changed?

The difference is that these problems and needs are now visible. You and other adults can see them, understand them and act upon them. As a result, you can work together to serve young people more effectively and faithfully as they mature in a confusing and complex world.

RESOURCES

The following publications may help you as you interpret and use your survey results:

All Grown Up and No Place to Go: Teenagers in Crisis. By Dr. David Elkind. Addison-Wesley, 1984.

An appropriate sequel to Dr. Elkind's *The Hurried Child*, this volume examines the many ways society influences young people and how they often feel emotionally abandoned by the very adults who are most important to them.

Bringing Up a Moral Child: A New Approach for Teaching Your Child to Be Kind, Just, and Responsible. By Michael Schulman and Eva Mekler. Addison-Wesley, 1985.

The first part of this useful book deals with how children develop consciences, and describes how parents can help their children learn moral behavior. The second section examines the societal forces that inhibit the development of concerned, just and moral adolescents. The book concludes by examining a range of moral issues.

Common Focus. Center for Early Adolescence, Carr Mill Mall, Suite 223, Carrboro, NC 27510.

This newsletter informs youth workers and educators about developments in early adolescence research.

Counseling Teenagers. By Dr. G. Keith Olson. Group Books, 1984.

This comprehensive reference book analyzes the transitions and characteristics of adolescence, and offers detailed information about how to deal with a variety of teenage problems and issues.

Emerging Trends. Princeton Religion Research Center, Publications Department, Box 310, 53 Bank St., Princeton, NJ 08542.

Reporting on Gallup research on religion, this newsletter analyzes the nature and depth of religious commitment around the world, including information on teenagers' faith.

Five Cries of Parents: New Help for Families on the Issues that Trouble Them Most. By Dr. Merton P. Strommen and A. Irene Strommen. Harper & Row, 1985.

This volume augments a massive collection of Search Institute research data on youth with the Strommens' own experience as parents and high school Bible study teachers. The book examines parents' need to understand their teenagers, and important dynamics of family life and faith.

Five Cries of Youth. By Dr. Merton P. Strommen. Harper & Row, 1979.

Though the original research in this book is from the early '70s, Dr. Strommen's insights into the needs of teenagers in the church still ring true.

GROUP Magazine. Box 202, Mt. Morris, IL 61054.

Covering a wide array of youth ministry concerns, this magazine includes numerous practical resources for youth workers. Its regular section titled News, Trends and Tips reports on current research about teenagers, religion and ministry.

Group's JR. HIGH MINISTRY Magazine. Box 407, Mt. Morris, IL 61054.

Each issue of this magazine for junior high ministries includes reports on research from Search Institute. The magazine focuses on the unique concerns of early adolescents.

The Hurried Child: Growing Up Too Fast Too Soon. By Dr. David Elkind. Addison-Wesley, 1981.

Rushing children through their childhoods, Dr. Elkind argues, damages their emotional and psychological development. The author focuses on the complicity of parents, schools and the media in the dynamics that rush children through adolescence to adulthood. The book also explores the value of growing up slowly.

The Private Life of the American Teenager. By Jane Norman and Dr. Myron Harris. Rawson, Wade, 1981.

Based on surveys of more than 160,000 teenagers and more than 100 extensive interviews with teenagers, this important book reports what teenagers say about such topics as parents, sex, drugs, peer pressure, religion and drinking.

The Quicksilver Years: The Hopes and Fears of Early Adolescence. By Dr. Peter L. Benson, Dorothy L. Williams and Arthur L. Johnson. Harper & Row, 1987.

This book reports the findings from a national Search Institute study of 8,000 fifth- to ninth-grade young people and 11,000 of their parents. Many chapters parallel sections of *Determining Needs in Your Youth Ministry*, so the analysis provides useful information for interpreting your own survey results.

Raising a Child Conservatively in a Sexually Permissive World. By Dr. Sol Gordon and Judith Gordon. Simon & Schuster, 1983.

This book focuses on adolescents' unfolding sexuality and advocates a unique approach to parenting. Though the ideas may not be in harmony with common practices, the authors believe their approach results in healthier and happier adolescents and adults.

Religion in America. Edited by Coleen McMurray. The Gallup Organization, Inc., 53 Bank St., Princeton, NJ 08542.

Compiled from Gallup research about religion in the United States, this periodically published volume analyzes data on a range of topics and trends, from religious preferences and church membership to evangelicalism and the electronic church.

Source. Search Institute, 122 W. Franklin, Suite 525, Minneapolis, MN 55404.

A bimonthly information resource on issues facing children, adolescents and families, this newsletter reports and analyzes current Search Institute research.

Why Teenagers Act the Way They Do. By Dr. G. Keith Olson. Group Books, 1987.

Dr. Olson examines the forces and personalities that shape adolescent behavior. He focuses on eight personality types, explaining how parents and leaders can work with and minister to different kinds of teenagers.

Youthworker Update. Youth Specialties, Inc., 1224 Greenfield Dr., El Cajon, CA 92021.

This newsletter for youth ministry summarizes recent research and writing about teenagers, the church and youth work.

SURVEY TOOLS

The following pages include all the research instruments you need to conduct your youth survey. The pages are perforated for easy use. You may photocopy any of the material in this section for local church use only. (See Chapter 1 for detailed instructions for how to use each instrument.)

Here's what we've included:

●**Youth survey** (20 copies). The six-page survey asks 162 questions about everything from school to family to moral values. Instruct the teenagers not to write in the survey so that it can be reused.

●**Answer sheet** (20 copies). The teenagers will record their answers on this simple form.

●**Tally sheet** (1 copy). Use this instrument to tabulate your survey results from the completed answer sheets. Give a copy of the tally sheet to each tally team.

●**Summary sheet** (1 copy). This tool consolidates the data from the tally sheets, allowing you to see highlights of the survey, problem areas in your youth group and ministry opportunities.

YOUTH SURVEY

Directions

This survey isn't about what you know.
It's about who you are—
what you think,
what you feel,
what you believe.

It's about your school,
your church,
your friends,
your family,
yourself.

It's about what is important to you in life—
what you do,
what you worry about,
what you enjoy.

Be honest in giving your answers. Your name will not be attached to the survey, so no one will know what you write. Your answers will be summarized together with the answers of other young people in your church. All of those answers together will provide important clues to the interests, beliefs, problems and hopes of your church's young people. It's important for youth ministry leaders to have those clues so they can do a better job of planning youth ministry for you and your friends.

Do not begin answering questions until you are instructed to do so. As soon as the survey administrator gives the signal to open this booklet to the first page, you may begin. Mark your answers on the answer sheet, not in this booklet.

For each question, decide which answer fits you best, then *circle the corresponding number or letter on the answer sheet*. Mark only one answer for each question. Do not spend a lot of time trying to decide between two answers; it's usually best to mark your first impression and go right on to the next question. There is no "right" or "wrong" answer to any question—so answer each question honestly.

When you have finished, fold your answer sheet in half and put it into the envelope provided by the survey administrator.

Thanks for helping.
Thanks for being *you*.

General Information

1. I am: **F.** Female
M. Male

2. My grade in school is:
7 8 9 10 11 12

A. What I Want in Life

Listed below are things that some people want in life. Read through the complete list without making any marks. Then go back and decide how important each one is to you. Your choices are:

> **V.** Very important
> **S.** Somewhat important
> **N.** Not very important

It is _____ to me . . .

3. To be good in music, drama or art.
4. To have a happy family life.
5. To make my parents proud of me.
6. To make my own decisions.
7. To do things that help people.
8. To feel safe and secure in my neighborhood.
9. To feel good about myself.
10. To be popular at school.
11. To have lots of fun and good times.
12. To understand my feelings.
13. To have lots of money.
14. To have God at the center of my life.
15. To have a world without hunger or poverty.
16. To get a good job when I am older.
17. To have things (such as clothes, records and so on) as nice as other kids have.
18. To do something important with my life.
19. To do well in school.
20. To have a world without war.
21. To be really good at sports.
22. To be different in some way from all the other teenagers I know.
23. To have friends I can count on.
24. To do whatever I want to do, when I want to do it.
25. To be part of a church.
26. To have clothes and hair that look good to other kids.

B. What I Worry About

How much do you worry about each of the following statements? Your choices are:

> **V.** Very much
> **S.** Somewhat
> **N.** Very little or not at all

I worry _____ . . .

27. About how my friends treat me.

28. That I might kill myself.
29. That I might not be able to get a good job when I am older.
30. That someone might force me to do sexual things I don't want to do.
31. About how well other teenagers like me.
32. That I might lose my best friend.
33. That one of my parents will hit me so hard that I will be badly hurt.
34. That I may die soon.
35. That a nuclear bomb might be dropped on our country.
36. About all the drugs and drinking I see around me.
37. That one of my parents might die.
38. About all the people who are hungry and poor in our country.
39. That I might get beaten up at school.
40. About whether my body is growing in a normal way.
41. About how much my mother or father drinks.
42. About how I'm doing in school.
43. About my looks.
44. That my friends might get me in trouble.
45. About all the violence in our country.
46. That my parents might get a divorce.

(Leave this number blank if your parents are already divorced, or if one of your parents is no longer living.)

C. My Family

For each of the following statements, mark the response that best matches your feelings. Your choices are:

> **A.** Strongly agree
> **B.** Agree
> **C.** Not sure
> **D.** Disagree
> **E.** Strongly disagree

I wish my parents (or guardians) would . . .

47. Give me more freedom.
48. Spend more time with me.
49. Yell at me less often.
50. Talk with me more about their views on important issues such as sex and drugs.
51. Be more interested in the things I care about.
52. Give me more responsibility.
53. Say "I love you" more often.
54. Trust me more.

Mark the appropriate response to the following statements and questions.

55. There is a lot of love in my family.
A. Very true
B. Somewhat true
C. Not true

56. How often does your family do projects *together* to help other people (such as collecting food for the hungry or helping a neighbor)?
A. At least once a month
B. Once in a while
C. Never

57. How often does your family talk together about God, the Bible or other religious things?
A. Every day
B. At least two or three times a week
C. At least once a week
D. At least once or twice a month
E. Never

58. How often do you hear your mother talk about her religious faith?
A. Every day
B. At least two or three times a week
C. At least once a week
D. At least once or twice a month
E. Never

59. How often do you hear your father talk about his religious faith?
A. Every day
B. At least two or three times a week
C. At least once a week
D. At least once or twice a month
E. Never

D. How I Feel About Myself

Tell how true each of the following statements is for you. Your options are:

> V. Very true
> S. Somewhat true
> N. Not true

60. On the whole, I like myself.
61. I spend a lot of time thinking about who I am.
62. No one really understands me.
63. I believe life has a purpose.
64. I feel good about my body.

E. My Future

For questions 65 to 70, indicate how likely it is that each statement will come true. Choose one of these answers for each question:

> E. Excellent chance
> G. Good chance
> F. Fair chance
> P. Poor chance
> N. No chance

I believe there is a(n) _____ that . . .

65. I will someday be married and have children.
66. I will go to college.

67. I will be very happy 10 years from now.
68. I will be active in church when I am 40.
69. I myself or someone close to me might get AIDS.
70. The world will be destroyed by a nuclear war sometime in the next 10 years.

F. My Friends

71. How many close friends (not relatives) do you have?
A. None
B. One or two
C. Three to five
D. Six to nine
E. Ten or more

72. I wish I could be better at making friends.
A. Strongly agree
B. Agree
C. Not sure
D. Disagree
E. Strongly disagree

73. I wish I could be better at being a friend to others.
A. Strongly agree
B. Agree
C. Not sure
D. Disagree
E. Strongly disagree

74. Some of my best friends belong to this church.
T. True
F. False

75. How often do you feel lonely?
A. Every day
B. Quite often, but not every day
C. Once in a while
D. Never

76. How often do your friends try to get you to do things you know are wrong?
A. Very often
B. Often
C. Sometimes
D. Once in a while
E. Never

77. Which of the following choices best describes your parents' feelings toward your friends?
A. My parents like all of my friends.
B. My parents like most of my friends, except for one or two.
C. My parents like about half of my friends, and half they don't.
D. My parents don't like most of my friends, but one or two are okay.
E. My parents don't like any of my friends.

G. Where I'd Go for Help

If you were in the following situations, to whom would you most likely turn for help or advice? For each situation, choose one of these answers:

> A. A parent or guardian
> B. A friend my own age
> C. An adult friend or relative
> D. A minister or youth worker
> E. Nobody

78. If I were having trouble in school, I would turn to _____.

79. If I were wondering how to handle my feelings, I would turn to _____.

80. If some of my friends started using alcohol or other drugs, I would turn to _____.

81. If I had questions about sex, I would turn to _____.

82. If I were feeling guilty about something I had done, I would turn to _____.

83. If I were deciding what to do with my life, I would turn to _____.

H. My Christian Faith

84. Overall, how important is religion in your life?
    V. Very important
    S. Somewhat important
    N. Not important

85. Compared to a year ago, would you say your faith is now more important, less important or about the same?
    M. More important
    L. Less important
    S. About the same

86. I am sure God loves me just as I am.
    T. True
    ?. Don't know
    F. False

87. Which of the following statements comes closest to your view of God?
    A. I know for sure that God exists.
    B. I am mostly sure that God exists.
    C. I'm not sure if God exists.
    D. I don't think there is a God.
    E. I am sure there is no such thing as God.

88. Which of the following statements is closest to your view of Jesus?
    A. Jesus is the Son of God who died on the cross and rose again.
    B. Jesus is the Son of God, but I doubt that he actually rose from the dead.
    C. Jesus was a great man who lived long ago, but I don't think he was the Son of God.
    D. Jesus never existed; his life is just a story people made up.

89. My religious beliefs greatly influence how I act at school and with my friends.
    M. Most of the time
    S. Some of the time
    R. Rarely or never

90. I believe God will stop loving me if I do a lot of wrong things.
    T. True
    ?. Not sure
    F. False

What do you think God wants you to do with your life? For each of the following actions, choose one of these responses:

> T. True
> ?. Not sure
> F. False

God wants me . . .
91. To pray.
92. To worship.
93. To read the Bible.
94. To help get rid of hunger, poverty and war.
95. To tell other people about Jesus.
96. To spend time helping other people.

I. What I Do

Please answer the following questions as honestly as you can. Remember, no one will ever find out how you answered.

Choose one of the following answers for questions 97 to 107:

> A. None
> B. Once or twice
> C. Three to five times
> D. Six to nine times
> E. Ten times or more

97. In the past twelve months, how many times have you been to a party where people your age were drinking alcohol?

98. During the past twelve months, how many times have you taken something from a store without paying for it?

99. During the past twelve months, how many times have you cheated on a test at school?

100. During the past twelve months, how many times have you intentionally damaged or destroyed property (for example, broken windows or furniture, put paint on walls or signs, or scratched or dented a car)?

101. During the past twelve months, how many times have you lied to one of your parents?

102. During the past twelve months, how many times have you hit or beat up another kid?

103. During the past twelve months, how many times have you drunk alcohol while you were alone or with friends your own age? (Do not include communion wine.)

104. During the past month, how many times have you drunk alcohol while you were alone or with friends your own age? (Do not include communion wine.)

105. How many times have you used marijuana (grass, pot) or hashish (hash, hash oil) in your lifetime?

106. How many times in the past two weeks have you had five or more drinks in a row? (A ''drink'' is a glass of wine, a bottle or can of beer, a shot of liquor or a mixed drink.)

107. How many times in your lifetime have you tried cocaine or crack?

108. In the past month, how much time did you spend helping people outside your family with special needs (for example, collecting food for hungry people, mowing lawns for people who can't do it themselves, or spending time with sick or disabled people)? Don't count work for which you were paid.
A. None
B. One or two hours
C. Three to five hours
D. Six to ten hours
E. Eleven hours or more

109. How much television do you watch on an average school day? Don't count weekends.
A. None
B. One hour or less
C. About two hours
D. About three or four hours
E. Five hours or more

J. School

110. How much time do you usually spend on homework each week?
A. None
B. One hour or less
C. Between one and three hours
D. Between three and five hours
E. Between five and ten hours
F. More than ten hours

111. I enjoy school.
M. Most of the time
S. Sometimes
N. Rarely or never

112. I try to do the best I can at school.
M. Most of the time
S. Sometimes
N. Rarely or never

113. How often, if ever, do you get in trouble at school?
M. Most of the time
S. Sometimes
N. Never

114. During the past four weeks, how many school days have you skipped or ''cut''?
A. None
B. One day
C. Two days
D. Three days or more

K. Right and Wrong

In your opinion, are each of the actions in questions 115 to 120 right or wrong? Here are the possible responses:

> R. Morally right
> ?. Not sure
> W. Morally wrong

115. Sexual intercourse between two unmarried 16-year-olds who love each other.

116. People trying to keep a minority family from moving into a neighborhood.

117. Cheating on a test at school.

118. Lying to one's parents.

119. Sixteen-year-olds drinking a couple of beers at a party.

120. Stealing a shirt from a store.

L. Male-Female Relationships

121. How many times in the past twelve months have you been out on a date (such as going to a party or movie with one person of the opposite sex)?
A. None
B. One or two times
C. Three to five times
D. Six to nine times
E. Ten to nineteen times
F. Twenty times or more

122. In the past twelve months, how many times have you kissed someone about your age who is of the opposite sex?
A. None
B. One or two times
C. Three to five times
D. Six to nine times
E. Ten to nineteen times
F. Twenty times or more

123. Is it difficult for you to talk with other kids of the opposite sex?
Y. Yes
N. No

124. Are you in love right now with someone about your age who is of the opposite sex?
Y. Yes
N. No

125. Do you like to do things with teenagers of the opposite sex?
A. Usually
B. Sometimes
C. Never

126. How often do you think about sex?
A. Very often
B. Sometimes
C. Never

127. Have you ever had sexual intercourse ("gone all the way" or "made love")?
   A. Never
   B. Yes, one time
   C. Yes, two to five times
   D. Yes, six times or more
   E. I don't know what sexual intercourse is.

M. My Church

128. How many adults in your church do you think know you well?
   A. None
   B. One or two
   C. Three to five
   D. Six to nine
   E. Ten or more

129. How much does your church help you answer important questions about your life?
   V. Very much
   S. Some
   L. A little
   N. Not at all

130. If you had an important question about life, how many adults in your church would you feel comfortable going to for help? Don't count your parents or other relatives.
   A. None
   B. One or two
   C. Three to five
   D. Six to nine
   E. Ten or more

131. How important is church to you?
   A. Very important
   B. Somewhat important
   C. Not important

132. Would you recommend your church to a friend who doesn't belong to another church?
   Y. Yes
   ?. Not sure
   N. No

N. My Feelings About My Church

For questions 133 to 138, circle the number that best describes the main "feeling" you get from your church. For example, if you believe that most people in your church think teenagers are important, but some don't, you might circle a 6 or 7 for question 133.

In my church . . .

133.	Kids are important	9 8 7 6 5 4 3 2 1	Kids aren't important
134.	I have many church friends.	9 8 7 6 5 4 3 2 1	I have no church friends.
135.	I learn a lot.	9 8 7 6 5 4 3 2 1	I don't learn anything.
136.	Questions are invited.	9 8 7 6 5 4 3 2 1	Questions aren't welcome.
137.	It's exciting.	9 8 7 6 5 4 3 2 1	It's boring.
138.	Everyone cares about me.	9 8 7 6 5 4 3 2 1	Nobody cares about me.

O. What I Want From My Church

When you think about what you want from your church, how important are each of the following to you? Your choices are:

> **5.** Extremely important
> **4.** Important
> **3.** Somewhat important
> **2.** Slightly important
> **1.** Not important

It is _____ to me . . .

139. To learn about the Bible.
140. To learn what it means to be a Christian.
141. To learn what is special about me.
142. To help my religious faith grow.
143. To make good friends.
144. To get to know adults who care about me.
145. To have opportunities to help other people.
146. To learn more about how I can make decisions about what is right and wrong.
147. To learn about sex and sexual values.
148. To learn about alcohol and other drugs, and what my values about them should be.
149. To have lots of fun and good times.
150. To learn what a Christian should do about big issues such as poverty and war.

P. How Well My Church Is Doing

Rate how well your church does in each of the areas listed in questions 151 to 162. Your choices are:

> **5.** Excellent
> **4.** Good
> **3.** Okay
> **2.** Fair
> **1.** Poor

How well does your church . . .

151. Help you learn about the Bible?
152. Help you learn what it means to be a Christian?
153. Help you learn what's special about you?
154. Help your religious faith grow?
155. Help you make friends?
156. Help you get to know adults who care about you?
157. Help you to help other people?
158. Help you learn about what is right or wrong?
159. Help you learn about sex and sexual values?
160. Help you learn about alcohol and other drugs, and what your values about them should be?
161. Provide lots of fun and good times?
162. Help you learn what a Christian should do about big issues such as poverty and war?

YOUTH SURVEY

Directions

This survey isn't about what you know.
It's about who you are—
what you think,
what you feel,
what you believe.

It's about your school,
your church,
your friends,
your family,
yourself.

It's about what is important to you in life—
what you do,
what you worry about,
what you enjoy.

Be honest in giving your answers. Your name will not be attached to the survey, so no one will know what you write. Your answers will be summarized together with the answers of other young people in your church. All of those answers together will provide important clues to the interests, beliefs, problems and hopes of your church's young people. It's important for youth ministry leaders to have those clues so they can do a better job of planning youth ministry for you and your friends.

Do not begin answering questions until you are instructed to do so. As soon as the survey administrator gives the signal to open this booklet to the first page, you may begin. Mark your answers on the answer sheet, not in this booklet.

For each question, decide which answer fits you best, then *circle the corresponding number or letter on the answer sheet*. Mark only one answer for each question. Do not spend a lot of time trying to decide between two answers; it's usually best to mark your first impression and go right on to the next question. There is no "right" or "wrong" answer to any question—so answer each question honestly.

When you have finished, fold your answer sheet in half and put it into the envelope provided by the survey administrator.

Thanks for helping.
Thanks for being *you*.

General Information

1. I am: **F.** Female
          M. Male

2. My grade in school is:
   7   8   9   10   11   12

A. What I Want in Life

Listed below are things that some people want in life. Read through the complete list without making any marks. Then go back and decide how important each one is to you. Your choices are:

> **V.** Very important
> **S.** Somewhat important
> **N.** Not very important

It is _____ to me . . .

3. To be good in music, drama or art.
4. To have a happy family life.
5. To make my parents proud of me.
6. To make my own decisions.
7. To do things that help people.
8. To feel safe and secure in my neighborhood.
9. To feel good about myself.
10. To be popular at school.
11. To have lots of fun and good times.
12. To understand my feelings.
13. To have lots of money.
14. To have God at the center of my life.
15. To have a world without hunger or poverty.
16. To get a good job when I am older.
17. To have things (such as clothes, records and so on) as nice as other kids have.
18. To do something important with my life.
19. To do well in school.
20. To have a world without war.
21. To be really good at sports.
22. To be different in some way from all the other teenagers I know.
23. To have friends I can count on.
24. To do whatever I want to do, when I want to do it.
25. To be part of a church.
26. To have clothes and hair that look good to other kids.

B. What I Worry About

How much do you worry about each of the following statements? Your choices are:

> **V.** Very much
> **S.** Somewhat
> **N.** Very little or not at all

I worry _____ . . .

27. About how my friends treat me.

28. That I might kill myself.
29. That I might not be able to get a good job when I am older.
30. That someone might force me to do sexual things I don't want to do.
31. About how well other teenagers like me.
32. That I might lose my best friend.
33. That one of my parents will hit me so hard that I will be badly hurt.
34. That I may die soon.
35. That a nuclear bomb might be dropped on our country.
36. About all the drugs and drinking I see around me.
37. That one of my parents might die.
38. About all the people who are hungry and poor in our country.
39. That I might get beaten up at school.
40. About whether my body is growing in a normal way.
41. About how much my mother or father drinks.
42. About how I'm doing in school.
43. About my looks.
44. That my friends might get me in trouble.
45. About all the violence in our country.
46. That my parents might get a divorce.
    (Leave this number blank if your parents are already divorced, or if one of your parents is no longer living.)

C. My Family

For each of the following statements, mark the response that best matches your feelings. Your choices are:

> **A.** Strongly agree
> **B.** Agree
> **C.** Not sure
> **D.** Disagree
> **E.** Strongly disagree

I wish my parents (or guardians) would . . .

47. Give me more freedom.
48. Spend more time with me.
49. Yell at me less often.
50. Talk with me more about their views on important issues such as sex and drugs.
51. Be more interested in the things I care about.
52. Give me more responsibility.
53. Say "I love you" more often.
54. Trust me more.

Mark the appropriate response to the following statements and questions.

55. There is a lot of love in my family.
    A. Very true
    B. Somewhat true
    C. Not true

56. How often does your family do projects *together* to help other people (such as collecting food for the hungry or helping a neighbor)?
   A. At least once a month
   B. Once in a while
   C. Never

57. How often does your family talk together about God, the Bible or other religious things?
   A. Every day
   B. At least two or three times a week
   C. At least once a week
   D. At least once or twice a month
   E. Never

58. How often do you hear your mother talk about her religious faith?
   A. Every day
   B. At least two or three times a week
   C. At least once a week
   D. At least once or twice a month
   E. Never

59. How often do you hear your father talk about his religious faith?
   A. Every day
   B. At least two or three times a week
   C. At least once a week
   D. At least once or twice a month
   E. Never

D. How I Feel About Myself

Tell how true each of the following statements is for you. Your options are:

> V. Very true
> S. Somewhat true
> N. Not true

60. On the whole, I like myself.
61. I spend a lot of time thinking about who I am.
62. No one really understands me.
63. I believe life has a purpose.
64. I feel good about my body.

E. My Future

For questions 65 to 70, indicate how likely it is that each statement will come true. Choose one of these answers for each question:

> E. Excellent chance
> G. Good chance
> F. Fair chance
> P. Poor chance
> N. No chance

I believe there is a(n) _____ that . . .
65. I will someday be married and have children.
66. I will go to college.

67. I will be very happy 10 years from now.
68. I will be active in church when I am 40.
69. I myself or someone close to me might get AIDS.
70. The world will be destroyed by a nuclear war sometime in the next 10 years.

F. My Friends

71. How many close friends (not relatives) do you have?
   A. None
   B. One or two
   C. Three to five
   D. Six to nine
   E. Ten or more

72. I wish I could be better at making friends.
   A. Strongly agree
   B. Agree
   C. Not sure
   D. Disagree
   E. Strongly disagree

73. I wish I could be better at being a friend to others.
   A. Strongly agree
   B. Agree
   C. Not sure
   D. Disagree
   E. Strongly disagree

74. Some of my best friends belong to this church.
   T. True
   F. False

75. How often do you feel lonely?
   A. Every day
   B. Quite often, but not every day
   C. Once in a while
   D. Never

76. How often do your friends try to get you to do things you know are wrong?
   A. Very often
   B. Often
   C. Sometimes
   D. Once in a while
   E. Never

77. Which of the following choices best describes your parents' feelings toward your friends?
   A. My parents like all of my friends.
   B. My parents like most of my friends, except for one or two.
   C. My parents like about half of my friends, and half they don't.
   D. My parents don't like most of my friends, but one or two are okay.
   E. My parents don't like any of my friends.

G. Where I'd Go for Help

If you were in the following situations, to whom would you most likely turn for help or advice? For each situation, choose one of these answers:

> **A.** A parent or guardian
> **B.** A friend my own age
> **C.** An adult friend or relative
> **D.** A minister or youth worker
> **E.** Nobody

78. If I were having trouble in school, I would turn to _____.

79. If I were wondering how to handle my feelings, I would turn to _____.

80. If some of my friends started using alcohol or other drugs, I would turn to _____.

81. If I had questions about sex, I would turn to _____.

82. If I were feeling guilty about something I had done, I would turn to _____.

83. If I were deciding what to do with my life, I would turn to _____.

H. My Christian Faith

84. Overall, how important is religion in your life?
   V. Very important
   S. Somewhat important
   N. Not important

85. Compared to a year ago, would you say your faith is now more important, less important or about the same?
   M. More important
   L. Less important
   S. About the same

86. I am sure God loves me just as I am.
   T. True
   ?. Don't know
   F. False

87. Which of the following statements comes closest to your view of God?
   A. I know for sure that God exists.
   B. I am mostly sure that God exists.
   C. I'm not sure if God exists.
   D. I don't think there is a God.
   E. I am sure there is no such thing as God.

88. Which of the following statements is closest to your view of Jesus?
   A. Jesus is the Son of God who died on the cross and rose again.
   B. Jesus is the Son of God, but I doubt that he actually rose from the dead.
   C. Jesus was a great man who lived long ago, but I don't think he was the Son of God.
   D. Jesus never existed; his life is just a story people made up.

89. My religious beliefs greatly influence how I act at school and with my friends.
   M. Most of the time
   S. Some of the time
   R. Rarely or never

90. I believe God will stop loving me if I do a lot of wrong things.
   T. True
   ?. Not sure
   F. False

What do you think God wants you to do with your life? For each of the following actions, choose one of these responses:

> **T.** True
> **?.** Not sure
> **F.** False

God wants me . . .

91. To pray.
92. To worship.
93. To read the Bible.
94. To help get rid of hunger, poverty and war.
95. To tell other people about Jesus.
96. To spend time helping other people.

I. What I Do

Please answer the following questions as honestly as you can. Remember, no one will ever find out how you answered.

Choose one of the following answers for questions 97 to 107:

> **A.** None
> **B.** Once or twice
> **C.** Three to five times
> **D.** Six to nine times
> **E.** Ten times or more

97. In the past twelve months, how many times have you been to a party where people your age were drinking alcohol?

98. During the past twelve months, how many times have you taken something from a store without paying for it?

99. During the past twelve months, how many times have you cheated on a test at school?

100. During the past twelve months, how many times have you intentionally damaged or destroyed property (for example, broken windows or furniture, put paint on walls or signs, or scratched or dented a car)?

101. During the past twelve months, how many times have you lied to one of your parents?

102. During the past twelve months, how many times have you hit or beat up another kid?

103. During the past twelve months, how many times have you drunk alcohol while you were alone or with friends your own age? (Do not include communion wine.)

104. During the past month, how many times have you drunk alcohol while you were alone or with friends your own age? (Do not include communion wine.)

105. How many times have you used marijuana (grass, pot) or hashish (hash, hash oil) in your lifetime?

106. How many times in the past two weeks have you had five or more drinks in a row? (A "drink" is a glass of wine, a bottle or can of beer, a shot of liquor or a mixed drink.)

107. How many times in your lifetime have you tried cocaine or crack?

108. In the past month, how much time did you spend helping people outside your family with special needs (for example, collecting food for hungry people, mowing lawns for people who can't do it themselves, or spending time with sick or disabled people)? Don't count work for which you were paid.
A. None
B. One or two hours
C. Three to five hours
D. Six to ten hours
E. Eleven hours or more

109. How much television do you watch on an average school day? Don't count weekends.
A. None
B. One hour or less
C. About two hours
D. About three or four hours
E. Five hours or more

J. School

110. How much time do you usually spend on homework each week?
A. None
B. One hour or less
C. Between one and three hours
D. Between three and five hours
E. Between five and ten hours
F. More than ten hours

111. I enjoy school.
M. Most of the time
S. Sometimes
N. Rarely or never

112. I try to do the best I can at school.
M. Most of the time
S. Sometimes
N. Rarely or never

113. How often, if ever, do you get in trouble at school?
M. Most of the time
S. Sometimes
N. Never

114. During the past four weeks, how many school days have you skipped or "cut"?
A. None
B. One day
C. Two days
D. Three days or more

K. Right and Wrong

In your opinion, are each of the actions in questions 115 to 120 right or wrong? Here are the possible responses:

R. Morally right
?. Not sure
W. Morally wrong

115. Sexual intercourse between two unmarried 16-year-olds who love each other.

116. People trying to keep a minority family from moving into a neighborhood.

117. Cheating on a test at school.

118. Lying to one's parents.

119. Sixteen-year-olds drinking a couple of beers at a party.

120. Stealing a shirt from a store.

L. Male-Female Relationships

121. How many times in the past twelve months have you been out on a date (such as going to a party or movie with one person of the opposite sex)?
A. None
B. One or two times
C. Three to five times
D. Six to nine times
E. Ten to nineteen times
F. Twenty times or more

122. In the past twelve months, how many times have you kissed someone about your age who is of the opposite sex?
A. None
B. One or two times
C. Three to five times
D. Six to nine times
E. Ten to nineteen times
F. Twenty times or more

123. Is it difficult for you to talk with other kids of the opposite sex?
Y. Yes
N. No

124. Are you in love right now with someone about your age who is of the opposite sex?
Y. Yes
N. No

125. Do you like to do things with teenagers of the opposite sex?
A. Usually
B. Sometimes
C. Never

126. How often do you think about sex?
A. Very often
B. Sometimes
C. Never

127. Have you ever had sexual intercourse ("gone all the way" or "made love")?
   A. Never
   B. Yes, one time
   C. Yes, two to five times
   D. Yes, six times or more
   E. I don't know what sexual intercourse is.

M. My Church

128. How many adults in your church do you think know you well?
   A. None
   B. One or two
   C. Three to five
   D. Six to nine
   E. Ten or more

129. How much does your church help you answer important questions about your life?
   V. Very much
   S. Some
   L. A little
   N. Not at all

130. If you had an important question about life, how many adults in your church would you feel comfortable going to for help? Don't count your parents or other relatives.
   A. None
   B. One or two
   C. Three to five
   D. Six to nine
   E. Ten or more

131. How important is church to you?
   A. Very important
   B. Somewhat important
   C. Not important

132. Would you recommend your church to a friend who doesn't belong to another church?
   Y. Yes
   ?. Not sure
   N. No

N. My Feelings About My Church

For questions 133 to 138, circle the number that best describes the main "feeling" you get from your church. For example, if you believe that most people in your church think teenagers are important, but some don't, you might circle a 6 or 7 for question 133.

In my church . . .

133. Kids are important	9 8 7 6 5 4 3 2 1	Kids aren't important
134. I have many church friends.	9 8 7 6 5 4 3 2 1	I have no church friends.
135. I learn a lot.	9 8 7 6 5 4 3 2 1	I don't learn anything.
136. Questions are invited.	9 8 7 6 5 4 3 2 1	Questions aren't welcome.
137. It's exciting.	9 8 7 6 5 4 3 2 1	It's boring.
138. Everyone cares about me.	9 8 7 6 5 4 3 2 1	Nobody cares about me.

O. What I Want From My Church

When you think about what you want from your church, how important are each of the following to you? Your choices are:

> **5.** Extremely important
> **4.** Important
> **3.** Somewhat important
> **2.** Slightly important
> **1.** Not important

It is _____ to me . . .

139. To learn about the Bible.
140. To learn what it means to be a Christian.
141. To learn what is special about me.
142. To help my religious faith grow.
143. To make good friends.
144. To get to know adults who care about me.
145. To have opportunities to help other people.
146. To learn more about how I can make decisions about what is right and wrong.
147. To learn about sex and sexual values.
148. To learn about alcohol and other drugs, and what my values about them should be.
149. To have lots of fun and good times.
150. To learn what a Christian should do about big issues such as poverty and war.

P. How Well My Church Is Doing

Rate how well your church does in each of the areas listed in questions 151 to 162. Your choices are:

> **5.** Excellent
> **4.** Good
> **3.** Okay
> **2.** Fair
> **1.** Poor

How well does your church . . .

151. Help you learn about the Bible?
152. Help you learn what it means to be a Christian?
153. Help you learn what's special about you?
154. Help your religious faith grow?
155. Help you make friends?
156. Help you get to know adults who care about you?
157. Help you to help other people?
158. Help you learn about what is right or wrong?
159. Help you learn about sex and sexual values?
160. Help you learn about alcohol and other drugs, and what your values about them should be?
161. Provide lots of fun and good times?
162. Help you learn what a Christian should do about big issues such as poverty and war?

YOUTH SURVEY

Directions

**This survey isn't about what you know.
It's about who you are—
what you think,
what you feel,
what you believe.**

**It's about your school,
your church,
your friends,
your family,
yourself.**

**It's about what is important to you in life—
what you do,
what you worry about,
what you enjoy.**

Be honest in giving your answers. Your name will not be attached to the survey, so no one will know what you write. Your answers will be summarized together with the answers of other young people in your church. All of those answers together will provide important clues to the interests, beliefs, problems and hopes of your church's young people. It's important for youth ministry leaders to have those clues so they can do a better job of planning youth ministry for you and your friends.

Do not begin answering questions until you are instructed to do so. As soon as the survey administrator gives the signal to open this booklet to the first page, you may begin. Mark your answers on the answer sheet, not in this booklet.

For each question, decide which answer fits you best, then *circle the corresponding number or letter on the answer sheet*. Mark only one answer for each question. Do not spend a lot of time trying to decide between two answers; it's usually best to mark your first impression and go right on to the next question. There is no "right" or "wrong" answer to any question—so answer each question honestly.

When you have finished, fold your answer sheet in half and put it into the envelope provided by the survey administrator.

**Thanks for helping.
Thanks for being *you*.**

General Information

1. I am: **F.** Female
M. Male

2. My grade in school is:
7 8 9 10 11 12

A. What I Want in Life

Listed below are things that some people want in life. Read through the complete list without making any marks. Then go back and decide how important each one is to you. Your choices are:

> **V.** Very important
> **S.** Somewhat important
> **N.** Not very important

It is _____ to me . . .

3. To be good in music, drama or art.
4. To have a happy family life.
5. To make my parents proud of me.
6. To make my own decisions.
7. To do things that help people.
8. To feel safe and secure in my neighborhood.
9. To feel good about myself.
10. To be popular at school.
11. To have lots of fun and good times.
12. To understand my feelings.
13. To have lots of money.
14. To have God at the center of my life.
15. To have a world without hunger or poverty.
16. To get a good job when I am older.
17. To have things (such as clothes, records and so on) as nice as other kids have.
18. To do something important with my life.
19. To do well in school.
20. To have a world without war.
21. To be really good at sports.
22. To be different in some way from all the other teenagers I know.
23. To have friends I can count on.
24. To do whatever I want to do, when I want to do it.
25. To be part of a church.
26. To have clothes and hair that look good to other kids.

B. What I Worry About

How much do you worry about each of the following statements? Your choices are:

> **V.** Very much
> **S.** Somewhat
> **N.** Very little or not at all

I worry _____ . . .

27. About how my friends treat me.

28. That I might kill myself.
29. That I might not be able to get a good job when I am older.
30. That someone might force me to do sexual things I don't want to do.
31. About how well other teenagers like me.
32. That I might lose my best friend.
33. That one of my parents will hit me so hard that I will be badly hurt.
34. That I may die soon.
35. That a nuclear bomb might be dropped on our country.
36. About all the drugs and drinking I see around me.
37. That one of my parents might die.
38. About all the people who are hungry and poor in our country.
39. That I might get beaten up at school.
40. About whether my body is growing in a normal way.
41. About how much my mother or father drinks.
42. About how I'm doing in school.
43. About my looks.
44. That my friends might get me in trouble.
45. About all the violence in our country.
46. That my parents might get a divorce.
(Leave this number blank if your parents are already divorced, or if one of your parents is no longer living.)

C. My Family

For each of the following statements, mark the response that best matches your feelings. Your choices are:

> **A.** Strongly agree
> **B.** Agree
> **C.** Not sure
> **D.** Disagree
> **E.** Strongly disagree

I wish my parents (or guardians) would . . .

47. Give me more freedom.
48. Spend more time with me.
49. Yell at me less often.
50. Talk with me more about their views on important issues such as sex and drugs.
51. Be more interested in the things I care about.
52. Give me more responsibility.
53. Say ''I love you'' more often.
54. Trust me more.

Mark the appropriate response to the following statements and questions.

55. There is a lot of love in my family.
A. Very true
B. Somewhat true
C. Not true

56. How often does your family do projects *together* to help other people (such as collecting food for the hungry or helping a neighbor)?
   A. At least once a month
   B. Once in a while
   C. Never

57. How often does your family talk together about God, the Bible or other religious things?
   A. Every day
   B. At least two or three times a week
   C. At least once a week
   D. At least once or twice a month
   E. Never

58. How often do you hear your mother talk about her religious faith?
   A. Every day
   B. At least two or three times a week
   C. At least once a week
   D. At least once or twice a month
   E. Never

59. How often do you hear your father talk about his religious faith?
   A. Every day
   B. At least two or three times a week
   C. At least once a week
   D. At least once or twice a month
   E. Never

D. How I Feel About Myself

Tell how true each of the following statements is for you. Your options are:

| V. Very true |
| S. Somewhat true |
| N. Not true |

60. On the whole, I like myself.
61. I spend a lot of time thinking about who I am.
62. No one really understands me.
63. I believe life has a purpose.
64. I feel good about my body.

E. My Future

For questions 65 to 70, indicate how likely it is that each statement will come true. Choose one of these answers for each question:

| E. Excellent chance |
| G. Good chance |
| F. Fair chance |
| P. Poor chance |
| N. No chance |

I believe there is a(n) _____ that . . .
   65. I will someday be married and have children.
   66. I will go to college.

67. I will be very happy 10 years from now.
68. I will be active in church when I am 40.
69. I myself or someone close to me might get AIDS.
70. The world will be destroyed by a nuclear war sometime in the next 10 years.

F. My Friends

71. How many close friends (not relatives) do you have?
   A. None
   B. One or two
   C. Three to five
   D. Six to nine
   E. Ten or more

72. I wish I could be better at making friends.
   A. Strongly agree
   B. Agree
   C. Not sure
   D. Disagree
   E. Strongly disagree

73. I wish I could be better at being a friend to others.
   A. Strongly agree
   B. Agree
   C. Not sure
   D. Disagree
   E. Strongly disagree

74. Some of my best friends belong to this church.
   T. True
   F. False

75. How often do you feel lonely?
   A. Every day
   B. Quite often, but not every day
   C. Once in a while
   D. Never

76. How often do your friends try to get you to do things you know are wrong?
   A. Very often
   B. Often
   C. Sometimes
   D. Once in a while
   E. Never

77. Which of the following choices best describes your parents' feelings toward your friends?
   A. My parents like all of my friends.
   B. My parents like most of my friends, except for one or two.
   C. My parents like about half of my friends, and half they don't.
   D. My parents don't like most of my friends, but one or two are okay.
   E. My parents don't like any of my friends.

G. Where I'd Go for Help

If you were in the following situations, to whom would you most likely turn for help or advice? For each situation, choose one of these answers:

> A. A parent or guardian
> B. A friend my own age
> C. An adult friend or relative
> D. A minister or youth worker
> E. Nobody

78. If I were having trouble in school, I would turn to _____.

79. If I were wondering how to handle my feelings, I would turn to _____.

80. If some of my friends started using alcohol or other drugs, I would turn to _____.

81. If I had questions about sex, I would turn to _____.

82. If I were feeling guilty about something I had done, I would turn to _____.

83. If I were deciding what to do with my life, I would turn to _____.

H. My Christian Faith

84. Overall, how important is religion in your life?
    V. Very important
    S. Somewhat important
    N. Not important

85. Compared to a year ago, would you say your faith is now more important, less important or about the same?
    M. More important
    L. Less important
    S. About the same

86. I am sure God loves me just as I am.
    T. True
    ?. Don't know
    F. False

87. Which of the following statements comes closest to your view of God?
    A. I know for sure that God exists.
    B. I am mostly sure that God exists.
    C. I'm not sure if God exists.
    D. I don't think there is a God.
    E. I am sure there is no such thing as God.

88. Which of the following statements is closest to your view of Jesus?
    A. Jesus is the Son of God who died on the cross and rose again.
    B. Jesus is the Son of God, but I doubt that he actually rose from the dead.
    C. Jesus was a great man who lived long ago, but I don't think he was the Son of God.
    D. Jesus never existed; his life is just a story people made up.

89. My religious beliefs greatly influence how I act at school and with my friends.
    M. Most of the time
    S. Some of the time
    R. Rarely or never

90. I believe God will stop loving me if I do a lot of wrong things.
    T. True
    ?. Not sure
    F. False

What do you think God wants you to do with your life? For each of the following actions, choose one of these responses:

> T. True
> ?. Not sure
> F. False

God wants me . . .
91. To pray.
92. To worship.
93. To read the Bible.
94. To help get rid of hunger, poverty and war.
95. To tell other people about Jesus.
96. To spend time helping other people.

I. What I Do

Please answer the following questions as honestly as you can. Remember, no one will ever find out how you answered.

Choose one of the following answers for questions 97 to 107:

> A. None
> B. Once or twice
> C. Three to five times
> D. Six to nine times
> E. Ten times or more

97. In the past twelve months, how many times have you been to a party where people your age were drinking alcohol?

98. During the past twelve months, how many times have you taken something from a store without paying for it?

99. During the past twelve months, how many times have you cheated on a test at school?

100. During the past twelve months, how many times have you intentionally damaged or destroyed property (for example, broken windows or furniture, put paint on walls or signs, or scratched or dented a car)?

101. During the past twelve months, how many times have you lied to one of your parents?

102. During the past twelve months, how many times have you hit or beat up another kid?

103. During the past twelve months, how many times have you drunk alcohol while you were alone or with friends your own age? (Do not include communion wine.)

104. During the past month, how many times have you drunk alcohol while you were alone or with friends your own age? (Do not include communion wine.)

105. How many times have you used marijuana (grass, pot) or hashish (hash, hash oil) in your lifetime?

106. How many times in the past two weeks have you had five or more drinks in a row? (A "drink" is a glass of wine, a bottle or can of beer, a shot of liquor or a mixed drink.)

107. How many times in your lifetime have you tried cocaine or crack?

108. In the past month, how much time did you spend helping people outside your family with special needs (for example, collecting food for hungry people, mowing lawns for people who can't do it themselves, or spending time with sick or disabled people)? Don't count work for which you were paid.
   A. None
   B. One or two hours
   C. Three to five hours
   D. Six to ten hours
   E. Eleven hours or more

109. How much television do you watch on an average school day? Don't count weekends.
   A. None
   B. One hour or less
   C. About two hours
   D. About three or four hours
   E. Five hours or more

J. School

110. How much time do you usually spend on homework each week?
   A. None
   B. One hour or less
   C. Between one and three hours
   D. Between three and five hours
   E. Between five and ten hours
   F. More than ten hours

111. I enjoy school.
   M. Most of the time
   S. Sometimes
   N. Rarely or never

112. I try to do the best I can at school.
   M. Most of the time
   S. Sometimes
   N. Rarely or never

113. How often, if ever, do you get in trouble at school?
   M. Most of the time
   S. Sometimes
   N. Never

114. During the past four weeks, how many school days have you skipped or "cut"?
   A. None
   B. One day
   C. Two days
   D. Three days or more

K. Right and Wrong

In your opinion, are each of the actions in questions 115 to 120 right or wrong? Here are the possible responses:

> R. Morally right
> ?. Not sure
> W. Morally wrong

115. Sexual intercourse between two unmarried 16-year-olds who love each other.

116. People trying to keep a minority family from moving into a neighborhood.

117. Cheating on a test at school.

118. Lying to one's parents.

119. Sixteen-year-olds drinking a couple of beers at a party.

120. Stealing a shirt from a store.

L. Male-Female Relationships

121. How many times in the past twelve months have you been out on a date (such as going to a party or movie with one person of the opposite sex)?
   A. None
   B. One or two times
   C. Three to five times
   D. Six to nine times
   E. Ten to nineteen times
   F. Twenty times or more

122. In the past twelve months, how many times have you kissed someone about your age who is of the opposite sex?
   A. None
   B. One or two times
   C. Three to five times
   D. Six to nine times
   E. Ten to nineteen times
   F. Twenty times or more

123. Is it difficult for you to talk with other kids of the opposite sex?
   Y. Yes
   N. No

124. Are you in love right now with someone about your age who is of the opposite sex?
   Y. Yes
   N. No

125. Do you like to do things with teenagers of the opposite sex?
   A. Usually
   B. Sometimes
   C. Never

126. How often do you think about sex?
   A. Very often
   B. Sometimes
   C. Never

127. Have you ever had sexual intercourse (''gone all the way'' or ''made love'')?
  A. Never
  B. Yes, one time
  C. Yes, two to five times
  D. Yes, six times or more
  E. I don't know what sexual intercourse is.

M. My Church

128. How many adults in your church do you think know you well?
  A. None
  B. One or two
  C. Three to five
  D. Six to nine
  E. Ten or more

129. How much does your church help you answer important questions about your life?
  V. Very much
  S. Some
  L. A little
  N. Not at all

130. If you had an important question about life, how many adults in your church would you feel comfortable going to for help? Don't count your parents or other relatives.
  A. None
  B. One or two
  C. Three to five
  D. Six to nine
  E. Ten or more

131. How important is church to you?
  A. Very important
  B. Somewhat important
  C. Not important

132. Would you recommend your church to a friend who doesn't belong to another church?
  Y. Yes
  ?. Not sure
  N. No

N. My Feelings About My Church

For questions 133 to 138, circle the number that best describes the main ''feeling'' you get from your church. For example, if you believe that most people in your church think teenagers are important, but some don't, you might circle a 6 or 7 for question 133.

In my church . . .

133.	Kids are important	9 8 7 6 5 4 3 2 1	Kids aren't important
134.	I have many church friends.	9 8 7 6 5 4 3 2 1	I have no church friends.
135.	I learn a lot.	9 8 7 6 5 4 3 2 1	I don't learn anything.
136.	Questions are invited.	9 8 7 6 5 4 3 2 1	Questions aren't welcome.
137.	It's exciting.	9 8 7 6 5 4 3 2 1	It's boring.
138.	Everyone cares about me.	9 8 7 6 5 4 3 2 1	Nobody cares about me.

O. What I Want From My Church

When you think about what you want from your church, how important are each of the following to you? Your choices are:

> **5.** Extremely important
> **4.** Important
> **3.** Somewhat important
> **2.** Slightly important
> **1.** Not important

It is _____ to me . . .

139. To learn about the Bible.
140. To learn what it means to be a Christian.
141. To learn what is special about me.
142. To help my religious faith grow.
143. To make good friends.
144. To get to know adults who care about me.
145. To have opportunities to help other people.
146. To learn more about how I can make decisions about what is right and wrong.
147. To learn about sex and sexual values.
148. To learn about alcohol and other drugs, and what my values about them should be.
149. To have lots of fun and good times.
150. To learn what a Christian should do about big issues such as poverty and war.

P. How Well My Church Is Doing

Rate how well your church does in each of the areas listed in questions 151 to 162. Your choices are:

> **5.** Excellent
> **4.** Good
> **3.** Okay
> **2.** Fair
> **1.** Poor

How well does your church . . .

151. Help you learn about the Bible?
152. Help you learn what it means to be a Christian?
153. Help you learn what's special about you?
154. Help your religious faith grow?
155. Help you make friends?
156. Help you get to know adults who care about you?
157. Help you to help other people?
158. Help you learn about what is right or wrong?
159. Help you learn about sex and sexual values?
160. Help you learn about alcohol and other drugs, and what your values about them should be?
161. Provide lots of fun and good times?
162. Help you learn what a Christian should do about big issues such as poverty and war?

Determining Needs in Your Youth Ministry

YOUTH SURVEY

Directions

This survey isn't about what you know.
It's about who you are—
what you think,
what you feel,
what you believe.

It's about your school,
your church,
your friends,
your family,
yourself.

It's about what is important to you in life—
what you do,
what you worry about,
what you enjoy.

Be honest in giving your answers. Your name will not be attached to the survey, so no one will know what you write. Your answers will be summarized together with the answers of other young people in your church. All of those answers together will provide important clues to the interests, beliefs, problems and hopes of your church's young people. It's important for youth ministry leaders to have those clues so they can do a better job of planning youth ministry for you and your friends.

Do not begin answering questions until you are instructed to do so. As soon as the survey administrator gives the signal to open this booklet to the first page, you may begin. Mark your answers on the answer sheet, not in this booklet.

For each question, decide which answer fits you best, then *circle the corresponding number or letter on the answer sheet*. Mark only one answer for each question. Do not spend a lot of time trying to decide between two answers; it's usually best to mark your first impression and go right on to the next question. There is no "right" or "wrong" answer to any question—so answer each question honestly.

When you have finished, fold your answer sheet in half and put it into the envelope provided by the survey administrator.

Thanks for helping.
Thanks for being *you*.

General Information

1. I am: **F.** Female
                M. Male

2. My grade in school is:
                7   8   9   10   11   12

A. What I Want in Life

Listed below are things that some people want in life. Read through the complete list without making any marks. Then go back and decide how important each one is to you. Your choices are:

> **V.** Very important
> **S.** Somewhat important
> **N.** Not very important

It is _____ to me . . .

3. To be good in music, drama or art.
4. To have a happy family life.
5. To make my parents proud of me.
6. To make my own decisions.
7. To do things that help people.
8. To feel safe and secure in my neighborhood.
9. To feel good about myself.
10. To be popular at school.
11. To have lots of fun and good times.
12. To understand my feelings.
13. To have lots of money.
14. To have God at the center of my life.
15. To have a world without hunger or poverty.
16. To get a good job when I am older.
17. To have things (such as clothes, records and so on) as nice as other kids have.
18. To do something important with my life.
19. To do well in school.
20. To have a world without war.
21. To be really good at sports.
22. To be different in some way from all the other teenagers I know.
23. To have friends I can count on.
24. To do whatever I want to do, when I want to do it.
25. To be part of a church.
26. To have clothes and hair that look good to other kids.

B. What I Worry About

How much do you worry about each of the following statements? Your choices are:

> **V.** Very much
> **S.** Somewhat
> **N.** Very little or not at all

I worry _____ . . .
27. About how my friends treat me.

28. That I might kill myself.
29. That I might not be able to get a good job when I am older.
30. That someone might force me to do sexual things I don't want to do.
31. About how well other teenagers like me.
32. That I might lose my best friend.
33. That one of my parents will hit me so hard that I will be badly hurt.
34. That I may die soon.
35. That a nuclear bomb might be dropped on our country.
36. About all the drugs and drinking I see around me.
37. That one of my parents might die.
38. About all the people who are hungry and poor in our country.
39. That I might get beaten up at school.
40. About whether my body is growing in a normal way.
41. About how much my mother or father drinks.
42. About how I'm doing in school.
43. About my looks.
44. That my friends might get me in trouble.
45. About all the violence in our country.
46. That my parents might get a divorce.
(Leave this number blank if your parents are already divorced, or if one of your parents is no longer living.)

C. My Family

For each of the following statements, mark the response that best matches your feelings. Your choices are:

> **A.** Strongly agree
> **B.** Agree
> **C.** Not sure
> **D.** Disagree
> **E.** Strongly disagree

I wish my parents (or guardians) would . . .
47. Give me more freedom.
48. Spend more time with me.
49. Yell at me less often.
50. Talk with me more about their views on important issues such as sex and drugs.
51. Be more interested in the things I care about.
52. Give me more responsibility.
53. Say "I love you" more often.
54. Trust me more.

Mark the appropriate response to the following statements and questions.

55. There is a lot of love in my family.
     A. Very true
     B. Somewhat true
     C. Not true

56. How often does your family do projects *together* to help other people (such as collecting food for the hungry or helping a neighbor)?
A. At least once a month
B. Once in a while
C. Never

57. How often does your family talk together about God, the Bible or other religious things?
A. Every day
B. At least two or three times a week
C. At least once a week
D. At least once or twice a month
E. Never

58. How often do you hear your mother talk about her religious faith?
A. Every day
B. At least two or three times a week
C. At least once a week
D. At least once or twice a month
E. Never

59. How often do you hear your father talk about his religious faith?
A. Every day
B. At least two or three times a week
C. At least once a week
D. At least once or twice a month
E. Never

D. How I Feel About Myself

Tell how true each of the following statements is for you. Your options are:

> V. Very true
> S. Somewhat true
> N. Not true

60. On the whole, I like myself.
61. I spend a lot of time thinking about who I am.
62. No one really understands me.
63. I believe life has a purpose.
64. I feel good about my body.

E. My Future

For questions 65 to 70, indicate how likely it is that each statement will come true. Choose one of these answers for each question:

> E. Excellent chance
> G. Good chance
> F. Fair chance
> P. Poor chance
> N. No chance

I believe there is a(n) _____ that . . .
65. I will someday be married and have children.
66. I will go to college.

67. I will be very happy 10 years from now.
68. I will be active in church when I am 40.
69. I myself or someone close to me might get AIDS.
70. The world will be destroyed by a nuclear war sometime in the next 10 years.

F. My Friends

71. How many close friends (not relatives) do you have?
A. None
B. One or two
C. Three to five
D. Six to nine
E. Ten or more

72. I wish I could be better at making friends.
A. Strongly agree
B. Agree
C. Not sure
D. Disagree
E. Strongly disagree

73. I wish I could be better at being a friend to others.
A. Strongly agree
B. Agree
C. Not sure
D. Disagree
E. Strongly disagree

74. Some of my best friends belong to this church.
T. True
F. False

75. How often do you feel lonely?
A. Every day
B. Quite often, but not every day
C. Once in a while
D. Never

76. How often do your friends try to get you to do things you know are wrong?
A. Very often
B. Often
C. Sometimes
D. Once in a while
E. Never

77. Which of the following choices best describes your parents' feelings toward your friends?
A. My parents like all of my friends.
B. My parents like most of my friends, except for one or two.
C. My parents like about half of my friends, and half they don't.
D. My parents don't like most of my friends, but one or two are okay.
E. My parents don't like any of my friends.

G. Where I'd Go for Help

If you were in the following situations, to whom would you most likely turn for help or advice? For each situation, choose one of these answers:

> A. A parent or guardian
> B. A friend my own age
> C. An adult friend or relative
> D. A minister or youth worker
> E. Nobody

78. If I were having trouble in school, I would turn to _____.

79. If I were wondering how to handle my feelings, I would turn to _____.

80. If some of my friends started using alcohol or other drugs, I would turn to _____.

81. If I had questions about sex, I would turn to _____.

82. If I were feeling guilty about something I had done, I would turn to _____.

83. If I were deciding what to do with my life, I would turn to _____.

H. My Christian Faith

84. Overall, how important is religion in your life?
    V. Very important
    S. Somewhat important
    N. Not important

85. Compared to a year ago, would you say your faith is now more important, less important or about the same?
    M. More important
    L. Less important
    S. About the same

86. I am sure God loves me just as I am.
    T. True
    ?. Don't know
    F. False

87. Which of the following statements comes closest to your view of God?
    A. I know for sure that God exists.
    B. I am mostly sure that God exists.
    C. I'm not sure if God exists.
    D. I don't think there is a God.
    E. I am sure there is no such thing as God.

88. Which of the following statements is closest to your view of Jesus?
    A. Jesus is the Son of God who died on the cross and rose again.
    B. Jesus is the Son of God, but I doubt that he actually rose from the dead.
    C. Jesus was a great man who lived long ago, but I don't think he was the Son of God.
    D. Jesus never existed; his life is just a story people made up.

89. My religious beliefs greatly influence how I act at school and with my friends.
    M. Most of the time
    S. Some of the time
    R. Rarely or never

90. I believe God will stop loving me if I do a lot of wrong things.
    T. True
    ?. Not sure
    F. False

What do you think God wants you to do with your life? For each of the following actions, choose one of these responses:

> T. True
> ?. Not sure
> F. False

God wants me . . .

91. To pray.
92. To worship.
93. To read the Bible.
94. To help get rid of hunger, poverty and war.
95. To tell other people about Jesus.
96. To spend time helping other people.

I. What I Do

Please answer the following questions as honestly as you can. Remember, no one will ever find out how you answered.

Choose one of the following answers for questions 97 to 107:

> A. None
> B. Once or twice
> C. Three to five times
> D. Six to nine times
> E. Ten times or more

97. In the past twelve months, how many times have you been to a party where people your age were drinking alcohol?

98. During the past twelve months, how many times have you taken something from a store without paying for it?

99. During the past twelve months, how many times have you cheated on a test at school?

100. During the past twelve months, how many times have you intentionally damaged or destroyed property (for example, broken windows or furniture, put paint on walls or signs, or scratched or dented a car)?

101. During the past twelve months, how many times have you lied to one of your parents?

102. During the past twelve months, how many times have you hit or beat up another kid?

103. During the past twelve months, how many times have you drunk alcohol while you were alone or with friends your own age? (Do not include communion wine.)

104. During the past month, how many times have you drunk alcohol while you were alone or with friends your own age? (Do not include communion wine.)

105. How many times have you used marijuana (grass, pot) or hashish (hash, hash oil) in your lifetime?

106. How many times in the past two weeks have you had five or more drinks in a row? (A "drink" is a glass of wine, a bottle or can of beer, a shot of liquor or a mixed drink.)

107. How many times in your lifetime have you tried cocaine or crack?

108. In the past month, how much time did you spend helping people outside your family with special needs (for example, collecting food for hungry people, mowing lawns for people who can't do it themselves, or spending time with sick or disabled people)? Don't count work for which you were paid.
   A. None
   B. One or two hours
   C. Three to five hours
   D. Six to ten hours
   E. Eleven hours or more

109. How much television do you watch on an average school day? Don't count weekends.
   A. None
   B. One hour or less
   C. About two hours
   D. About three or four hours
   E. Five hours or more

J. School

110. How much time do you usually spend on homework each week?
   A. None
   B. One hour or less
   C. Between one and three hours
   D. Between three and five hours
   E. Between five and ten hours
   F. More than ten hours

111. I enjoy school.
   M. Most of the time
   S. Sometimes
   N. Rarely or never

112. I try to do the best I can at school.
   M. Most of the time
   S. Sometimes
   N. Rarely or never

113. How often, if ever, do you get in trouble at school?
   M. Most of the time
   S. Sometimes
   N. Never

114. During the past four weeks, how many school days have you skipped or "cut"?
   A. None
   B. One day
   C. Two days
   D. Three days or more

K. Right and Wrong

In your opinion, are each of the actions in questions 115 to 120 right or wrong? Here are the possible responses:

   R. Morally right
   ?. Not sure
   W. Morally wrong

115. Sexual intercourse between two unmarried 16-year-olds who love each other.

116. People trying to keep a minority family from moving into a neighborhood.

117. Cheating on a test at school.

118. Lying to one's parents.

119. Sixteen-year-olds drinking a couple of beers at a party.

120. Stealing a shirt from a store.

L. Male-Female Relationships

121. How many times in the past twelve months have you been out on a date (such as going to a party or movie with one person of the opposite sex)?
   A. None
   B. One or two times
   C. Three to five times
   D. Six to nine times
   E. Ten to nineteen times
   F. Twenty times or more

122. In the past twelve months, how many times have you kissed someone about your age who is of the opposite sex?
   A. None
   B. One or two times
   C. Three to five times
   D. Six to nine times
   E. Ten to nineteen times
   F. Twenty times or more

123. Is it difficult for you to talk with other kids of the opposite sex?
   Y. Yes
   N. No

124. Are you in love right now with someone about your age who is of the opposite sex?
   Y. Yes
   N. No

125. Do you like to do things with teenagers of the opposite sex?
   A. Usually
   B. Sometimes
   C. Never

126. How often do you think about sex?
   A. Very often
   B. Sometimes
   C. Never

127. Have you ever had sexual intercourse ("gone all the way" or "made love")?
   A. Never
   B. Yes, one time
   C. Yes, two to five times
   D. Yes, six times or more
   E. I don't know what sexual intercourse is.

M. My Church

128. How many adults in your church do you think know you well?
   A. None
   B. One or two
   C. Three to five
   D. Six to nine
   E. Ten or more

129. How much does your church help you answer important questions about your life?
   V. Very much
   S. Some
   L. A little
   N. Not at all

130. If you had an important question about life, how many adults in your church would you feel comfortable going to for help? Don't count your parents or other relatives.
   A. None
   B. One or two
   C. Three to five
   D. Six to nine
   E. Ten or more

131. How important is church to you?
   A. Very important
   B. Somewhat important
   C. Not important

132. Would you recommend your church to a friend who doesn't belong to another church?
   Y. Yes
   ?. Not sure
   N. No

N. My Feelings About My Church

For questions 133 to 138, circle the number that best describes the main "feeling" you get from your church. For example, if you believe that most people in your church think teenagers are important, but some don't, you might circle a 6 or 7 for question 133.

In my church . . .

133.	Kids are important	9 8 7 6 5 4 3 2 1	Kids aren't important
134.	I have many church friends.	9 8 7 6 5 4 3 2 1	I have no church friends.
135.	I learn a lot.	9 8 7 6 5 4 3 2 1	I don't learn anything.
136.	Questions are invited.	9 8 7 6 5 4 3 2 1	Questions aren't welcome.
137.	It's exciting.	9 8 7 6 5 4 3 2 1	It's boring.
138.	Everyone cares about me.	9 8 7 6 5 4 3 2 1	Nobody cares about me.

O. What I Want From My Church

When you think about what you want from your church, how important are each of the following to you? Your choices are:

> 5. Extremely important
> 4. Important
> 3. Somewhat important
> 2. Slightly important
> 1. Not important

It is _____ to me . . .

139. To learn about the Bible.
140. To learn what it means to be a Christian.
141. To learn what is special about me.
142. To help my religious faith grow.
143. To make good friends.
144. To get to know adults who care about me.
145. To have opportunities to help other people.
146. To learn more about how I can make decisions about what is right and wrong.
147. To learn about sex and sexual values.
148. To learn about alcohol and other drugs, and what my values about them should be.
149. To have lots of fun and good times.
150. To learn what a Christian should do about big issues such as poverty and war.

P. How Well My Church Is Doing

Rate how well your church does in each of the areas listed in questions 151 to 162. Your choices are:

> 5. Excellent
> 4. Good
> 3. Okay
> 2. Fair
> 1. Poor

How well does your church . . .

151. Help you learn about the Bible?
152. Help you learn what it means to be a Christian?
153. Help you learn what's special about you?
154. Help your religious faith grow?
155. Help you make friends?
156. Help you get to know adults who care about you?
157. Help you to help other people?
158. Help you learn about what is right or wrong?
159. Help you learn about sex and sexual values?
160. Help you learn about alcohol and other drugs, and what your values about them should be?
161. Provide lots of fun and good times?
162. Help you learn what a Christian should do about big issues such as poverty and war?

YOUTH SURVEY

Directions

**This survey isn't about what you know.
It's about who you are—
what you think,
what you feel,
what you believe.**

**It's about your school,
your church,
your friends,
your family,
yourself.**

**It's about what is important to you in life—
what you do,
what you worry about,
what you enjoy.**

Be honest in giving your answers. Your name will not be attached to the survey, so no one will know what you write. Your answers will be summarized together with the answers of other young people in your church. All of those answers together will provide important clues to the interests, beliefs, problems and hopes of your church's young people. It's important for youth ministry leaders to have those clues so they can do a better job of planning youth ministry for you and your friends.

Do not begin answering questions until you are instructed to do so. As soon as the survey administrator gives the signal to open this booklet to the first page, you may begin. Mark your answers on the answer sheet, not in this booklet.

For each question, decide which answer fits you best, then *circle the corresponding number or letter on the answer sheet*. Mark only one answer for each question. Do not spend a lot of time trying to decide between two answers; it's usually best to mark your first impression and go right on to the next question. There is no "right" or "wrong" answer to any question—so answer each question honestly.

When you have finished, fold your answer sheet in half and put it into the envelope provided by the survey administrator.

Thanks for helping.
Thanks for being *you*.

General Information

1. I am: **F.** Female
            M. Male
2. My grade in school is:
            7   8   9   10   11   12

A. What I Want in Life

Listed below are things that some people want in life. Read through the complete list without making any marks. Then go back and decide how important each one is to you. Your choices are:

> **V.** Very important
> **S.** Somewhat important
> **N.** Not very important

It is _____ to me . . .

3. To be good in music, drama or art.
4. To have a happy family life.
5. To make my parents proud of me.
6. To make my own decisions.
7. To do things that help people.
8. To feel safe and secure in my neighborhood.
9. To feel good about myself.
10. To be popular at school.
11. To have lots of fun and good times.
12. To understand my feelings.
13. To have lots of money.
14. To have God at the center of my life.
15. To have a world without hunger or poverty.
16. To get a good job when I am older.
17. To have things (such as clothes, records and so on) as nice as other kids have.
18. To do something important with my life.
19. To do well in school.
20. To have a world without war.
21. To be really good at sports.
22. To be different in some way from all the other teenagers I know.
23. To have friends I can count on.
24. To do whatever I want to do, when I want to do it.
25. To be part of a church.
26. To have clothes and hair that look good to other kids.

B. What I Worry About

How much do you worry about each of the following statements? Your choices are:

> **V.** Very much
> **S.** Somewhat
> **N.** Very little or not at all

I worry _____ . . .

27. About how my friends treat me.
28. That I might kill myself.
29. That I might not be able to get a good job when I am older.
30. That someone might force me to do sexual things I don't want to do.
31. About how well other teenagers like me.
32. That I might lose my best friend.
33. That one of my parents will hit me so hard that I will be badly hurt.
34. That I may die soon.
35. That a nuclear bomb might be dropped on our country.
36. About all the drugs and drinking I see around me.
37. That one of my parents might die.
38. About all the people who are hungry and poor in our country.
39. That I might get beaten up at school.
40. About whether my body is growing in a normal way.
41. About how much my mother or father drinks.
42. About how I'm doing in school.
43. About my looks.
44. That my friends might get me in trouble.
45. About all the violence in our country.
46. That my parents might get a divorce.
    (Leave this number blank if your parents are already divorced, or if one of your parents is no longer living.)

C. My Family

For each of the following statements, mark the response that best matches your feelings. Your choices are:

> **A.** Strongly agree
> **B.** Agree
> **C.** Not sure
> **D.** Disagree
> **E.** Strongly disagree

I wish my parents (or guardians) would . . .

47. Give me more freedom.
48. Spend more time with me.
49. Yell at me less often.
50. Talk with me more about their views on important issues such as sex and drugs.
51. Be more interested in the things I care about.
52. Give me more responsibility.
53. Say "I love you" more often.
54. Trust me more.

Mark the appropriate response to the following statements and questions.

55. There is a lot of love in my family.
    A. Very true
    B. Somewhat true
    C. Not true

56. How often does your family do projects *together* to help other people (such as collecting food for the hungry or helping a neighbor)?
   A. At least once a month
   B. Once in a while
   C. Never

57. How often does your family talk together about God, the Bible or other religious things?
   A. Every day
   B. At least two or three times a week
   C. At least once a week
   D. At least once or twice a month
   E. Never

58. How often do you hear your mother talk about her religious faith?
   A. Every day
   B. At least two or three times a week
   C. At least once a week
   D. At least once or twice a month
   E. Never

59. How often do you hear your father talk about his religious faith?
   A. Every day
   B. At least two or three times a week
   C. At least once a week
   D. At least once or twice a month
   E. Never

D. How I Feel About Myself

Tell how true each of the following statements is for you. Your options are:

> V. Very true
> S. Somewhat true
> N. Not true

60. On the whole, I like myself.
61. I spend a lot of time thinking about who I am.
62. No one really understands me.
63. I believe life has a purpose.
64. I feel good about my body.

E. My Future

For questions 65 to 70, indicate how likely it is that each statement will come true. Choose one of these answers for each question:

> E. Excellent chance
> G. Good chance
> F. Fair chance
> P. Poor chance
> N. No chance

I believe there is a(n) _____ that . . .
65. I will someday be married and have children.
66. I will go to college.

67. I will be very happy 10 years from now.
68. I will be active in church when I am 40.
69. I myself or someone close to me might get AIDS.
70. The world will be destroyed by a nuclear war sometime in the next 10 years.

F. My Friends

71. How many close friends (not relatives) do you have?
   A. None
   B. One or two
   C. Three to five
   D. Six to nine
   E. Ten or more

72. I wish I could be better at making friends.
   A. Strongly agree
   B. Agree
   C. Not sure
   D. Disagree
   E. Strongly disagree

73. I wish I could be better at being a friend to others.
   A. Strongly agree
   B. Agree
   C. Not sure
   D. Disagree
   E. Strongly disagree

74. Some of my best friends belong to this church.
   T. True
   F. False

75. How often do you feel lonely?
   A. Every day
   B. Quite often, but not every day
   C. Once in a while
   D. Never

76. How often do your friends try to get you to do things you know are wrong?
   A. Very often
   B. Often
   C. Sometimes
   D. Once in a while
   E. Never

77. Which of the following choices best describes your parents' feelings toward your friends?
   A. My parents like all of my friends.
   B. My parents like most of my friends, except for one or two.
   C. My parents like about half of my friends, and half they don't.
   D. My parents don't like most of my friends, but one or two are okay.
   E. My parents don't like any of my friends.

G. Where I'd Go for Help

If you were in the following situations, to whom would you most likely turn for help or advice? For each situation, choose one of these answers:

> **A.** A parent or guardian
> **B.** A friend my own age
> **C.** An adult friend or relative
> **D.** A minister or youth worker
> **E.** Nobody

78. If I were having trouble in school, I would turn to _____.

79. If I were wondering how to handle my feelings, I would turn to _____.

80. If some of my friends started using alcohol or other drugs, I would turn to _____.

81. If I had questions about sex, I would turn to _____.

82. If I were feeling guilty about something I had done, I would turn to _____.

83. If I were deciding what to do with my life, I would turn to _____.

H. My Christian Faith

84. Overall, how important is religion in your life?
    V. Very important
    S. Somewhat important
    N. Not important

85. Compared to a year ago, would you say your faith is now more important, less important or about the same?
    M. More important
    L. Less important
    S. About the same

86. I am sure God loves me just as I am.
    T. True
    ?. Don't know
    F. False

87. Which of the following statements comes closest to your view of God?
    A. I know for sure that God exists.
    B. I am mostly sure that God exists.
    C. I'm not sure if God exists.
    D. I don't think there is a God.
    E. I am sure there is no such thing as God.

88. Which of the following statements is closest to your view of Jesus?
    A. Jesus is the Son of God who died on the cross and rose again.
    B. Jesus is the Son of God, but I doubt that he actually rose from the dead.
    C. Jesus was a great man who lived long ago, but I don't think he was the Son of God.
    D. Jesus never existed; his life is just a story people made up.

89. My religious beliefs greatly influence how I act at school and with my friends.
    M. Most of the time
    S. Some of the time
    R. Rarely or never

90. I believe God will stop loving me if I do a lot of wrong things.
    T. True
    ?. Not sure
    F. False

What do you think God wants you to do with your life? For each of the following actions, choose one of these responses:

> **T.** True
> **?.** Not sure
> **F.** False

God wants me . . .
91. To pray.
92. To worship.
93. To read the Bible.
94. To help get rid of hunger, poverty and war.
95. To tell other people about Jesus.
96. To spend time helping other people.

I. What I Do

Please answer the following questions as honestly as you can. Remember, no one will ever find out how you answered.

Choose one of the following answers for questions 97 to 107:

> **A.** None
> **B.** Once or twice
> **C.** Three to five times
> **D.** Six to nine times
> **E.** Ten times or more

97. In the past twelve months, how many times have you been to a party where people your age were drinking alcohol?

98. During the past twelve months, how many times have you taken something from a store without paying for it?

99. During the past twelve months, how many times have you cheated on a test at school?

100. During the past twelve months, how many times have you intentionally damaged or destroyed property (for example, broken windows or furniture, put paint on walls or signs, or scratched or dented a car)?

101. During the past twelve months, how many times have you lied to one of your parents?

102. During the past twelve months, how many times have you hit or beat up another kid?

103. During the past twelve months, how many times have you drunk alcohol while you were alone or with friends your own age? (Do not include communion wine.)

104. During the past month, how many times have you drunk alcohol while you were alone or with friends your own age? (Do not include communion wine.)

105. How many times have you used marijuana (grass, pot) or hashish (hash, hash oil) in your lifetime?

106. How many times in the past two weeks have you had five or more drinks in a row? (A "drink" is a glass of wine, a bottle or can of beer, a shot of liquor or a mixed drink.)

107. How many times in your lifetime have you tried cocaine or crack?

108. In the past month, how much time did you spend helping people outside your family with special needs (for example, collecting food for hungry people, mowing lawns for people who can't do it themselves, or spending time with sick or disabled people)? Don't count work for which you were paid.
   A. None
   B. One or two hours
   C. Three to five hours
   D. Six to ten hours
   E. Eleven hours or more

109. How much television do you watch on an average school day? Don't count weekends.
   A. None
   B. One hour or less
   C. About two hours
   D. About three or four hours
   E. Five hours or more

J. School

110. How much time do you usually spend on homework each week?
   A. None
   B. One hour or less
   C. Between one and three hours
   D. Between three and five hours
   E. Between five and ten hours
   F. More than ten hours

111. I enjoy school.
   M. Most of the time
   S. Sometimes
   N. Rarely or never

112. I try to do the best I can at school.
   M. Most of the time
   S. Sometimes
   N. Rarely or never

113. How often, if ever, do you get in trouble at school?
   M. Most of the time
   S. Sometimes
   N. Never

114. During the past four weeks, how many school days have you skipped or "cut"?
   A. None
   B. One day
   C. Two days
   D. Three days or more

K. Right and Wrong

In your opinion, are each of the actions in questions 115 to 120 right or wrong? Here are the possible responses:

R. Morally right
?. Not sure
W. Morally wrong

115. Sexual intercourse between two unmarried 16-year-olds who love each other.

116. People trying to keep a minority family from moving into a neighborhood.

117. Cheating on a test at school.

118. Lying to one's parents.

119. Sixteen-year-olds drinking a couple of beers at a party.

120. Stealing a shirt from a store.

L. Male-Female Relationships

121. How many times in the past twelve months have you been out on a date (such as going to a party or movie with one person of the opposite sex)?
   A. None
   B. One or two times
   C. Three to five times
   D. Six to nine times
   E. Ten to nineteen times
   F. Twenty times or more

122. In the past twelve months, how many times have you kissed someone about your age who is of the opposite sex?
   A. None
   B. One or two times
   C. Three to five times
   D. Six to nine times
   E. Ten to nineteen times
   F. Twenty times or more

123. Is it difficult for you to talk with other kids of the opposite sex?
   Y. Yes
   N. No

124. Are you in love right now with someone about your age who is of the opposite sex?
   Y. Yes
   N. No

125. Do you like to do things with teenagers of the opposite sex?
   A. Usually
   B. Sometimes
   C. Never

126. How often do you think about sex?
   A. Very often
   B. Sometimes
   C. Never

127. Have you ever had sexual intercourse ("gone all the way" or "made love")?
- **A.** Never
- **B.** Yes, one time
- **C.** Yes, two to five times
- **D.** Yes, six times or more
- **E.** I don't know what sexual intercourse is.

M. My Church

128. How many adults in your church do you think know you well?
- **A.** None
- **B.** One or two
- **C.** Three to five
- **D.** Six to nine
- **E.** Ten or more

129. How much does your church help you answer important questions about your life?
- **V.** Very much
- **S.** Some
- **L.** A little
- **N.** Not at all

130. If you had an important question about life, how many adults in your church would you feel comfortable going to for help? Don't count your parents or other relatives.
- **A.** None
- **B.** One or two
- **C.** Three to five
- **D.** Six to nine
- **E.** Ten or more

131. How important is church to you?
- **A.** Very important
- **B.** Somewhat important
- **C.** Not important

132. Would you recommend your church to a friend who doesn't belong to another church?
- **Y.** Yes
- **?.** Not sure
- **N.** No

N. My Feelings About My Church

For questions 133 to 138, circle the number that best describes the main "feeling" you get from your church. For example, if you believe that most people in your church think teenagers are important, but some don't, you might circle a 6 or 7 for question 133.

In my church . . .

133.	Kids are important	9 8 7 6 5 4 3 2 1	Kids aren't important
134.	I have many church friends.	9 8 7 6 5 4 3 2 1	I have no church friends.
135.	I learn a lot.	9 8 7 6 5 4 3 2 1	I don't learn anything.
136.	Questions are invited.	9 8 7 6 5 4 3 2 1	Questions aren't welcome.
137.	It's exciting.	9 8 7 6 5 4 3 2 1	It's boring.
138.	Everyone cares about me.	9 8 7 6 5 4 3 2 1	Nobody cares about me.

O. What I Want From My Church

When you think about what you want from your church, how important are each of the following to you? Your choices are:

> **5.** Extremely important
> **4.** Important
> **3.** Somewhat important
> **2.** Slightly important
> **1.** Not important

It is _____ to me . . .

139. To learn about the Bible.
140. To learn what it means to be a Christian.
141. To learn what is special about me.
142. To help my religious faith grow.
143. To make good friends.
144. To get to know adults who care about me.
145. To have opportunities to help other people.
146. To learn more about how I can make decisions about what is right and wrong.
147. To learn about sex and sexual values.
148. To learn about alcohol and other drugs, and what my values about them should be.
149. To have lots of fun and good times.
150. To learn what a Christian should do about big issues such as poverty and war.

P. How Well My Church Is Doing

Rate how well your church does in each of the areas listed in questions 151 to 162. Your choices are:

> **5.** Excellent
> **4.** Good
> **3.** Okay
> **2.** Fair
> **1.** Poor

How well does your church . . .
151. Help you learn about the Bible?
152. Help you learn what it means to be a Christian?
153. Help you learn what's special about you?
154. Help your religious faith grow?
155. Help you make friends?
156. Help you get to know adults who care about you?
157. Help you to help other people?
158. Help you learn about what is right or wrong?
159. Help you learn about sex and sexual values?
160. Help you learn about alcohol and other drugs, and what your values about them should be?
161. Provide lots of fun and good times?
162. Help you learn what a Christian should do about big issues such as poverty and war?

YOUTH SURVEY

Directions

**This survey isn't about what you know.
It's about who you are—
what you think,
what you feel,
what you believe.**

**It's about your school,
your church,
your friends,
your family,
yourself.**

**It's about what is important to you in life—
what you do,
what you worry about,
what you enjoy.**

Be honest in giving your answers. Your name will not be attached to the survey, so no one will know what you write. Your answers will be summarized together with the answers of other young people in your church. All of those answers together will provide important clues to the interests, beliefs, problems and hopes of your church's young people. It's important for youth ministry leaders to have those clues so they can do a better job of planning youth ministry for you and your friends.

Do not begin answering questions until you are instructed to do so. As soon as the survey administrator gives the signal to open this booklet to the first page, you may begin. Mark your answers on the answer sheet, not in this booklet.

For each question, decide which answer fits you best, then *circle the corresponding number or letter on the answer sheet*. Mark only one answer for each question. Do not spend a lot of time trying to decide between two answers; it's usually best to mark your first impression and go right on to the next question. There is no "right" or "wrong" answer to any question—so answer each question honestly.

When you have finished, fold your answer sheet in half and put it into the envelope provided by the survey administrator.

**Thanks for helping.
Thanks for being *you*.**

General Information

1. I am: **F.** Female
             M. Male
2. My grade in school is:
        7   8   9   10   11   12

A. What I Want in Life

Listed below are things that some people want in life. Read through the complete list without making any marks. Then go back and decide how important each one is to you. Your choices are:

> **V.** Very important
> **S.** Somewhat important
> **N.** Not very important

It is _____ to me . . .

3. To be good in music, drama or art.
4. To have a happy family life.
5. To make my parents proud of me.
6. To make my own decisions.
7. To do things that help people.
8. To feel safe and secure in my neighborhood.
9. To feel good about myself.
10. To be popular at school.
11. To have lots of fun and good times.
12. To understand my feelings.
13. To have lots of money.
14. To have God at the center of my life.
15. To have a world without hunger or poverty.
16. To get a good job when I am older.
17. To have things (such as clothes, records and so on) as nice as other kids have.
18. To do something important with my life.
19. To do well in school.
20. To have a world without war.
21. To be really good at sports.
22. To be different in some way from all the other teenagers I know.
23. To have friends I can count on.
24. To do whatever I want to do, when I want to do it.
25. To be part of a church.
26. To have clothes and hair that look good to other kids.

B. What I Worry About

How much do you worry about each of the following statements? Your choices are:

> **V.** Very much
> **S.** Somewhat
> **N.** Very little or not at all

I worry _____ . . .
27. About how my friends treat me.

28. That I might kill myself.
29. That I might not be able to get a good job when I am older.
30. That someone might force me to do sexual things I don't want to do.
31. About how well other teenagers like me.
32. That I might lose my best friend.
33. That one of my parents will hit me so hard that I will be badly hurt.
34. That I may die soon.
35. That a nuclear bomb might be dropped on our country.
36. About all the drugs and drinking I see around me.
37. That one of my parents might die.
38. About all the people who are hungry and poor in our country.
39. That I might get beaten up at school.
40. About whether my body is growing in a normal way.
41. About how much my mother or father drinks.
42. About how I'm doing in school.
43. About my looks.
44. That my friends might get me in trouble.
45. About all the violence in our country.
46. That my parents might get a divorce.
        (Leave this number blank if your parents are already divorced, or if one of your parents is no longer living.)

C. My Family

For each of the following statements, mark the response that best matches your feelings. Your choices are:

> **A.** Strongly agree
> **B.** Agree
> **C.** Not sure
> **D.** Disagree
> **E.** Strongly disagree

I wish my parents (or guardians) would . . .
47. Give me more freedom.
48. Spend more time with me.
49. Yell at me less often.
50. Talk with me more about their views on important issues such as sex and drugs.
51. Be more interested in the things I care about.
52. Give me more responsibility.
53. Say "I love you" more often.
54. Trust me more.

Mark the appropriate response to the following statements and questions.

55. There is a lot of love in my family.
        A. Very true
        B. Somewhat true
        C. Not true

56. How often does your family do projects *together* to help other people (such as collecting food for the hungry or helping a neighbor)?
A. At least once a month
B. Once in a while
C. Never

57. How often does your family talk together about God, the Bible or other religious things?
A. Every day
B. At least two or three times a week
C. At least once a week
D. At least once or twice a month
E. Never

58. How often do you hear your mother talk about her religious faith?
A. Every day
B. At least two or three times a week
C. At least once a week
D. At least once or twice a month
E. Never

59. How often do you hear your father talk about his religious faith?
A. Every day
B. At least two or three times a week
C. At least once a week
D. At least once or twice a month
E. Never

D. How I Feel About Myself

Tell how true each of the following statements is for you. Your options are:

> **V.** Very true
> **S.** Somewhat true
> **N.** Not true

60. On the whole, I like myself.
61. I spend a lot of time thinking about who I am.
62. No one really understands me.
63. I believe life has a purpose.
64. I feel good about my body.

E. My Future

For questions 65 to 70, indicate how likely it is that each statement will come true. Choose one of these answers for each question:

> **E.** Excellent chance
> **G.** Good chance
> **F.** Fair chance
> **P.** Poor chance
> **N.** No chance

I believe there is a(n) _____ that . . .
65. I will someday be married and have children.
66. I will go to college.

67. I will be very happy 10 years from now.
68. I will be active in church when I am 40.
69. I myself or someone close to me might get AIDS.
70. The world will be destroyed by a nuclear war sometime in the next 10 years.

F. My Friends

71. How many close friends (not relatives) do you have?
A. None
B. One or two
C. Three to five
D. Six to nine
E. Ten or more

72. I wish I could be better at making friends.
A. Strongly agree
B. Agree
C. Not sure
D. Disagree
E. Strongly disagree

73. I wish I could be better at being a friend to others.
A. Strongly agree
B. Agree
C. Not sure
D. Disagree
E. Strongly disagree

74. Some of my best friends belong to this church.
T. True
F. False

75. How often do you feel lonely?
A. Every day
B. Quite often, but not every day
C. Once in a while
D. Never

76. How often do your friends try to get you to do things you know are wrong?
A. Very often
B. Often
C. Sometimes
D. Once in a while
E. Never

77. Which of the following choices best describes your parents' feelings toward your friends?
A. My parents like all of my friends.
B. My parents like most of my friends, except for one or two.
C. My parents like about half of my friends, and half they don't.
D. My parents don't like most of my friends, but one or two are okay.
E. My parents don't like any of my friends.

G. Where I'd Go for Help

If you were in the following situations, to whom would you most likely turn for help or advice? For each situation, choose one of these answers:

> **A.** A parent or guardian
> **B.** A friend my own age
> **C.** An adult friend or relative
> **D.** A minister or youth worker
> **E.** Nobody

78. If I were having trouble in school, I would turn to _____.
79. If I were wondering how to handle my feelings, I would turn to _____.
80. If some of my friends started using alcohol or other drugs, I would turn to _____.
81. If I had questions about sex, I would turn to _____.
82. If I were feeling guilty about something I had done, I would turn to _____.
83. If I were deciding what to do with my life, I would turn to _____.

H. My Christian Faith

84. Overall, how important is religion in your life?
    V. Very important
    S. Somewhat important
    N. Not important
85. Compared to a year ago, would you say your faith is now more important, less important or about the same?
    M. More important
    L. Less important
    S. About the same
86. I am sure God loves me just as I am.
    T. True
    ?. Don't know
    F. False
87. Which of the following statements comes closest to your view of God?
    A. I know for sure that God exists.
    B. I am mostly sure that God exists.
    C. I'm not sure if God exists.
    D. I don't think there is a God.
    E. I am sure there is no such thing as God.
88. Which of the following statements is closest to your view of Jesus?
    A. Jesus is the Son of God who died on the cross and rose again.
    B. Jesus is the Son of God, but I doubt that he actually rose from the dead.
    C. Jesus was a great man who lived long ago, but I don't think he was the Son of God.
    D. Jesus never existed; his life is just a story people made up.

89. My religious beliefs greatly influence how I act at school and with my friends.
    M. Most of the time
    S. Some of the time
    R. Rarely or never
90. I believe God will stop loving me if I do a lot of wrong things.
    T. True
    ?. Not sure
    F. False

What do you think God wants you to do with your life? For each of the following actions, choose one of these responses:

> **T.** True
> **?.** Not sure
> **F.** False

God wants me . . .
91. To pray.
92. To worship.
93. To read the Bible.
94. To help get rid of hunger, poverty and war.
95. To tell other people about Jesus.
96. To spend time helping other people.

I. What I Do

Please answer the following questions as honestly as you can. Remember, no one will ever find out how you answered.

Choose one of the following answers for questions 97 to 107:

> **A.** None
> **B.** Once or twice
> **C.** Three to five times
> **D.** Six to nine times
> **E.** Ten times or more

97. In the past twelve months, how many times have you been to a party where people your age were drinking alcohol?
98. During the past twelve months, how many times have you taken something from a store without paying for it?
99. During the past twelve months, how many times have you cheated on a test at school?
100. During the past twelve months, how many times have you intentionally damaged or destroyed property (for example, broken windows or furniture, put paint on walls or signs, or scratched or dented a car)?
101. During the past twelve months, how many times have you lied to one of your parents?
102. During the past twelve months, how many times have you hit or beat up another kid?
103. During the past twelve months, how many times have you drunk alcohol while you were alone or with friends your own age? (Do not include communion wine.)

104. During the past month, how many times have you drunk alcohol while you were alone or with friends your own age? (Do not include communion wine.)

105. How many times have you used marijuana (grass, pot) or hashish (hash, hash oil) in your lifetime?

106. How many times in the past two weeks have you had five or more drinks in a row? (A "drink" is a glass of wine, a bottle or can of beer, a shot of liquor or a mixed drink.)

107. How many times in your lifetime have you tried cocaine or crack?

108. In the past month, how much time did you spend helping people outside your family with special needs (for example, collecting food for hungry people, mowing lawns for people who can't do it themselves, or spending time with sick or disabled people)? Don't count work for which you were paid.
A. None
B. One or two hours
C. Three to five hours
D. Six to ten hours
E. Eleven hours or more

109. How much television do you watch on an average school day? Don't count weekends.
A. None
B. One hour or less
C. About two hours
D. About three or four hours
E. Five hours or more

J. School

110. How much time do you usually spend on homework each week?
A. None
B. One hour or less
C. Between one and three hours
D. Between three and five hours
E. Between five and ten hours
F. More than ten hours

111. I enjoy school.
M. Most of the time
S. Sometimes
N. Rarely or never

112. I try to do the best I can at school.
M. Most of the time
S. Sometimes
N. Rarely or never

113. How often, if ever, do you get in trouble at school?
M. Most of the time
S. Sometimes
N. Never

114. During the past four weeks, how many school days have you skipped or "cut"?
A. None
B. One day
C. Two days
D. Three days or more

K. Right and Wrong

In your opinion, are each of the actions in questions 115 to 120 right or wrong? Here are the possible responses:

> **R.** Morally right
> **?.** Not sure
> **W.** Morally wrong

115. Sexual intercourse between two unmarried 16-year-olds who love each other.

116. People trying to keep a minority family from moving into a neighborhood.

117. Cheating on a test at school.

118. Lying to one's parents.

119. Sixteen-year-olds drinking a couple of beers at a party.

120. Stealing a shirt from a store.

L. Male-Female Relationships

121. How many times in the past twelve months have you been out on a date (such as going to a party or movie with one person of the opposite sex)?
A. None
B. One or two times
C. Three to five times
D. Six to nine times
E. Ten to nineteen times
F. Twenty times or more

122. In the past twelve months, how many times have you kissed someone about your age who is of the opposite sex?
A. None
B. One or two times
C. Three to five times
D. Six to nine times
E. Ten to nineteen times
F. Twenty times or more

123. Is it difficult for you to talk with other kids of the opposite sex?
Y. Yes
N. No

124. Are you in love right now with someone about your age who is of the opposite sex?
Y. Yes
N. No

125. Do you like to do things with teenagers of the opposite sex?
A. Usually
B. Sometimes
C. Never

126. How often do you think about sex?
A. Very often
B. Sometimes
C. Never

127. Have you ever had sexual intercourse ("gone all the way" or "made love")?
- **A.** Never
- **B.** Yes, one time
- **C.** Yes, two to five times
- **D.** Yes, six times or more
- **E.** I don't know what sexual intercourse is.

M. My Church

128. How many adults in your church do you think know you well?
- **A.** None
- **B.** One or two
- **C.** Three to five
- **D.** Six to nine
- **E.** Ten or more

129. How much does your church help you answer important questions about your life?
- **V.** Very much
- **S.** Some
- **L.** A little
- **N.** Not at all

130. If you had an important question about life, how many adults in your church would you feel comfortable going to for help? Don't count your parents or other relatives.
- **A.** None
- **B.** One or two
- **C.** Three to five
- **D.** Six to nine
- **E.** Ten or more

131. How important is church to you?
- **A.** Very important
- **B.** Somewhat important
- **C.** Not important

132. Would you recommend your church to a friend who doesn't belong to another church?
- **Y.** Yes
- **?.** Not sure
- **N.** No

N. My Feelings About My Church

For questions 133 to 138, circle the number that best describes the main "feeling" you get from your church. For example, if you believe that most people in your church think teenagers are important, but some don't, you might circle a 6 or 7 for question 133.

In my church . . .

133.	Kids are important	9 8 7 6 5 4 3 2 1	Kids aren't important
134.	I have many church friends.	9 8 7 6 5 4 3 2 1	I have no church friends.
135.	I learn a lot.	9 8 7 6 5 4 3 2 1	I don't learn anything.
136.	Questions are invited.	9 8 7 6 5 4 3 2 1	Questions aren't welcome.
137.	It's exciting.	9 8 7 6 5 4 3 2 1	It's boring.
138.	Everyone cares about me.	9 8 7 6 5 4 3 2 1	Nobody cares about me.

O. What I Want From My Church

When you think about what you want from your church, how important are each of the following to you? Your choices are:

> **5.** Extremely important
> **4.** Important
> **3.** Somewhat important
> **2.** Slightly important
> **1.** Not important

It is _____ to me . . .

139. To learn about the Bible.
140. To learn what it means to be a Christian.
141. To learn what is special about me.
142. To help my religious faith grow.
143. To make good friends.
144. To get to know adults who care about me.
145. To have opportunities to help other people.
146. To learn more about how I can make decisions about what is right and wrong.
147. To learn about sex and sexual values.
148. To learn about alcohol and other drugs, and what my values about them should be.
149. To have lots of fun and good times.
150. To learn what a Christian should do about big issues such as poverty and war.

P. How Well My Church Is Doing

Rate how well your church does in each of the areas listed in questions 151 to 162. Your choices are:

> **5.** Excellent
> **4.** Good
> **3.** Okay
> **2.** Fair
> **1.** Poor

How well does your church . . .

151. Help you learn about the Bible?
152. Help you learn what it means to be a Christian?
153. Help you learn what's special about you?
154. Help your religious faith grow?
155. Help you make friends?
156. Help you get to know adults who care about you?
157. Help you to help other people?
158. Help you learn about what is right or wrong?
159. Help you learn about sex and sexual values?
160. Help you learn about alcohol and other drugs, and what your values about them should be?
161. Provide lots of fun and good times?
162. Help you learn what a Christian should do about big issues such as poverty and war?

Determining Needs in Your Youth Ministry

YOUTH SURVEY

Directions

**This survey isn't about what you know.
It's about who you are—
what you think,
what you feel,
what you believe.**

**It's about your school,
your church,
your friends,
your family,
yourself.**

**It's about what is important to you in life—
what you do,
what you worry about,
what you enjoy.**

Be honest in giving your answers. Your name will not be attached to the survey, so no one will know what you write. Your answers will be summarized together with the answers of other young people in your church. All of those answers together will provide important clues to the interests, beliefs, problems and hopes of your church's young people. It's important for youth ministry leaders to have those clues so they can do a better job of planning youth ministry for you and your friends.

Do not begin answering questions until you are instructed to do so. As soon as the survey administrator gives the signal to open this booklet to the first page, you may begin. Mark your answers on the answer sheet, not in this booklet.

For each question, decide which answer fits you best, then *circle the corresponding number or letter on the answer sheet*. Mark only one answer for each question. Do not spend a lot of time trying to decide between two answers; it's usually best to mark your first impression and go right on to the next question. There is no "right" or "wrong" answer to any question—so answer each question honestly.

When you have finished, fold your answer sheet in half and put it into the envelope provided by the survey administrator.

Thanks for helping.
Thanks for being *you*.

General Information

1. I am: **F.** Female
M. Male

2. My grade in school is:
7 8 9 10 11 12

A. What I Want in Life

Listed below are things that some people want in life. Read through the complete list without making any marks. Then go back and decide how important each one is to you. Your choices are:

> **V.** Very important
> **S.** Somewhat important
> **N.** Not very important

It is _____ to me . . .

3. To be good in music, drama or art.
4. To have a happy family life.
5. To make my parents proud of me.
6. To make my own decisions.
7. To do things that help people.
8. To feel safe and secure in my neighborhood.
9. To feel good about myself.
10. To be popular at school.
11. To have lots of fun and good times.
12. To understand my feelings.
13. To have lots of money.
14. To have God at the center of my life.
15. To have a world without hunger or poverty.
16. To get a good job when I am older.
17. To have things (such as clothes, records and so on) as nice as other kids have.
18. To do something important with my life.
19. To do well in school.
20. To have a world without war.
21. To be really good at sports.
22. To be different in some way from all the other teenagers I know.
23. To have friends I can count on.
24. To do whatever I want to do, when I want to do it.
25. To be part of a church.
26. To have clothes and hair that look good to other kids.

B. What I Worry About

How much do you worry about each of the following statements? Your choices are:

> **V.** Very much
> **S.** Somewhat
> **N.** Very little or not at all

I worry _____ . . .
27. About how my friends treat me.

28. That I might kill myself.
29. That I might not be able to get a good job when I am older.
30. That someone might force me to do sexual things I don't want to do.
31. About how well other teenagers like me.
32. That I might lose my best friend.
33. That one of my parents will hit me so hard that I will be badly hurt.
34. That I may die soon.
35. That a nuclear bomb might be dropped on our country.
36. About all the drugs and drinking I see around me.
37. That one of my parents might die.
38. About all the people who are hungry and poor in our country.
39. That I might get beaten up at school.
40. About whether my body is growing in a normal way.
41. About how much my mother or father drinks.
42. About how I'm doing in school.
43. About my looks.
44. That my friends might get me in trouble.
45. About all the violence in our country.
46. That my parents might get a divorce.
(Leave this number blank if your parents are already divorced, or if one of your parents is no longer living.)

C. My Family

For each of the following statements, mark the response that best matches your feelings. Your choices are:

> **A.** Strongly agree
> **B.** Agree
> **C.** Not sure
> **D.** Disagree
> **E.** Strongly disagree

I wish my parents (or guardians) would . . .
47. Give me more freedom.
48. Spend more time with me.
49. Yell at me less often.
50. Talk with me more about their views on important issues such as sex and drugs.
51. Be more interested in the things I care about.
52. Give me more responsibility.
53. Say "I love you" more often.
54. Trust me more.

Mark the appropriate response to the following statements and questions.

55. There is a lot of love in my family.
A. Very true
B. Somewhat true
C. Not true

56. How often does your family do projects *together* to help other people (such as collecting food for the hungry or helping a neighbor)?
    A. At least once a month
    B. Once in a while
    C. Never

57. How often does your family talk together about God, the Bible or other religious things?
    A. Every day
    B. At least two or three times a week
    C. At least once a week
    D. At least once or twice a month
    E. Never

58. How often do you hear your mother talk about her religious faith?
    A. Every day
    B. At least two or three times a week
    C. At least once a week
    D. At least once or twice a month
    E. Never

59. How often do you hear your father talk about his religious faith?
    A. Every day
    B. At least two or three times a week
    C. At least once a week
    D. At least once or twice a month
    E. Never

D. How I Feel About Myself

Tell how true each of the following statements is for you. Your options are:

> V. Very true
> S. Somewhat true
> N. Not true

60. On the whole, I like myself.
61. I spend a lot of time thinking about who I am.
62. No one really understands me.
63. I believe life has a purpose.
64. I feel good about my body.

E. My Future

For questions 65 to 70, indicate how likely it is that each statement will come true. Choose one of these answers for each question:

> E. Excellent chance
> G. Good chance
> F. Fair chance
> P. Poor chance
> N. No chance

I believe there is a(n) _____ *that . . .*

65. I will someday be married and have children.
66. I will go to college.

67. I will be very happy 10 years from now.
68. I will be active in church when I am 40.
69. I myself or someone close to me might get AIDS.
70. The world will be destroyed by a nuclear war sometime in the next 10 years.

F. My Friends

71. How many close friends (not relatives) do you have?
    A. None
    B. One or two
    C. Three to five
    D. Six to nine
    E. Ten or more

72. I wish I could be better at making friends.
    A. Strongly agree
    B. Agree
    C. Not sure
    D. Disagree
    E. Strongly disagree

73. I wish I could be better at being a friend to others.
    A. Strongly agree
    B. Agree
    C. Not sure
    D. Disagree
    E. Strongly disagree

74. Some of my best friends belong to this church.
    T. True
    F. False

75. How often do you feel lonely?
    A. Every day
    B. Quite often, but not every day
    C. Once in a while
    D. Never

76. How often do your friends try to get you to do things you know are wrong?
    A. Very often
    B. Often
    C. Sometimes
    D. Once in a while
    E. Never

77. Which of the following choices best describes your parents' feelings toward your friends?
    A. My parents like all of my friends.
    B. My parents like most of my friends, except for one or two.
    C. My parents like about half of my friends, and half they don't.
    D. My parents don't like most of my friends, but one or two are okay.
    E. My parents don't like any of my friends.

G. Where I'd Go for Help

If you were in the following situations, to whom would you most likely turn for help or advice? For each situation, choose one of these answers:

> A. A parent or guardian
> B. A friend my own age
> C. An adult friend or relative
> D. A minister or youth worker
> E. Nobody

78. If I were having trouble in school, I would turn to _____.

79. If I were wondering how to handle my feelings, I would turn to _____.

80. If some of my friends started using alcohol or other drugs, I would turn to _____.

81. If I had questions about sex, I would turn to _____.

82. If I were feeling guilty about something I had done, I would turn to _____.

83. If I were deciding what to do with my life, I would turn to _____.

H. My Christian Faith

84. Overall, how important is religion in your life?
    V. Very important
    S. Somewhat important
    N. Not important

85. Compared to a year ago, would you say your faith is now more important, less important or about the same?
    M. More important
    L. Less important
    S. About the same

86. I am sure God loves me just as I am.
    T. True
    ?. Don't know
    F. False

87. Which of the following statements comes closest to your view of God?
    A. I know for sure that God exists.
    B. I am mostly sure that God exists.
    C. I'm not sure if God exists.
    D. I don't think there is a God.
    E. I am sure there is no such thing as God.

88. Which of the following statements is closest to your view of Jesus?
    A. Jesus is the Son of God who died on the cross and rose again.
    B. Jesus is the Son of God, but I doubt that he actually rose from the dead.
    C. Jesus was a great man who lived long ago, but I don't think he was the Son of God.
    D. Jesus never existed; his life is just a story people made up.

89. My religious beliefs greatly influence how I act at school and with my friends.
    M. Most of the time
    S. Some of the time
    R. Rarely or never

90. I believe God will stop loving me if I do a lot of wrong things.
    T. True
    ?. Not sure
    F. False

What do you think God wants you to do with your life? For each of the following actions, choose one of these responses:

> T. True
> ?. Not sure
> F. False

God wants me . . .

91. To pray.
92. To worship.
93. To read the Bible.
94. To help get rid of hunger, poverty and war.
95. To tell other people about Jesus.
96. To spend time helping other people.

I. What I Do

Please answer the following questions as honestly as you can. Remember, no one will ever find out how you answered.

Choose one of the following answers for questions 97 to 107:

> A. None
> B. Once or twice
> C. Three to five times
> D. Six to nine times
> E. Ten times or more

97. In the past twelve months, how many times have you been to a party where people your age were drinking alcohol?

98. During the past twelve months, how many times have you taken something from a store without paying for it?

99. During the past twelve months, how many times have you cheated on a test at school?

100. During the past twelve months, how many times have you intentionally damaged or destroyed property (for example, broken windows or furniture, put paint on walls or signs, or scratched or dented a car)?

101. During the past twelve months, how many times have you lied to one of your parents?

102. During the past twelve months, how many times have you hit or beat up another kid?

103. During the past twelve months, how many times have you drunk alcohol while you were alone or with friends your own age? (Do not include communion wine.)

104. During the past month, how many times have you drunk alcohol while you were alone or with friends your own age? (Do not include communion wine.)

105. How many times have you used marijuana (grass, pot) or hashish (hash, hash oil) in your lifetime?

106. How many times in the past two weeks have you had five or more drinks in a row? (A "drink" is a glass of wine, a bottle or can of beer, a shot of liquor or a mixed drink.)

107. How many times in your lifetime have you tried cocaine or crack?

108. In the past month, how much time did you spend helping people outside your family with special needs (for example, collecting food for hungry people, mowing lawns for people who can't do it themselves, or spending time with sick or disabled people)? Don't count work for which you were paid.
   A. None
   B. One or two hours
   C. Three to five hours
   D. Six to ten hours
   E. Eleven hours or more

109. How much television do you watch on an average school day? Don't count weekends.
   A. None
   B. One hour or less
   C. About two hours
   D. About three or four hours
   E. Five hours or more

J. School

110. How much time do you usually spend on homework each week?
   A. None
   B. One hour or less
   C. Between one and three hours
   D. Between three and five hours
   E. Between five and ten hours
   F. More than ten hours

111. I enjoy school.
   M. Most of the time
   S. Sometimes
   N. Rarely or never

112. I try to do the best I can at school.
   M. Most of the time
   S. Sometimes
   N. Rarely or never

113. How often, if ever, do you get in trouble at school?
   M. Most of the time
   S. Sometimes
   N. Never

114. During the past four weeks, how many school days have you skipped or "cut"?
   A. None
   B. One day
   C. Two days
   D. Three days or more

K. Right and Wrong

In your opinion, are each of the actions in questions 115 to 120 right or wrong? Here are the possible responses:

   R. Morally right
   ?. Not sure
   W. Morally wrong

115. Sexual intercourse between two unmarried 16-year-olds who love each other.

116. People trying to keep a minority family from moving into a neighborhood.

117. Cheating on a test at school.

118. Lying to one's parents.

119. Sixteen-year-olds drinking a couple of beers at a party.

120. Stealing a shirt from a store.

L. Male-Female Relationships

121. How many times in the past twelve months have you been out on a date (such as going to a party or movie with one person of the opposite sex)?
   A. None
   B. One or two times
   C. Three to five times
   D. Six to nine times
   E. Ten to nineteen times
   F. Twenty times or more

122. In the past twelve months, how many times have you kissed someone about your age who is of the opposite sex?
   A. None
   B. One or two times
   C. Three to five times
   D. Six to nine times
   E. Ten to nineteen times
   F. Twenty times or more

123. Is it difficult for you to talk with other kids of the opposite sex?
   Y. Yes
   N. No

124. Are you in love right now with someone about your age who is of the opposite sex?
   Y. Yes
   N. No

125. Do you like to do things with teenagers of the opposite sex?
   A. Usually
   B. Sometimes
   C. Never

126. How often do you think about sex?
   A. Very often
   B. Sometimes
   C. Never

127. Have you ever had sexual intercourse ("gone all the way" or "made love")?
  A. Never
  B. Yes, one time
  C. Yes, two to five times
  D. Yes, six times or more
  E. I don't know what sexual intercourse is.

M. My Church

128. How many adults in your church do you think know you well?
  A. None
  B. One or two
  C. Three to five
  D. Six to nine
  E. Ten or more

129. How much does your church help you answer important questions about your life?
  V. Very much
  S. Some
  L. A little
  N. Not at all

130. If you had an important question about life, how many adults in your church would you feel comfortable going to for help? Don't count your parents or other relatives.
  A. None
  B. One or two
  C. Three to five
  D. Six to nine
  E. Ten or more

131. How important is church to you?
  A. Very important
  B. Somewhat important
  C. Not important

132. Would you recommend your church to a friend who doesn't belong to another church?
  Y. Yes
  ?. Not sure
  N. No

N. My Feelings About My Church

For questions 133 to 138, circle the number that best describes the main "feeling" you get from your church. For example, if you believe that most people in your church think teenagers are important, but some don't, you might circle a 6 or 7 for question 133.

In my church . . .

133.	Kids are important	9 8 7 6 5 4 3 2 1	Kids aren't important
134.	I have many church friends.	9 8 7 6 5 4 3 2 1	I have no church friends.
135.	I learn a lot.	9 8 7 6 5 4 3 2 1	I don't learn anything.
136.	Questions are invited.	9 8 7 6 5 4 3 2 1	Questions aren't welcome.
137.	It's exciting.	9 8 7 6 5 4 3 2 1	It's boring.
138.	Everyone cares about me.	9 8 7 6 5 4 3 2 1	Nobody cares about me.

O. What I Want From My Church

When you think about what you want from your church, how important are each of the following to you? Your choices are:

> 5. Extremely important
> 4. Important
> 3. Somewhat important
> 2. Slightly important
> 1. Not important

It is _____ to me . . .

139. To learn about the Bible.
140. To learn what it means to be a Christian.
141. To learn what is special about me.
142. To help my religious faith grow.
143. To make good friends.
144. To get to know adults who care about me.
145. To have opportunities to help other people.
146. To learn more about how I can make decisions about what is right and wrong.
147. To learn about sex and sexual values.
148. To learn about alcohol and other drugs, and what my values about them should be.
149. To have lots of fun and good times.
150. To learn what a Christian should do about big issues such as poverty and war.

P. How Well My Church Is Doing

Rate how well your church does in each of the areas listed in questions 151 to 162. Your choices are:

> 5. Excellent
> 4. Good
> 3. Okay
> 2. Fair
> 1. Poor

How well does your church . . .

151. Help you learn about the Bible?
152. Help you learn what it means to be a Christian?
153. Help you learn what's special about you?
154. Help your religious faith grow?
155. Help you make friends?
156. Help you get to know adults who care about you?
157. Help you to help other people?
158. Help you learn about what is right or wrong?
159. Help you learn about sex and sexual values?
160. Help you learn about alcohol and other drugs, and what your values about them should be?
161. Provide lots of fun and good times?
162. Help you learn what a Christian should do about big issues such as poverty and war?

YOUTH SURVEY

Directions

**This survey isn't about what you know.
It's about who you are—
what you think,
what you feel,
what you believe.**

**It's about your school,
your church,
your friends,
your family,
yourself.**

**It's about what is important to you in life—
what you do,
what you worry about,
what you enjoy.**

Be honest in giving your answers. Your name will not be attached to the survey, so no one will know what you write. Your answers will be summarized together with the answers of other young people in your church. All of those answers together will provide important clues to the interests, beliefs, problems and hopes of your church's young people. It's important for youth ministry leaders to have those clues so they can do a better job of planning youth ministry for you and your friends.

Do not begin answering questions until you are instructed to do so. As soon as the survey administrator gives the signal to open this booklet to the first page, you may begin. Mark your answers on the answer sheet, not in this booklet.

For each question, decide which answer fits you best, then *circle the corresponding number or letter on the answer sheet*. Mark only one answer for each question. Do not spend a lot of time trying to decide between two answers; it's usually best to mark your first impression and go right on to the next question. There is no "right" or "wrong" answer to any question—so answer each question honestly.

When you have finished, fold your answer sheet in half and put it into the envelope provided by the survey administrator.

Thanks for helping.
Thanks for being *you*.

General Information

1. I am: **F.** Female
  M. Male

2. My grade in school is:
  7   8   9   10   11   12

A. What I Want in Life

Listed below are things that some people want in life. Read through the complete list without making any marks. Then go back and decide how important each one is to you. Your choices are:

> **V.** Very important
> **S.** Somewhat important
> **N.** Not very important

It is _____ to me . . .

3. To be good in music, drama or art.
4. To have a happy family life.
5. To make my parents proud of me.
6. To make my own decisions.
7. To do things that help people.
8. To feel safe and secure in my neighborhood.
9. To feel good about myself.
10. To be popular at school.
11. To have lots of fun and good times.
12. To understand my feelings.
13. To have lots of money.
14. To have God at the center of my life.
15. To have a world without hunger or poverty.
16. To get a good job when I am older.
17. To have things (such as clothes, records and so on) as nice as other kids have.
18. To do something important with my life.
19. To do well in school.
20. To have a world without war.
21. To be really good at sports.
22. To be different in some way from all the other teenagers I know.
23. To have friends I can count on.
24. To do whatever I want to do, when I want to do it.
25. To be part of a church.
26. To have clothes and hair that look good to other kids.

B. What I Worry About

How much do you worry about each of the following statements? Your choices are:

> **V.** Very much
> **S.** Somewhat
> **N.** Very little or not at all

I worry _____ . . .
27. About how my friends treat me.

28. That I might kill myself.
29. That I might not be able to get a good job when I am older.
30. That someone might force me to do sexual things I don't want to do.
31. About how well other teenagers like me.
32. That I might lose my best friend.
33. That one of my parents will hit me so hard that I will be badly hurt.
34. That I may die soon.
35. That a nuclear bomb might be dropped on our country.
36. About all the drugs and drinking I see around me.
37. That one of my parents might die.
38. About all the people who are hungry and poor in our country.
39. That I might get beaten up at school.
40. About whether my body is growing in a normal way.
41. About how much my mother or father drinks.
42. About how I'm doing in school.
43. About my looks.
44. That my friends might get me in trouble.
45. About all the violence in our country.
46. That my parents might get a divorce.
  (Leave this number blank if your parents are already divorced, or if one of your parents is no longer living.)

C. My Family

For each of the following statements, mark the response that best matches your feelings. Your choices are:

> **A.** Strongly agree
> **B.** Agree
> **C.** Not sure
> **D.** Disagree
> **E.** Strongly disagree

I wish my parents (or guardians) would . . .
47. Give me more freedom.
48. Spend more time with me.
49. Yell at me less often.
50. Talk with me more about their views on important issues such as sex and drugs.
51. Be more interested in the things I care about.
52. Give me more responsibility.
53. Say "I love you" more often.
54. Trust me more.

Mark the appropriate response to the following statements and questions.

55. There is a lot of love in my family.
  A. Very true
  B. Somewhat true
  C. Not true

56. How often does your family do projects *together* to help other people (such as collecting food for the hungry or helping a neighbor)?
  A. At least once a month
  B. Once in a while
  C. Never

57. How often does your family talk together about God, the Bible or other religious things?
  A. Every day
  B. At least two or three times a week
  C. At least once a week
  D. At least once or twice a month
  E. Never

58. How often do you hear your mother talk about her religious faith?
  A. Every day
  B. At least two or three times a week
  C. At least once a week
  D. At least once or twice a month
  E. Never

59. How often do you hear your father talk about his religious faith?
  A. Every day
  B. At least two or three times a week
  C. At least once a week
  D. At least once or twice a month
  E. Never

D. How I Feel About Myself

Tell how true each of the following statements is for you. Your options are:

> **V.** Very true
> **S.** Somewhat true
> **N.** Not true

60. On the whole, I like myself.
61. I spend a lot of time thinking about who I am.
62. No one really understands me.
63. I believe life has a purpose.
64. I feel good about my body.

E. My Future

For questions 65 to 70, indicate how likely it is that each statement will come true. Choose one of these answers for each question:

> **E.** Excellent chance
> **G.** Good chance
> **F.** Fair chance
> **P.** Poor chance
> **N.** No chance

I believe there is a(n) _____ that . . .
65. I will someday be married and have children.
66. I will go to college.

67. I will be very happy 10 years from now.
68. I will be active in church when I am 40.
69. I myself or someone close to me might get AIDS.
70. The world will be destroyed by a nuclear war sometime in the next 10 years.

F. My Friends

71. How many close friends (not relatives) do you have?
  A. None
  B. One or two
  C. Three to five
  D. Six to nine
  E. Ten or more

72. I wish I could be better at making friends.
  A. Strongly agree
  B. Agree
  C. Not sure
  D. Disagree
  E. Strongly disagree

73. I wish I could be better at being a friend to others.
  A. Strongly agree
  B. Agree
  C. Not sure
  D. Disagree
  E. Strongly disagree

74. Some of my best friends belong to this church.
  T. True
  F. False

75. How often do you feel lonely?
  A. Every day
  B. Quite often, but not every day
  C. Once in a while
  D. Never

76. How often do your friends try to get you to do things you know are wrong?
  A. Very often
  B. Often
  C. Sometimes
  D. Once in a while
  E. Never

77. Which of the following choices best describes your parents' feelings toward your friends?
  A. My parents like all of my friends.
  B. My parents like most of my friends, except for one or two.
  C. My parents like about half of my friends, and half they don't.
  D. My parents don't like most of my friends, but one or two are okay.
  E. My parents don't like any of my friends.

G. Where I'd Go for Help

If you were in the following situations, to whom would you most likely turn for help or advice? For each situation, choose one of these answers:

> **A.** A parent or guardian
> **B.** A friend my own age
> **C.** An adult friend or relative
> **D.** A minister or youth worker
> **E.** Nobody

78. If I were having trouble in school, I would turn to _____.

79. If I were wondering how to handle my feelings, I would turn to _____.

80. If some of my friends started using alcohol or other drugs, I would turn to _____.

81. If I had questions about sex, I would turn to _____.

82. If I were feeling guilty about something I had done, I would turn to _____.

83. If I were deciding what to do with my life, I would turn to _____.

H. My Christian Faith

84. Overall, how important is religion in your life?
V. Very important
S. Somewhat important
N. Not important

85. Compared to a year ago, would you say your faith is now more important, less important or about the same?
M. More important
L. Less important
S. About the same

86. I am sure God loves me just as I am.
T. True
?. Don't know
F. False

87. Which of the following statements comes closest to your view of God?
A. I know for sure that God exists.
B. I am mostly sure that God exists.
C. I'm not sure if God exists.
D. I don't think there is a God.
E. I am sure there is no such thing as God.

88. Which of the following statements is closest to your view of Jesus?
A. Jesus is the Son of God who died on the cross and rose again.
B. Jesus is the Son of God, but I doubt that he actually rose from the dead.
C. Jesus was a great man who lived long ago, but I don't think he was the Son of God.
D. Jesus never existed; his life is just a story people made up.

89. My religious beliefs greatly influence how I act at school and with my friends.
M. Most of the time
S. Some of the time
R. Rarely or never

90. I believe God will stop loving me if I do a lot of wrong things.
T. True
?. Not sure
F. False

What do you think God wants you to do with your life? For each of the following actions, choose one of these responses:

> **T.** True
> **?.** Not sure
> **F.** False

God wants me . . .
91. To pray.
92. To worship.
93. To read the Bible.
94. To help get rid of hunger, poverty and war.
95. To tell other people about Jesus.
96. To spend time helping other people.

I. What I Do

Please answer the following questions as honestly as you can. Remember, no one will ever find out how you answered.

Choose one of the following answers for questions 97 to 107:

> **A.** None
> **B.** Once or twice
> **C.** Three to five times
> **D.** Six to nine times
> **E.** Ten times or more

97. In the past twelve months, how many times have you been to a party where people your age were drinking alcohol?

98. During the past twelve months, how many times have you taken something from a store without paying for it?

99. During the past twelve months, how many times have you cheated on a test at school?

100. During the past twelve months, how many times have you intentionally damaged or destroyed property (for example, broken windows or furniture, put paint on walls or signs, or scratched or dented a car)?

101. During the past twelve months, how many times have you lied to one of your parents?

102. During the past twelve months, how many times have you hit or beat up another kid?

103. During the past twelve months, how many times have you drunk alcohol while you were alone or with friends your own age? (Do not include communion wine.)

104. During the past month, how many times have you drunk alcohol while you were alone or with friends your own age? (Do not include communion wine.)

105. How many times have you used marijuana (grass, pot) or hashish (hash, hash oil) in your lifetime?

106. How many times in the past two weeks have you had five or more drinks in a row? (A "drink" is a glass of wine, a bottle or can of beer, a shot of liquor or a mixed drink.)

107. How many times in your lifetime have you tried cocaine or crack?

108. In the past month, how much time did you spend helping people outside your family with special needs (for example, collecting food for hungry people, mowing lawns for people who can't do it themselves, or spending time with sick or disabled people)? Don't count work for which you were paid.
   A. None
   B. One or two hours
   C. Three to five hours
   D. Six to ten hours
   E. Eleven hours or more

109. How much television do you watch on an average school day? Don't count weekends.
   A. None
   B. One hour or less
   C. About two hours
   D. About three or four hours
   E. Five hours or more

J. School

110. How much time do you usually spend on homework each week?
   A. None
   B. One hour or less
   C. Between one and three hours
   D. Between three and five hours
   E. Between five and ten hours
   F. More than ten hours

111. I enjoy school.
   M. Most of the time
   S. Sometimes
   N. Rarely or never

112. I try to do the best I can at school.
   M. Most of the time
   S. Sometimes
   N. Rarely or never

113. How often, if ever, do you get in trouble at school?
   M. Most of the time
   S. Sometimes
   N. Never

114. During the past four weeks, how many school days have you skipped or "cut"?
   A. None
   B. One day
   C. Two days
   D. Three days or more

K. Right and Wrong

In your opinion, are each of the actions in questions 115 to 120 right or wrong? Here are the possible responses:

R. Morally right
?. Not sure
W. Morally wrong

115. Sexual intercourse between two unmarried 16-year-olds who love each other.

116. People trying to keep a minority family from moving into a neighborhood.

117. Cheating on a test at school.

118. Lying to one's parents.

119. Sixteen-year-olds drinking a couple of beers at a party.

120. Stealing a shirt from a store.

L. Male-Female Relationships

121. How many times in the past twelve months have you been out on a date (such as going to a party or movie with one person of the opposite sex)?
   A. None
   B. One or two times
   C. Three to five times
   D. Six to nine times
   E. Ten to nineteen times
   F. Twenty times or more

122. In the past twelve months, how many times have you kissed someone about your age who is of the opposite sex?
   A. None
   B. One or two times
   C. Three to five times
   D. Six to nine times
   E. Ten to nineteen times
   F. Twenty times or more

123. Is it difficult for you to talk with other kids of the opposite sex?
   Y. Yes
   N. No

124. Are you in love right now with someone about your age who is of the opposite sex?
   Y. Yes
   N. No

125. Do you like to do things with teenagers of the opposite sex?
   A. Usually
   B. Sometimes
   C. Never

126. How often do you think about sex?
   A. Very often
   B. Sometimes
   C. Never

127. Have you ever had sexual intercourse ("gone all the way" or "made love")?

A. Never

B. Yes, one time

C. Yes, two to five times

D. Yes, six times or more

E. I don't know what sexual intercourse is.

M. My Church

128. How many adults in your church do you think know you well?

A. None

B. One or two

C. Three to five

D. Six to nine

E. Ten or more

129. How much does your church help you answer important questions about your life?

V. Very much

S. Some

L. A little

N. Not at all

130. If you had an important question about life, how many adults in your church would you feel comfortable going to for help? Don't count your parents or other relatives.

A. None

B. One or two

C. Three to five

D. Six to nine

E. Ten or more

131. How important is church to you?

A. Very important

B. Somewhat important

C. Not important

132. Would you recommend your church to a friend who doesn't belong to another church?

Y. Yes

?. Not sure

N. No

N. My Feelings About My Church

For questions 133 to 138, circle the number that best describes the main "feeling" you get from your church. For example, if you believe that most people in your church think teenagers are important, but some don't, you might circle a 6 or 7 for question 133.

In my church . . .

133.	Kids are important	9 8 7 6 5 4 3 2 1	Kids aren't important
134.	I have many church friends.	9 8 7 6 5 4 3 2 1	I have no church friends.
135.	I learn a lot.	9 8 7 6 5 4 3 2 1	I don't learn anything.
136.	Questions are invited.	9 8 7 6 5 4 3 2 1	Questions aren't welcome.
137.	It's exciting.	9 8 7 6 5 4 3 2 1	It's boring.
138.	Everyone cares about me.	9 8 7 6 5 4 3 2 1	Nobody cares about me.

O. What I Want From My Church

When you think about what you want from your church, how important are each of the following to you? Your choices are:

> 5. Extremely important
> 4. Important
> 3. Somewhat important
> 2. Slightly important
> 1. Not important

It is _____ to me . . .

139. To learn about the Bible.

140. To learn what it means to be a Christian.

141. To learn what is special about me.

142. To help my religious faith grow.

143. To make good friends.

144. To get to know adults who care about me.

145. To have opportunities to help other people.

146. To learn more about how I can make decisions about what is right and wrong.

147. To learn about sex and sexual values.

148. To learn about alcohol and other drugs, and what my values about them should be.

149. To have lots of fun and good times.

150. To learn what a Christian should do about big issues such as poverty and war.

P. How Well My Church Is Doing

Rate how well your church does in each of the areas listed in questions 151 to 162. Your choices are:

> 5. Excellent
> 4. Good
> 3. Okay
> 2. Fair
> 1. Poor

How well does your church . . .

151. Help you learn about the Bible?

152. Help you learn what it means to be a Christian?

153. Help you learn what's special about you?

154. Help your religious faith grow?

155. Help you make friends?

156. Help you get to know adults who care about you?

157. Help you to help other people?

158. Help you learn about what is right or wrong?

159. Help you learn about sex and sexual values?

160. Help you learn about alcohol and other drugs, and what your values about them should be?

161. Provide lots of fun and good times?

162. Help you learn what a Christian should do about big issues such as poverty and war?

YOUTH SURVEY

Directions

**This survey isn't about what you know.
It's about who you are—
what you think,
what you feel,
what you believe.**

**It's about your school,
your church,
your friends,
your family,
yourself.**

**It's about what is important to you in life—
what you do,
what you worry about,
what you enjoy.**

Be honest in giving your answers. Your name will not be attached to the survey, so no one will know what you write. Your answers will be summarized together with the answers of other young people in your church. All of those answers together will provide important clues to the interests, beliefs, problems and hopes of your church's young people. It's important for youth ministry leaders to have those clues so they can do a better job of planning youth ministry for you and your friends.

Do not begin answering questions until you are instructed to do so. As soon as the survey administrator gives the signal to open this booklet to the first page, you may begin. Mark your answers on the answer sheet, not in this booklet.

For each question, decide which answer fits you best, then *circle the corresponding number or letter on the answer sheet*. Mark only one answer for each question. Do not spend a lot of time trying to decide between two answers; it's usually best to mark your first impression and go right on to the next question. There is no "right" or "wrong" answer to any question—so answer each question honestly.

When you have finished, fold your answer sheet in half and put it into the envelope provided by the survey administrator.

Thanks for helping.
Thanks for being *you*.

General Information

1. I am: **F.** Female
    M. Male

2. My grade in school is:
    7 8 9 10 11 12

A. What I Want in Life

Listed below are things that some people want in life. Read through the complete list without making any marks. Then go back and decide how important each one is to you. Your choices are:

> **V.** Very important
> **S.** Somewhat important
> **N.** Not very important

It is _____ to me . . .

3. To be good in music, drama or art.
4. To have a happy family life.
5. To make my parents proud of me.
6. To make my own decisions.
7. To do things that help people.
8. To feel safe and secure in my neighborhood.
9. To feel good about myself.
10. To be popular at school.
11. To have lots of fun and good times.
12. To understand my feelings.
13. To have lots of money.
14. To have God at the center of my life.
15. To have a world without hunger or poverty.
16. To get a good job when I am older.
17. To have things (such as clothes, records and so on) as nice as other kids have.
18. To do something important with my life.
19. To do well in school.
20. To have a world without war.
21. To be really good at sports.
22. To be different in some way from all the other teenagers I know.
23. To have friends I can count on.
24. To do whatever I want to do, when I want to do it.
25. To be part of a church.
26. To have clothes and hair that look good to other kids.

B. What I Worry About

How much do you worry about each of the following statements? Your choices are:

> **V.** Very much
> **S.** Somewhat
> **N.** Very little or not at all

I worry _____ . . .
27. About how my friends treat me.

28. That I might kill myself.
29. That I might not be able to get a good job when I am older.
30. That someone might force me to do sexual things I don't want to do.
31. About how well other teenagers like me.
32. That I might lose my best friend.
33. That one of my parents will hit me so hard that I will be badly hurt.
34. That I may die soon.
35. That a nuclear bomb might be dropped on our country.
36. About all the drugs and drinking I see around me.
37. That one of my parents might die.
38. About all the people who are hungry and poor in our country.
39. That I might get beaten up at school.
40. About whether my body is growing in a normal way.
41. About how much my mother or father drinks.
42. About how I'm doing in school.
43. About my looks.
44. That my friends might get me in trouble.
45. About all the violence in our country.
46. That my parents might get a divorce.
    (Leave this number blank if your parents are already divorced, or if one of your parents is no longer living.)

C. My Family

For each of the following statements, mark the response that best matches your feelings. Your choices are:

> **A.** Strongly agree
> **B.** Agree
> **C.** Not sure
> **D.** Disagree
> **E.** Strongly disagree

I wish my parents (or guardians) would . . .
47. Give me more freedom.
48. Spend more time with me.
49. Yell at me less often.
50. Talk with me more about their views on important issues such as sex and drugs.
51. Be more interested in the things I care about.
52. Give me more responsibility.
53. Say "I love you" more often.
54. Trust me more.

Mark the appropriate response to the following statements and questions.

55. There is a lot of love in my family.
    A. Very true
    B. Somewhat true
    C. Not true

56. How often does your family do projects *together* to help other people (such as collecting food for the hungry or helping a neighbor)?
   A. At least once a month
   B. Once in a while
   C. Never

57. How often does your family talk together about God, the Bible or other religious things?
   A. Every day
   B. At least two or three times a week
   C. At least once a week
   D. At least once or twice a month
   E. Never

58. How often do you hear your mother talk about her religious faith?
   A. Every day
   B. At least two or three times a week
   C. At least once a week
   D. At least once or twice a month
   E. Never

59. How often do you hear your father talk about his religious faith?
   A. Every day
   B. At least two or three times a week
   C. At least once a week
   D. At least once or twice a month
   E. Never

D. How I Feel About Myself

Tell how true each of the following statements is for you. Your options are:

> V. Very true
> S. Somewhat true
> N. Not true

60. On the whole, I like myself.
61. I spend a lot of time thinking about who I am.
62. No one really understands me.
63. I believe life has a purpose.
64. I feel good about my body.

E. My Future

For questions 65 to 70, indicate how likely it is that each statement will come true. Choose one of these answers for each question:

> E. Excellent chance
> G. Good chance
> F. Fair chance
> P. Poor chance
> N. No chance

I believe there is a(n) _____ that . . .
65. I will someday be married and have children.
66. I will go to college.

67. I will be very happy 10 years from now.
68. I will be active in church when I am 40.
69. I myself or someone close to me might get AIDS.
70. The world will be destroyed by a nuclear war sometime in the next 10 years.

F. My Friends

71. How many close friends (not relatives) do you have?
   A. None
   B. One or two
   C. Three to five
   D. Six to nine
   E. Ten or more

72. I wish I could be better at making friends.
   A. Strongly agree
   B. Agree
   C. Not sure
   D. Disagree
   E. Strongly disagree

73. I wish I could be better at being a friend to others.
   A. Strongly agree
   B. Agree
   C. Not sure
   D. Disagree
   E. Strongly disagree

74. Some of my best friends belong to this church.
   T. True
   F. False

75. How often do you feel lonely?
   A. Every day
   B. Quite often, but not every day
   C. Once in a while
   D. Never

76. How often do your friends try to get you to do things you know are wrong?
   A. Very often
   B. Often
   C. Sometimes
   D. Once in a while
   E. Never

77. Which of the following choices best describes your parents' feelings toward your friends?
   A. My parents like all of my friends.
   B. My parents like most of my friends, except for one or two.
   C. My parents like about half of my friends, and half they don't.
   D. My parents don't like most of my friends, but one or two are okay.
   E. My parents don't like any of my friends.

G. Where I'd Go for Help

If you were in the following situations, to whom would you most likely turn for help or advice? For each situation, choose one of these answers:

> A. A parent or guardian
> B. A friend my own age
> C. An adult friend or relative
> D. A minister or youth worker
> E. Nobody

78. If I were having trouble in school, I would turn to _____.

79. If I were wondering how to handle my feelings, I would turn to _____.

80. If some of my friends started using alcohol or other drugs, I would turn to _____.

81. If I had questions about sex, I would turn to _____.

82. If I were feeling guilty about something I had done, I would turn to _____.

83. If I were deciding what to do with my life, I would turn to _____.

H. My Christian Faith

84. Overall, how important is religion in your life?
    V. Very important
    S. Somewhat important
    N. Not important

85. Compared to a year ago, would you say your faith is now more important, less important or about the same?
    M. More important
    L. Less important
    S. About the same

86. I am sure God loves me just as I am.
    T. True
    ?. Don't know
    F. False

87. Which of the following statements comes closest to your view of God?
    A. I know for sure that God exists.
    B. I am mostly sure that God exists.
    C. I'm not sure if God exists.
    D. I don't think there is a God.
    E. I am sure there is no such thing as God.

88. Which of the following statements is closest to your view of Jesus?
    A. Jesus is the Son of God who died on the cross and rose again.
    B. Jesus is the Son of God, but I doubt that he actually rose from the dead.
    C. Jesus was a great man who lived long ago, but I don't think he was the Son of God.
    D. Jesus never existed; his life is just a story people made up.

89. My religious beliefs greatly influence how I act at school and with my friends.
    M. Most of the time
    S. Some of the time
    R. Rarely or never

90. I believe God will stop loving me if I do a lot of wrong things.
    T. True
    ?. Not sure
    F. False

What do you think God wants you to do with your life? For each of the following actions, choose one of these responses:

> T. True
> ?. Not sure
> F. False

God wants me . . .
91. To pray.
92. To worship.
93. To read the Bible.
94. To help get rid of hunger, poverty and war.
95. To tell other people about Jesus.
96. To spend time helping other people.

I. What I Do

Please answer the following questions as honestly as you can. Remember, no one will ever find out how you answered.

Choose one of the following answers for questions 97 to 107:

> A. None
> B. Once or twice
> C. Three to five times
> D. Six to nine times
> E. Ten times or more

97. In the past twelve months, how many times have you been to a party where people your age were drinking alcohol?

98. During the past twelve months, how many times have you taken something from a store without paying for it?

99. During the past twelve months, how many times have you cheated on a test at school?

100. During the past twelve months, how many times have you intentionally damaged or destroyed property (for example, broken windows or furniture, put paint on walls or signs, or scratched or dented a car)?

101. During the past twelve months, how many times have you lied to one of your parents?

102. During the past twelve months, how many times have you hit or beat up another kid?

103. During the past twelve months, how many times have you drunk alcohol while you were alone or with friends your own age? (Do not include communion wine.)

104. During the past month, how many times have you drunk alcohol while you were alone or with friends your own age? (Do not include communion wine.)

105. How many times have you used marijuana (grass, pot) or hashish (hash, hash oil) in your lifetime?

106. How many times in the past two weeks have you had five or more drinks in a row? (A "drink" is a glass of wine, a bottle or can of beer, a shot of liquor or a mixed drink.)

107. How many times in your lifetime have you tried cocaine or crack?

108. In the past month, how much time did you spend helping people outside your family with special needs (for example, collecting food for hungry people, mowing lawns for people who can't do it themselves, or spending time with sick or disabled people)? Don't count work for which you were paid.
   A. None
   B. One or two hours
   C. Three to five hours
   D. Six to ten hours
   E. Eleven hours or more

109. How much television do you watch on an average school day? Don't count weekends.
   A. None
   B. One hour or less
   C. About two hours
   D. About three or four hours
   E. Five hours or more

J. School

110. How much time do you usually spend on homework each week?
   A. None
   B. One hour or less
   C. Between one and three hours
   D. Between three and five hours
   E. Between five and ten hours
   F. More than ten hours

111. I enjoy school.
   M. Most of the time
   S. Sometimes
   N. Rarely or never

112. I try to do the best I can at school.
   M. Most of the time
   S. Sometimes
   N. Rarely or never

113. How often, if ever, do you get in trouble at school?
   M. Most of the time
   S. Sometimes
   N. Never

114. During the past four weeks, how many school days have you skipped or "cut"?
   A. None
   B. One day
   C. Two days
   D. Three days or more

K. Right and Wrong

In your opinion, are each of the actions in questions 115 to 120 right or wrong? Here are the possible responses:

> R. Morally right
> ?. Not sure
> W. Morally wrong

115. Sexual intercourse between two unmarried 16-year-olds who love each other.

116. People trying to keep a minority family from moving into a neighborhood.

117. Cheating on a test at school.

118. Lying to one's parents.

119. Sixteen-year-olds drinking a couple of beers at a party.

120. Stealing a shirt from a store.

L. Male-Female Relationships

121. How many times in the past twelve months have you been out on a date (such as going to a party or movie with one person of the opposite sex)?
   A. None
   B. One or two times
   C. Three to five times
   D. Six to nine times
   E. Ten to nineteen times
   F. Twenty times or more

122. In the past twelve months, how many times have you kissed someone about your age who is of the opposite sex?
   A. None
   B. One or two times
   C. Three to five times
   D. Six to nine times
   E. Ten to nineteen times
   F. Twenty times or more

123. Is it difficult for you to talk with other kids of the opposite sex?
   Y. Yes
   N. No

124. Are you in love right now with someone about your age who is of the opposite sex?
   Y. Yes
   N. No

125. Do you like to do things with teenagers of the opposite sex?
   A. Usually
   B. Sometimes
   C. Never

126. How often do you think about sex?
   A. Very often
   B. Sometimes
   C. Never

127. Have you ever had sexual intercourse ("gone all the way" or "made love")?
A. Never
B. Yes, one time
C. Yes, two to five times
D. Yes, six times or more
E. I don't know what sexual intercourse is.

M. My Church

128. How many adults in your church do you think know you well?
A. None
B. One or two
C. Three to five
D. Six to nine
E. Ten or more

129. How much does your church help you answer important questions about your life?
V. Very much
S. Some
L. A little
N. Not at all

130. If you had an important question about life, how many adults in your church would you feel comfortable going to for help? Don't count your parents or other relatives.
A. None
B. One or two
C. Three to five
D. Six to nine
E. Ten or more

131. How important is church to you?
A. Very important
B. Somewhat important
C. Not important

132. Would you recommend your church to a friend who doesn't belong to another church?
Y. Yes
?. Not sure
N. No

N. My Feelings About My Church

For questions 133 to 138, circle the number that best describes the main "feeling" you get from your church. For example, if you believe that most people in your church think teenagers are important, but some don't, you might circle a 6 or 7 for question 133.

In my church . . .

133. Kids are important	9 8 7 6 5 4 3 2 1	Kids aren't important
134. I have many church friends.	9 8 7 6 5 4 3 2 1	I have no church friends.
135. I learn a lot.	9 8 7 6 5 4 3 2 1	I don't learn anything.
136. Questions are invited.	9 8 7 6 5 4 3 2 1	Questions aren't welcome.
137. It's exciting.	9 8 7 6 5 4 3 2 1	It's boring.
138. Everyone cares about me.	9 8 7 6 5 4 3 2 1	Nobody cares about me.

O. What I Want From My Church

When you think about what you want from your church, how important are each of the following to you? Your choices are:

> 5. Extremely important
> 4. Important
> 3. Somewhat important
> 2. Slightly important
> 1. Not important

It is _____ to me . . .

139. To learn about the Bible.
140. To learn what it means to be a Christian.
141. To learn what is special about me.
142. To help my religious faith grow.
143. To make good friends.
144. To get to know adults who care about me.
145. To have opportunities to help other people.
146. To learn more about how I can make decisions about what is right and wrong.
147. To learn about sex and sexual values.
148. To learn about alcohol and other drugs, and what my values about them should be.
149. To have lots of fun and good times.
150. To learn what a Christian should do about big issues such as poverty and war.

P. How Well My Church Is Doing

Rate how well your church does in each of the areas listed in questions 151 to 162. Your choices are:

> 5. Excellent
> 4. Good
> 3. Okay
> 2. Fair
> 1. Poor

How well does your church . . .

151. Help you learn about the Bible?
152. Help you learn what it means to be a Christian?
153. Help you learn what's special about you?
154. Help your religious faith grow?
155. Help you make friends?
156. Help you get to know adults who care about you?
157. Help you to help other people?
158. Help you learn about what is right or wrong?
159. Help you learn about sex and sexual values?
160. Help you learn about alcohol and other drugs, and what your values about them should be?
161. Provide lots of fun and good times?
162. Help you learn what a Christian should do about big issues such as poverty and war?

YOUTH SURVEY

Directions

This survey isn't about what you know.
It's about who you are—
what you think,
what you feel,
what you believe.

It's about your school,
your church,
your friends,
your family,
yourself.

It's about what is important to you in life—
what you do,
what you worry about,
what you enjoy.

Be honest in giving your answers. Your name will not be attached to the survey, so no one will know what you write. Your answers will be summarized together with the answers of other young people in your church. All of those answers together will provide important clues to the interests, beliefs, problems and hopes of your church's young people. It's important for youth ministry leaders to have those clues so they can do a better job of planning youth ministry for you and your friends.

Do not begin answering questions until you are instructed to do so. As soon as the survey administrator gives the signal to open this booklet to the first page, you may begin. Mark your answers on the answer sheet, not in this booklet.

For each question, decide which answer fits you best, then *circle the corresponding number or letter on the answer sheet*. Mark only one answer for each question. Do not spend a lot of time trying to decide between two answers; it's usually best to mark your first impression and go right on to the next question. There is no "right" or "wrong" answer to any question—so answer each question honestly.

When you have finished, fold your answer sheet in half and put it into the envelope provided by the survey administrator.

Thanks for helping.
Thanks for being *you*.

General Information

1. I am: **F.** Female
                   M. Male

2. My grade in school is:
   7   8   9   10   11   12

A. What I Want in Life

Listed below are things that some people want in life.
Read through the complete list without making any
marks. Then go back and decide how important each
one is to you. Your choices are:

> **V.** Very important
> **S.** Somewhat important
> **N.** Not very important

It is _____ to me . . .

3. To be good in music, drama or art.
4. To have a happy family life.
5. To make my parents proud of me.
6. To make my own decisions.
7. To do things that help people.
8. To feel safe and secure in my neighborhood.
9. To feel good about myself.
10. To be popular at school.
11. To have lots of fun and good times.
12. To understand my feelings.
13. To have lots of money.
14. To have God at the center of my life.
15. To have a world without hunger or poverty.
16. To get a good job when I am older.
17. To have things (such as clothes, records and so on)
      as nice as other kids have.
18. To do something important with my life.
19. To do well in school.
20. To have a world without war.
21. To be really good at sports.
22. To be different in some way from all the other
      teenagers I know.
23. To have friends I can count on.
24. To do whatever I want to do, when I want to do it.
25. To be part of a church.
26. To have clothes and hair that look good to other kids.

B. What I Worry About

How much do you worry about each of the following
statements? Your choices are:

> **V.** Very much
> **S.** Somewhat
> **N.** Very little or not at all

I worry _____ . . .

27. About how my friends treat me.

28. That I might kill myself.
29. That I might not be able to get a good job when I am
      older.
30. That someone might force me to do sexual things I
      don't want to do.
31. About how well other teenagers like me.
32. That I might lose my best friend.
33. That one of my parents will hit me so hard that I will
      be badly hurt.
34. That I may die soon.
35. That a nuclear bomb might be dropped on our
      country.
36. About all the drugs and drinking I see around me.
37. That one of my parents might die.
38. About all the people who are hungry and poor in our
      country.
39. That I might get beaten up at school.
40. About whether my body is growing in a normal way.
41. About how much my mother or father drinks.
42. About how I'm doing in school.
43. About my looks.
44. That my friends might get me in trouble.
45. About all the violence in our country.
46. That my parents might get a divorce.
   **(Leave this number blank if your parents are al-
   ready divorced, or if one of your parents is no
   longer living.)**

C. My Family

For each of the following statements, mark the response
that best matches your feelings. Your choices are:

> **A.** Strongly agree
> **B.** Agree
> **C.** Not sure
> **D.** Disagree
> **E.** Strongly disagree

I wish my parents (or guardians) would . . .

47. Give me more freedom.
48. Spend more time with me.
49. Yell at me less often.
50. Talk with me more about their views on important is-
      sues such as sex and drugs.
51. Be more interested in the things I care about.
52. Give me more responsibility.
53. Say "I love you" more often.
54. Trust me more.

Mark the appropriate response to the following statements and questions.

55. There is a lot of love in my family.
   A. Very true
   B. Somewhat true
   C. Not true

56. How often does your family do projects *together* to help other people (such as collecting food for the hungry or helping a neighbor)?
   A. At least once a month
   B. Once in a while
   C. Never

57. How often does your family talk together about God, the Bible or other religious things?
   A. Every day
   B. At least two or three times a week
   C. At least once a week
   D. At least once or twice a month
   E. Never

58. How often do you hear your mother talk about her religious faith?
   A. Every day
   B. At least two or three times a week
   C. At least once a week
   D. At least once or twice a month
   E. Never

59. How often do you hear your father talk about his religious faith?
   A. Every day
   B. At least two or three times a week
   C. At least once a week
   D. At least once or twice a month
   E. Never

D. How I Feel About Myself

Tell how true each of the following statements is for you. Your options are:

> **V.** Very true
> **S.** Somewhat true
> **N.** Not true

60. On the whole, I like myself.
61. I spend a lot of time thinking about who I am.
62. No one really understands me.
63. I believe life has a purpose.
64. I feel good about my body.

E. My Future

For questions 65 to 70, indicate how likely it is that each statement will come true. Choose one of these answers for each question:

> **E.** Excellent chance
> **G.** Good chance
> **F.** Fair chance
> **P.** Poor chance
> **N.** No chance

I believe there is a(n) _____ that . . .

65. I will someday be married and have children.
66. I will go to college.

67. I will be very happy 10 years from now.
68. I will be active in church when I am 40.
69. I myself or someone close to me might get AIDS.
70. The world will be destroyed by a nuclear war sometime in the next 10 years.

F. My Friends

71. How many close friends (not relatives) do you have?
   A. None
   B. One or two
   C. Three to five
   D. Six to nine
   E. Ten or more

72. I wish I could be better at making friends.
   A. Strongly agree
   B. Agree
   C. Not sure
   D. Disagree
   E. Strongly disagree

73. I wish I could be better at being a friend to others.
   A. Strongly agree
   B. Agree
   C. Not sure
   D. Disagree
   E. Strongly disagree

74. Some of my best friends belong to this church.
   T. True
   F. False

75. How often do you feel lonely?
   A. Every day
   B. Quite often, but not every day
   C. Once in a while
   D. Never

76. How often do your friends try to get you to do things you know are wrong?
   A. Very often
   B. Often
   C. Sometimes
   D. Once in a while
   E. Never

77. Which of the following choices best describes your parents' feelings toward your friends?
   A. My parents like all of my friends.
   B. My parents like most of my friends, except for one or two.
   C. My parents like about half of my friends, and half they don't.
   D. My parents don't like most of my friends, but one or two are okay.
   E. My parents don't like any of my friends.

G. Where I'd Go for Help

If you were in the following situations, to whom would you most likely turn for help or advice? For each situation, choose one of these answers:

> **A.** A parent or guardian
> **B.** A friend my own age
> **C.** An adult friend or relative
> **D.** A minister or youth worker
> **E.** Nobody

78. If I were having trouble in school, I would turn to _____.

79. If I were wondering how to handle my feelings, I would turn to _____.

80. If some of my friends started using alcohol or other drugs, I would turn to _____.

81. If I had questions about sex, I would turn to _____.

82. If I were feeling guilty about something I had done, I would turn to _____.

83. If I were deciding what to do with my life, I would turn to _____.

H. My Christian Faith

84. Overall, how important is religion in your life?
    V. Very important
    S. Somewhat important
    N. Not important

85. Compared to a year ago, would you say your faith is now more important, less important or about the same?
    M. More important
    L. Less important
    S. About the same

86. I am sure God loves me just as I am.
    T. True
    ?. Don't know
    F. False

87. Which of the following statements comes closest to your view of God?
    A. I know for sure that God exists.
    B. I am mostly sure that God exists.
    C. I'm not sure if God exists.
    D. I don't think there is a God.
    E. I am sure there is no such thing as God.

88. Which of the following statements is closest to your view of Jesus?
    A. Jesus is the Son of God who died on the cross and rose again.
    B. Jesus is the Son of God, but I doubt that he actually rose from the dead.
    C. Jesus was a great man who lived long ago, but I don't think he was the Son of God.
    D. Jesus never existed; his life is just a story people made up.

89. My religious beliefs greatly influence how I act at school and with my friends.
    M. Most of the time
    S. Some of the time
    R. Rarely or never

90. I believe God will stop loving me if I do a lot of wrong things.
    T. True
    ?. Not sure
    F. False

What do you think God wants you to do with your life? For each of the following actions, choose one of these responses:

> **T.** True
> **?.** Not sure
> **F.** False

God wants me . . .

91. To pray.

92. To worship.

93. To read the Bible.

94. To help get rid of hunger, poverty and war.

95. To tell other people about Jesus.

96. To spend time helping other people.

I. What I Do

Please answer the following questions as honestly as you can. Remember, no one will ever find out how you answered.

Choose one of the following answers for questions 97 to 107:

> **A.** None
> **B.** Once or twice
> **C.** Three to five times
> **D.** Six to nine times
> **E.** Ten times or more

97. In the past twelve months, how many times have you been to a party where people your age were drinking alcohol?

98. During the past twelve months, how many times have you taken something from a store without paying for it?

99. During the past twelve months, how many times have you cheated on a test at school?

100. During the past twelve months, how many times have you intentionally damaged or destroyed property (for example, broken windows or furniture, put paint on walls or signs, or scratched or dented a car)?

101. During the past twelve months, how many times have you lied to one of your parents?

102. During the past twelve months, how many times have you hit or beat up another kid?

103. During the past twelve months, how many times have you drunk alcohol while you were alone or with friends your own age? (Do not include communion wine.)

104. During the past month, how many times have you drunk alcohol while you were alone or with friends your own age? (Do not include communion wine.)

105. How many times have you used marijuana (grass, pot) or hashish (hash, hash oil) in your lifetime?

106. How many times in the past two weeks have you had five or more drinks in a row? (A "drink" is a glass of wine, a bottle or can of beer, a shot of liquor or a mixed drink.)

107. How many times in your lifetime have you tried cocaine or crack?

108. In the past month, how much time did you spend helping people outside your family with special needs (for example, collecting food for hungry people, mowing lawns for people who can't do it themselves, or spending time with sick or disabled people)? Don't count work for which you were paid.
A. None
B. One or two hours
C. Three to five hours
D. Six to ten hours
E. Eleven hours or more

109. How much television do you watch on an average school day? Don't count weekends.
A. None
B. One hour or less
C. About two hours
D. About three or four hours
E. Five hours or more

J. School

110. How much time do you usually spend on homework each week?
A. None
B. One hour or less
C. Between one and three hours
D. Between three and five hours
E. Between five and ten hours
F. More than ten hours

111. I enjoy school.
M. Most of the time
S. Sometimes
N. Rarely or never

112. I try to do the best I can at school.
M. Most of the time
S. Sometimes
N. Rarely or never

113. How often, if ever, do you get in trouble at school?
M. Most of the time
S. Sometimes
N. Never

114. During the past four weeks, how many school days have you skipped or "cut"?
A. None
B. One day
C. Two days
D. Three days or more

K. Right and Wrong

In your opinion, are each of the actions in questions 115 to 120 right or wrong? Here are the possible responses:

> R. Morally right
> ?. Not sure
> W. Morally wrong

115. Sexual intercourse between two unmarried 16-year-olds who love each other.

116. People trying to keep a minority family from moving into a neighborhood.

117. Cheating on a test at school.

118. Lying to one's parents.

119. Sixteen-year-olds drinking a couple of beers at a party.

120. Stealing a shirt from a store.

L. Male-Female Relationships

121. How many times in the past twelve months have you been out on a date (such as going to a party or movie with one person of the opposite sex)?
A. None
B. One or two times
C. Three to five times
D. Six to nine times
E. Ten to nineteen times
F. Twenty times or more

122. In the past twelve months, how many times have you kissed someone about your age who is of the opposite sex?
A. None
B. One or two times
C. Three to five times
D. Six to nine times
E. Ten to nineteen times
F. Twenty times or more

123. Is it difficult for you to talk with other kids of the opposite sex?
Y. Yes
N. No

124. Are you in love right now with someone about your age who is of the opposite sex?
Y. Yes
N. No

125. Do you like to do things with teenagers of the opposite sex?
A. Usually
B. Sometimes
C. Never

126. How often do you think about sex?
A. Very often
B. Sometimes
C. Never

127. Have you ever had sexual intercourse ("gone all the way" or "made love")?
- **A.** Never
- **B.** Yes, one time
- **C.** Yes, two to five times
- **D.** Yes, six times or more
- **E.** I don't know what sexual intercourse is.

M. My Church

128. How many adults in your church do you think know you well?
- **A.** None
- **B.** One or two
- **C.** Three to five
- **D.** Six to nine
- **E.** Ten or more

129. How much does your church help you answer important questions about your life?
- **V.** Very much
- **S.** Some
- **L.** A little
- **N.** Not at all

130. If you had an important question about life, how many adults in your church would you feel comfortable going to for help? Don't count your parents or other relatives.
- **A.** None
- **B.** One or two
- **C.** Three to five
- **D.** Six to nine
- **E.** Ten or more

131. How important is church to you?
- **A.** Very important
- **B.** Somewhat important
- **C.** Not important

132. Would you recommend your church to a friend who doesn't belong to another church?
- **Y.** Yes
- **?.** Not sure
- **N.** No

N. My Feelings About My Church

For questions 133 to 138, circle the number that best describes the main "feeling" you get from your church. For example, if you believe that most people in your church think teenagers are important, but some don't, you might circle a 6 or 7 for question 133.

In my church . . .

133. Kids are important	9 8 7 6 5 4 3 2 1	Kids aren't important
134. I have many church friends.	9 8 7 6 5 4 3 2 1	I have no church friends.
135. I learn a lot.	9 8 7 6 5 4 3 2 1	I don't learn anything.
136. Questions are invited.	9 8 7 6 5 4 3 2 1	Questions aren't welcome.
137. It's exciting.	9 8 7 6 5 4 3 2 1	It's boring.
138. Everyone cares about me.	9 8 7 6 5 4 3 2 1	Nobody cares about me.

O. What I Want From My Church

When you think about what you want from your church, how important are each of the following to you? Your choices are:

> **5.** Extremely important
> **4.** Important
> **3.** Somewhat important
> **2.** Slightly important
> **1.** Not important

It is _____ to me . . .

139. To learn about the Bible.
140. To learn what it means to be a Christian.
141. To learn what is special about me.
142. To help my religious faith grow.
143. To make good friends.
144. To get to know adults who care about me.
145. To have opportunities to help other people.
146. To learn more about how I can make decisions about what is right and wrong.
147. To learn about sex and sexual values.
148. To learn about alcohol and other drugs, and what my values about them should be.
149. To have lots of fun and good times.
150. To learn what a Christian should do about big issues such as poverty and war.

P. How Well My Church Is Doing

Rate how well your church does in each of the areas listed in questions 151 to 162. Your choices are:

> **5.** Excellent
> **4.** Good
> **3.** Okay
> **2.** Fair
> **1.** Poor

How well does your church . . .

151. Help you learn about the Bible?
152. Help you learn what it means to be a Christian?
153. Help you learn what's special about you?
154. Help your religious faith grow?
155. Help you make friends?
156. Help you get to know adults who care about you?
157. Help you to help other people?
158. Help you learn about what is right or wrong?
159. Help you learn about sex and sexual values?
160. Help you learn about alcohol and other drugs, and what your values about them should be?
161. Provide lots of fun and good times?
162. Help you learn what a Christian should do about big issues such as poverty and war?

YOUTH SURVEY

Directions

**This survey isn't about what you know.
It's about who you are—
what you think,
what you feel,
what you believe.**

**It's about your school,
your church,
your friends,
your family,
yourself.**

**It's about what is important to you in life—
what you do,
what you worry about,
what you enjoy.**

Be honest in giving your answers. Your name will not be attached to the survey, so no one will know what you write. Your answers will be summarized together with the answers of other young people in your church. All of those answers together will provide important clues to the interests, beliefs, problems and hopes of your church's young people. It's important for youth ministry leaders to have those clues so they can do a better job of planning youth ministry for you and your friends.

Do not begin answering questions until you are instructed to do so. As soon as the survey administrator gives the signal to open this booklet to the first page, you may begin. Mark your answers on the answer sheet, not in this booklet.

For each question, decide which answer fits you best, then *circle the corresponding number or letter on the answer sheet*. Mark only one answer for each question. Do not spend a lot of time trying to decide between two answers; it's usually best to mark your first impression and go right on to the next question. There is no "right" or "wrong" answer to any question—so answer each question honestly.

When you have finished, fold your answer sheet in half and put it into the envelope provided by the survey administrator.

Thanks for helping.
Thanks for being *you*.

General Information

1. I am: **F.** Female
            M. Male

2. My grade in school is:
       7   8   9   10   11   12

A. What I Want in Life

Listed below are things that some people want in life. Read through the complete list without making any marks. Then go back and decide how important each one is to you. Your choices are:

> **V.** Very important
> **S.** Somewhat important
> **N.** Not very important

It is _____ *to me . . .*

3. To be good in music, drama or art.
4. To have a happy family life.
5. To make my parents proud of me.
6. To make my own decisions.
7. To do things that help people.
8. To feel safe and secure in my neighborhood.
9. To feel good about myself.
10. To be popular at school.
11. To have lots of fun and good times.
12. To understand my feelings.
13. To have lots of money.
14. To have God at the center of my life.
15. To have a world without hunger or poverty.
16. To get a good job when I am older.
17. To have things (such as clothes, records and so on) as nice as other kids have.
18. To do something important with my life.
19. To do well in school.
20. To have a world without war.
21. To be really good at sports.
22. To be different in some way from all the other teenagers I know.
23. To have friends I can count on.
24. To do whatever I want to do, when I want to do it.
25. To be part of a church.
26. To have clothes and hair that look good to other kids.

B. What I Worry About

How much do you worry about each of the following statements? Your choices are:

> **V.** Very much
> **S.** Somewhat
> **N.** Very little or not at all

I worry _____ *. . .*

27. About how my friends treat me.

28. That I might kill myself.
29. That I might not be able to get a good job when I am older.
30. That someone might force me to do sexual things I don't want to do.
31. About how well other teenagers like me.
32. That I might lose my best friend.
33. That one of my parents will hit me so hard that I will be badly hurt.
34. That I may die soon.
35. That a nuclear bomb might be dropped on our country.
36. About all the drugs and drinking I see around me.
37. That one of my parents might die.
38. About all the people who are hungry and poor in our country.
39. That I might get beaten up at school.
40. About whether my body is growing in a normal way.
41. About how much my mother or father drinks.
42. About how I'm doing in school.
43. About my looks.
44. That my friends might get me in trouble.
45. About all the violence in our country.
46. That my parents might get a divorce.
    (Leave this number blank if your parents are already divorced, or if one of your parents is no longer living.)

C. My Family

For each of the following statements, mark the response that best matches your feelings. Your choices are:

> **A.** Strongly agree
> **B.** Agree
> **C.** Not sure
> **D.** Disagree
> **E.** Strongly disagree

I wish my parents (or guardians) would . . .

47. Give me more freedom.
48. Spend more time with me.
49. Yell at me less often.
50. Talk with me more about their views on important issues such as sex and drugs.
51. Be more interested in the things I care about.
52. Give me more responsibility.
53. Say "I love you" more often.
54. Trust me more.

Mark the appropriate response to the following statements and questions.

55. There is a lot of love in my family.
    A. Very true
    B. Somewhat true
    C. Not true

56. How often does your family do projects *together* to help other people (such as collecting food for the hungry or helping a neighbor)?
- **A.** At least once a month
- **B.** Once in a while
- **C.** Never

57. How often does your family talk together about God, the Bible or other religious things?
- **A.** Every day
- **B.** At least two or three times a week
- **C.** At least once a week
- **D.** At least once or twice a month
- **E.** Never

58. How often do you hear your mother talk about her religious faith?
- **A.** Every day
- **B.** At least two or three times a week
- **C.** At least once a week
- **D.** At least once or twice a month
- **E.** Never

59. How often do you hear your father talk about his religious faith?
- **A.** Every day
- **B.** At least two or three times a week
- **C.** At least once a week
- **D.** At least once or twice a month
- **E.** Never

D. How I Feel About Myself

Tell how true each of the following statements is for you. Your options are:

> **V.** Very true
> **S.** Somewhat true
> **N.** Not true

60. On the whole, I like myself.
61. I spend a lot of time thinking about who I am.
62. No one really understands me.
63. I believe life has a purpose.
64. I feel good about my body.

E. My Future

For questions 65 to 70, indicate how likely it is that each statement will come true. Choose one of these answers for each question:

> **E.** Excellent chance
> **G.** Good chance
> **F.** Fair chance
> **P.** Poor chance
> **N.** No chance

I believe there is a(n) _____ that . . .

65. I will someday be married and have children.
66. I will go to college.

67. I will be very happy 10 years from now.
68. I will be active in church when I am 40.
69. I myself or someone close to me might get AIDS.
70. The world will be destroyed by a nuclear war sometime in the next 10 years.

F. My Friends

71. How many close friends (not relatives) do you have?
- **A.** None
- **B.** One or two
- **C.** Three to five
- **D.** Six to nine
- **E.** Ten or more

72. I wish I could be better at making friends.
- **A.** Strongly agree
- **B.** Agree
- **C.** Not sure
- **D.** Disagree
- **E.** Strongly disagree

73. I wish I could be better at being a friend to others.
- **A.** Strongly agree
- **B.** Agree
- **C.** Not sure
- **D.** Disagree
- **E.** Strongly disagree

74. Some of my best friends belong to this church.
- **T.** True
- **F.** False

75. How often do you feel lonely?
- **A.** Every day
- **B.** Quite often, but not every day
- **C.** Once in a while
- **D.** Never

76. How often do your friends try to get you to do things you know are wrong?
- **A.** Very often
- **B.** Often
- **C.** Sometimes
- **D.** Once in a while
- **E.** Never

77. Which of the following choices best describes your parents' feelings toward your friends?
- **A.** My parents like all of my friends.
- **B.** My parents like most of my friends, except for one or two.
- **C.** My parents like about half of my friends, and half they don't.
- **D.** My parents don't like most of my friends, but one or two are okay.
- **E.** My parents don't like any of my friends.

G. Where I'd Go for Help

If you were in the following situations, to whom would you most likely turn for help or advice? For each situation, choose one of these answers:

> **A.** A parent or guardian
> **B.** A friend my own age
> **C.** An adult friend or relative
> **D.** A minister or youth worker
> **E.** Nobody

78. If I were having trouble in school, I would turn to _____.

79. If I were wondering how to handle my feelings, I would turn to _____.

80. If some of my friends started using alcohol or other drugs, I would turn to _____.

81. If I had questions about sex, I would turn to _____.

82. If I were feeling guilty about something I had done, I would turn to _____.

83. If I were deciding what to do with my life, I would turn to _____.

H. My Christian Faith

84. Overall, how important is religion in your life?
    V. Very important
    S. Somewhat important
    N. Not important

85. Compared to a year ago, would you say your faith is now more important, less important or about the same?
    M. More important
    L. Less important
    S. About the same

86. I am sure God loves me just as I am.
    T. True
    ?. Don't know
    F. False

87. Which of the following statements comes closest to your view of God?
    A. I know for sure that God exists.
    B. I am mostly sure that God exists.
    C. I'm not sure if God exists.
    D. I don't think there is a God.
    E. I am sure there is no such thing as God.

88. Which of the following statements is closest to your view of Jesus?
    A. Jesus is the Son of God who died on the cross and rose again.
    B. Jesus is the Son of God, but I doubt that he actually rose from the dead.
    C. Jesus was a great man who lived long ago, but I don't think he was the Son of God.
    D. Jesus never existed; his life is just a story people made up.

89. My religious beliefs greatly influence how I act at school and with my friends.
    M. Most of the time
    S. Some of the time
    R. Rarely or never

90. I believe God will stop loving me if I do a lot of wrong things.
    T. True
    ?. Not sure
    F. False

What do you think God wants you to do with your life? For each of the following actions, choose one of these responses:

> **T.** True
> **?.** Not sure
> **F.** False

God wants me . . .
91. To pray.
92. To worship.
93. To read the Bible.
94. To help get rid of hunger, poverty and war.
95. To tell other people about Jesus.
96. To spend time helping other people.

I. What I Do

Please answer the following questions as honestly as you can. Remember, no one will ever find out how you answered.

Choose one of the following answers for questions 97 to 107:

> **A.** None
> **B.** Once or twice
> **C.** Three to five times
> **D.** Six to nine times
> **E.** Ten times or more

97. In the past twelve months, how many times have you been to a party where people your age were drinking alcohol?

98. During the past twelve months, how many times have you taken something from a store without paying for it?

99. During the past twelve months, how many times have you cheated on a test at school?

100. During the past twelve months, how many times have you intentionally damaged or destroyed property (for example, broken windows or furniture, put paint on walls or signs, or scratched or dented a car)?

101. During the past twelve months, how many times have you lied to one of your parents?

102. During the past twelve months, how many times have you hit or beat up another kid?

103. During the past twelve months, how many times have you drunk alcohol while you were alone or with friends your own age? (Do not include communion wine.)

104. During the past month, how many times have you drunk alcohol while you were alone or with friends your own age? (Do not include communion wine.)

105. How many times have you used marijuana (grass, pot) or hashish (hash, hash oil) in your lifetime?

106. How many times in the past two weeks have you had five or more drinks in a row? (A "drink" is a glass of wine, a bottle or can of beer, a shot of liquor or a mixed drink.)

107. How many times in your lifetime have you tried cocaine or crack?

108. In the past month, how much time did you spend helping people outside your family with special needs (for example, collecting food for hungry people, mowing lawns for people who can't do it themselves, or spending time with sick or disabled people)? Don't count work for which you were paid.
   A. None
   B. One or two hours
   C. Three to five hours
   D. Six to ten hours
   E. Eleven hours or more

109. How much television do you watch on an average school day? Don't count weekends.
   A. None
   B. One hour or less
   C. About two hours
   D. About three or four hours
   E. Five hours or more

J. School

110. How much time do you usually spend on homework each week?
   A. None
   B. One hour or less
   C. Between one and three hours
   D. Between three and five hours
   E. Between five and ten hours
   F. More than ten hours

111. I enjoy school.
   M. Most of the time
   S. Sometimes
   N. Rarely or never

112. I try to do the best I can at school.
   M. Most of the time
   S. Sometimes
   N. Rarely or never

113. How often, if ever, do you get in trouble at school?
   M. Most of the time
   S. Sometimes
   N. Never

114. During the past four weeks, how many school days have you skipped or "cut"?
   A. None
   B. One day
   C. Two days
   D. Three days or more

K. Right and Wrong

In your opinion, are each of the actions in questions 115 to 120 right or wrong? Here are the possible responses:

   R. Morally right
   ?. Not sure
   W. Morally wrong

115. Sexual intercourse between two unmarried 16-year-olds who love each other.

116. People trying to keep a minority family from moving into a neighborhood.

117. Cheating on a test at school.

118. Lying to one's parents.

119. Sixteen-year-olds drinking a couple of beers at a party.

120. Stealing a shirt from a store.

L. Male-Female Relationships

121. How many times in the past twelve months have you been out on a date (such as going to a party or movie with one person of the opposite sex)?
   A. None
   B. One or two times
   C. Three to five times
   D. Six to nine times
   E. Ten to nineteen times
   F. Twenty times or more

122. In the past twelve months, how many times have you kissed someone about your age who is of the opposite sex?
   A. None
   B. One or two times
   C. Three to five times
   D. Six to nine times
   E. Ten to nineteen times
   F. Twenty times or more

123. Is it difficult for you to talk with other kids of the opposite sex?
   Y. Yes
   N. No

124. Are you in love right now with someone about your age who is of the opposite sex?
   Y. Yes
   N. No

125. Do you like to do things with teenagers of the opposite sex?
   A. Usually
   B. Sometimes
   C. Never

126. How often do you think about sex?
   A. Very often
   B. Sometimes
   C. Never

127. Have you ever had sexual intercourse ("gone all the way" or "made love")?
A. Never
B. Yes, one time
C. Yes, two to five times
D. Yes, six times or more
E. I don't know what sexual intercourse is.

M. My Church

128. How many adults in your church do you think know you well?
A. None
B. One or two
C. Three to five
D. Six to nine
E. Ten or more

129. How much does your church help you answer important questions about your life?
V. Very much
S. Some
L. A little
N. Not at all

130. If you had an important question about life, how many adults in your church would you feel comfortable going to for help? Don't count your parents or other relatives.
A. None
B. One or two
C. Three to five
D. Six to nine
E. Ten or more

131. How important is church to you?
A. Very important
B. Somewhat important
C. Not important

132. Would you recommend your church to a friend who doesn't belong to another church?
Y. Yes
?. Not sure
N. No

N. My Feelings About My Church

For questions 133 to 138, circle the number that best describes the main "feeling" you get from your church. For example, if you believe that most people in your church think teenagers are important, but some don't, you might circle a 6 or 7 for question 133.

In my church . . .

133.	Kids are important	9 8 7 6 5 4 3 2 1	Kids aren't important
134.	I have many church friends.	9 8 7 6 5 4 3 2 1	I have no church friends.
135.	I learn a lot.	9 8 7 6 5 4 3 2 1	I don't learn anything.
136.	Questions are invited.	9 8 7 6 5 4 3 2 1	Questions aren't welcome.
137.	It's exciting.	9 8 7 6 5 4 3 2 1	It's boring.
138.	Everyone cares about me.	9 8 7 6 5 4 3 2 1	Nobody cares about me.

O. What I Want From My Church

When you think about what you want from your church, how important are each of the following to you? Your choices are:

> 5. Extremely important
> 4. Important
> 3. Somewhat important
> 2. Slightly important
> 1. Not important

It is _____ to me . . .

139. To learn about the Bible.
140. To learn what it means to be a Christian.
141. To learn what is special about me.
142. To help my religious faith grow.
143. To make good friends.
144. To get to know adults who care about me.
145. To have opportunities to help other people.
146. To learn more about how I can make decisions about what is right and wrong.
147. To learn about sex and sexual values.
148. To learn about alcohol and other drugs, and what my values about them should be.
149. To have lots of fun and good times.
150. To learn what a Christian should do about big issues such as poverty and war.

P. How Well My Church Is Doing

Rate how well your church does in each of the areas listed in questions 151 to 162. Your choices are:

> 5. Excellent
> 4. Good
> 3. Okay
> 2. Fair
> 1. Poor

How well does your church . . .

151. Help you learn about the Bible?
152. Help you learn what it means to be a Christian?
153. Help you learn what's special about you?
154. Help your religious faith grow?
155. Help you make friends?
156. Help you get to know adults who care about you?
157. Help you to help other people?
158. Help you learn about what is right or wrong?
159. Help you learn about sex and sexual values?
160. Help you learn about alcohol and other drugs, and what your values about them should be?
161. Provide lots of fun and good times?
162. Help you learn what a Christian should do about big issues such as poverty and war?

YOUTH SURVEY

Directions

**This survey isn't about what you know.
It's about who you are—
what you think,
what you feel,
what you believe.**

**It's about your school,
your church,
your friends,
your family,
yourself.**

**It's about what is important to you in life—
what you do,
what you worry about,
what you enjoy.**

Be honest in giving your answers. Your name will not be attached to the survey, so no one will know what you write. Your answers will be summarized together with the answers of other young people in your church. All of those answers together will provide important clues to the interests, beliefs, problems and hopes of your church's young people. It's important for youth ministry leaders to have those clues so they can do a better job of planning youth ministry for you and your friends.

Do not begin answering questions until you are instructed to do so. As soon as the survey administrator gives the signal to open this booklet to the first page, you may begin. Mark your answers on the answer sheet, not in this booklet.

For each question, decide which answer fits you best, then *circle the corresponding number or letter on the answer sheet*. Mark only one answer for each question. Do not spend a lot of time trying to decide between two answers; it's usually best to mark your first impression and go right on to the next question. There is no "right" or "wrong" answer to any question—so answer each question honestly.

When you have finished, fold your answer sheet in half and put it into the envelope provided by the survey administrator.

Thanks for helping.
Thanks for being *you*.

General Information

1. I am: **F.** Female
              M. Male
2. My grade in school is:
             7   8   9   10   11   12

A. What I Want in Life

Listed below are things that some people want in life. Read through the complete list without making any marks. Then go back and decide how important each one is to you. Your choices are:

> **V.** Very important
> **S.** Somewhat important
> **N.** Not very important

It is _____ to me . . .

3. To be good in music, drama or art.
4. To have a happy family life.
5. To make my parents proud of me.
6. To make my own decisions.
7. To do things that help people.
8. To feel safe and secure in my neighborhood.
9. To feel good about myself.
10. To be popular at school.
11. To have lots of fun and good times.
12. To understand my feelings.
13. To have lots of money.
14. To have God at the center of my life.
15. To have a world without hunger or poverty.
16. To get a good job when I am older.
17. To have things (such as clothes, records and so on) as nice as other kids have.
18. To do something important with my life.
19. To do well in school.
20. To have a world without war.
21. To be really good at sports.
22. To be different in some way from all the other teenagers I know.
23. To have friends I can count on.
24. To do whatever I want to do, when I want to do it.
25. To be part of a church.
26. To have clothes and hair that look good to other kids.

B. What I Worry About

How much do you worry about each of the following statements? Your choices are:

> **V.** Very much
> **S.** Somewhat
> **N.** Very little or not at all

I worry _____ . . .

27. About how my friends treat me.
28. That I might kill myself.
29. That I might not be able to get a good job when I am older.
30. That someone might force me to do sexual things I don't want to do.
31. About how well other teenagers like me.
32. That I might lose my best friend.
33. That one of my parents will hit me so hard that I will be badly hurt.
34. That I may die soon.
35. That a nuclear bomb might be dropped on our country.
36. About all the drugs and drinking I see around me.
37. That one of my parents might die.
38. About all the people who are hungry and poor in our country.
39. That I might get beaten up at school.
40. About whether my body is growing in a normal way.
41. About how much my mother or father drinks.
42. About how I'm doing in school.
43. About my looks.
44. That my friends might get me in trouble.
45. About all the violence in our country.
46. That my parents might get a divorce.
    (Leave this number blank if your parents are already divorced, or if one of your parents is no longer living.)

C. My Family

For each of the following statements, mark the response that best matches your feelings. Your choices are:

> **A.** Strongly agree
> **B.** Agree
> **C.** Not sure
> **D.** Disagree
> **E.** Strongly disagree

I wish my parents (or guardians) would . . .

47. Give me more freedom.
48. Spend more time with me.
49. Yell at me less often.
50. Talk with me more about their views on important issues such as sex and drugs.
51. Be more interested in the things I care about.
52. Give me more responsibility.
53. Say "I love you" more often.
54. Trust me more.

Mark the appropriate response to the following statements and questions.

55. There is a lot of love in my family.
    A. Very true
    B. Somewhat true
    C. Not true

56. How often does your family do projects *together* to help other people (such as collecting food for the hungry or helping a neighbor)?
   A. At least once a month
   B. Once in a while
   C. Never

57. How often does your family talk together about God, the Bible or other religious things?
   A. Every day
   B. At least two or three times a week
   C. At least once a week
   D. At least once or twice a month
   E. Never

58. How often do you hear your mother talk about her religious faith?
   A. Every day
   B. At least two or three times a week
   C. At least once a week
   D. At least once or twice a month
   E. Never

59. How often do you hear your father talk about his religious faith?
   A. Every day
   B. At least two or three times a week
   C. At least once a week
   D. At least once or twice a month
   E. Never

D. How I Feel About Myself

Tell how true each of the following statements is for you. Your options are:

> **V.** Very true
> **S.** Somewhat true
> **N.** Not true

60. On the whole, I like myself.
61. I spend a lot of time thinking about who I am.
62. No one really understands me.
63. I believe life has a purpose.
64. I feel good about my body.

E. My Future

For questions 65 to 70, indicate how likely it is that each statement will come true. Choose one of these answers for each question:

> **E.** Excellent chance
> **G.** Good chance
> **F.** Fair chance
> **P.** Poor chance
> **N.** No chance

I believe there is a(n) _____ that . . .

65. I will someday be married and have children.
66. I will go to college.

67. I will be very happy 10 years from now.
68. I will be active in church when I am 40.
69. I myself or someone close to me might get AIDS.
70. The world will be destroyed by a nuclear war sometime in the next 10 years.

F. My Friends

71. How many close friends (not relatives) do you have?
   A. None
   B. One or two
   C. Three to five
   D. Six to nine
   E. Ten or more

72. I wish I could be better at making friends.
   A. Strongly agree
   B. Agree
   C. Not sure
   D. Disagree
   E. Strongly disagree

73. I wish I could be better at being a friend to others.
   A. Strongly agree
   B. Agree
   C. Not sure
   D. Disagree
   E. Strongly disagree

74. Some of my best friends belong to this church.
   T. True
   F. False

75. How often do you feel lonely?
   A. Every day
   B. Quite often, but not every day
   C. Once in a while
   D. Never

76. How often do your friends try to get you to do things you know are wrong?
   A. Very often
   B. Often
   C. Sometimes
   D. Once in a while
   E. Never

77. Which of the following choices best describes your parents' feelings toward your friends?
   A. My parents like all of my friends.
   B. My parents like most of my friends, except for one or two.
   C. My parents like about half of my friends, and half they don't.
   D. My parents don't like most of my friends, but one or two are okay.
   E. My parents don't like any of my friends.

G. Where I'd Go for Help

If you were in the following situations, to whom would you most likely turn for help or advice? For each situation, choose one of these answers:

> **A.** A parent or guardian
> **B.** A friend my own age
> **C.** An adult friend or relative
> **D.** A minister or youth worker
> **E.** Nobody

78. If I were having trouble in school, I would turn to _____.

79. If I were wondering how to handle my feelings, I would turn to _____.

80. If some of my friends started using alcohol or other drugs, I would turn to _____.

81. If I had questions about sex, I would turn to _____.

82. If I were feeling guilty about something I had done, I would turn to _____.

83. If I were deciding what to do with my life, I would turn to _____.

H. My Christian Faith

84. Overall, how important is religion in your life?
    V. Very important
    S. Somewhat important
    N. Not important

85. Compared to a year ago, would you say your faith is now more important, less important or about the same?
    M. More important
    L. Less important
    S. About the same

86. I am sure God loves me just as I am.
    T. True
    ?. Don't know
    F. False

87. Which of the following statements comes closest to your view of God?
    A. I know for sure that God exists.
    B. I am mostly sure that God exists.
    C. I'm not sure if God exists.
    D. I don't think there is a God.
    E. I am sure there is no such thing as God.

88. Which of the following statements is closest to your view of Jesus?
    A. Jesus is the Son of God who died on the cross and rose again.
    B. Jesus is the Son of God, but I doubt that he actually rose from the dead.
    C. Jesus was a great man who lived long ago, but I don't think he was the Son of God.
    D. Jesus never existed; his life is just a story people made up.

89. My religious beliefs greatly influence how I act at school and with my friends.
    M. Most of the time
    S. Some of the time
    R. Rarely or never

90. I believe God will stop loving me if I do a lot of wrong things.
    T. True
    ?. Not sure
    F. False

What do you think God wants you to do with your life? For each of the following actions, choose one of these responses:

> **T.** True
> **?.** Not sure
> **F.** False

God wants me . . .

91. To pray.
92. To worship.
93. To read the Bible.
94. To help get rid of hunger, poverty and war.
95. To tell other people about Jesus.
96. To spend time helping other people.

I. What I Do

Please answer the following questions as honestly as you can. Remember, no one will ever find out how you answered.

Choose one of the following answers for questions 97 to 107:

> **A.** None
> **B.** Once or twice
> **C.** Three to five times
> **D.** Six to nine times
> **E.** Ten times or more

97. In the past twelve months, how many times have you been to a party where people your age were drinking alcohol?

98. During the past twelve months, how many times have you taken something from a store without paying for it?

99. During the past twelve months, how many times have you cheated on a test at school?

100. During the past twelve months, how many times have you intentionally damaged or destroyed property (for example, broken windows or furniture, put paint on walls or signs, or scratched or dented a car)?

101. During the past twelve months, how many times have you lied to one of your parents?

102. During the past twelve months, how many times have you hit or beat up another kid?

103. During the past twelve months, how many times have you drunk alcohol while you were alone or with friends your own age? (Do not include communion wine.)

104. During the past month, how many times have you drunk alcohol while you were alone or with friends your own age? (Do not include communion wine.)

105. How many times have you used marijuana (grass, pot) or hashish (hash, hash oil) in your lifetime?

106. How many times in the past two weeks have you had five or more drinks in a row? (A "drink" is a glass of wine, a bottle or can of beer, a shot of liquor or a mixed drink.)

107. How many times in your lifetime have you tried cocaine or crack?

108. In the past month, how much time did you spend helping people outside your family with special needs (for example, collecting food for hungry people, mowing lawns for people who can't do it themselves, or spending time with sick or disabled people)? Don't count work for which you were paid.
   A. None
   B. One or two hours
   C. Three to five hours
   D. Six to ten hours
   E. Eleven hours or more

109. How much television do you watch on an average school day? Don't count weekends.
   A. None
   B. One hour or less
   C. About two hours
   D. About three or four hours
   E. Five hours or more

J. School

110. How much time do you usually spend on homework each week?
   A. None
   B. One hour or less
   C. Between one and three hours
   D. Between three and five hours
   E. Between five and ten hours
   F. More than ten hours

111. I enjoy school.
   M. Most of the time
   S. Sometimes
   N. Rarely or never

112. I try to do the best I can at school.
   M. Most of the time
   S. Sometimes
   N. Rarely or never

113. How often, if ever, do you get in trouble at school?
   M. Most of the time
   S. Sometimes
   N. Never

114. During the past four weeks, how many school days have you skipped or "cut"?
   A. None
   B. One day
   C. Two days
   D. Three days or more

K. Right and Wrong

In your opinion, are each of the actions in questions 115 to 120 right or wrong? Here are the possible responses:

> R. Morally right
> ?. Not sure
> W. Morally wrong

115. Sexual intercourse between two unmarried 16-year-olds who love each other.

116. People trying to keep a minority family from moving into a neighborhood.

117. Cheating on a test at school.

118. Lying to one's parents.

119. Sixteen-year-olds drinking a couple of beers at a party.

120. Stealing a shirt from a store.

L. Male-Female Relationships

121. How many times in the past twelve months have you been out on a date (such as going to a party or movie with one person of the opposite sex)?
   A. None
   B. One or two times
   C. Three to five times
   D. Six to nine times
   E. Ten to nineteen times
   F. Twenty times or more

122. In the past twelve months, how many times have you kissed someone about your age who is of the opposite sex?
   A. None
   B. One or two times
   C. Three to five times
   D. Six to nine times
   E. Ten to nineteen times
   F. Twenty times or more

123. Is it difficult for you to talk with other kids of the opposite sex?
   Y. Yes
   N. No

124. Are you in love right now with someone about your age who is of the opposite sex?
   Y. Yes
   N. No

125. Do you like to do things with teenagers of the opposite sex?
   A. Usually
   B. Sometimes
   C. Never

126. How often do you think about sex?
   A. Very often
   B. Sometimes
   C. Never

127. Have you ever had sexual intercourse ("gone all the way" or "made love")?
 A. Never
 B. Yes, one time
 C. Yes, two to five times
 D. Yes, six times or more
 E. I don't know what sexual intercourse is.

M. My Church

128. How many adults in your church do you think know you well?
 A. None
 B. One or two
 C. Three to five
 D. Six to nine
 E. Ten or more

129. How much does your church help you answer important questions about your life?
 V. Very much
 S. Some
 L. A little
 N. Not at all

130. If you had an important question about life, how many adults in your church would you feel comfortable going to for help? Don't count your parents or other relatives.
 A. None
 B. One or two
 C. Three to five
 D. Six to nine
 E. Ten or more

131. How important is church to you?
 A. Very important
 B. Somewhat important
 C. Not important

132. Would you recommend your church to a friend who doesn't belong to another church?
 Y. Yes
 ?. Not sure
 N. No

N. My Feelings About My Church

For questions 133 to 138, circle the number that best describes the main "feeling" you get from your church. For example, if you believe that most people in your church think teenagers are important, but some don't, you might circle a 6 or 7 for question 133.

In my church . . .

133.	Kids are important	9 8 7 6 5 4 3 2 1	Kids aren't important
134.	I have many church friends.	9 8 7 6 5 4 3 2 1	I have no church friends.
135.	I learn a lot.	9 8 7 6 5 4 3 2 1	I don't learn anything.
136.	Questions are invited.	9 8 7 6 5 4 3 2 1	Questions aren't welcome.
137.	It's exciting.	9 8 7 6 5 4 3 2 1	It's boring.
138.	Everyone cares about me.	9 8 7 6 5 4 3 2 1	Nobody cares about me.

O. What I Want From My Church

When you think about what you want from your church, how important are each of the following to you? Your choices are:

> **5.** Extremely important
> **4.** Important
> **3.** Somewhat important
> **2.** Slightly important
> **1.** Not important

It is _____ to me . . .
139. To learn about the Bible.
140. To learn what it means to be a Christian.
141. To learn what is special about me.
142. To help my religious faith grow.
143. To make good friends.
144. To get to know adults who care about me.
145. To have opportunities to help other people.
146. To learn more about how I can make decisions about what is right and wrong.
147. To learn about sex and sexual values.
148. To learn about alcohol and other drugs, and what my values about them should be.
149. To have lots of fun and good times.
150. To learn what a Christian should do about big issues such as poverty and war.

P. How Well My Church Is Doing

Rate how well your church does in each of the areas listed in questions 151 to 162. Your choices are:

> **5.** Excellent
> **4.** Good
> **3.** Okay
> **2.** Fair
> **1.** Poor

How well does your church . . .
151. Help you learn about the Bible?
152. Help you learn what it means to be a Christian?
153. Help you learn what's special about you?
154. Help your religious faith grow?
155. Help you make friends?
156. Help you get to know adults who care about you?
157. Help you to help other people?
158. Help you learn about what is right or wrong?
159. Help you learn about sex and sexual values?
160. Help you learn about alcohol and other drugs, and what your values about them should be?
161. Provide lots of fun and good times?
162. Help you learn what a Christian should do about big issues such as poverty and war?

Determining Needs in Your Youth Ministry

YOUTH SURVEY

Directions

**This survey isn't about what you know.
It's about who you are—
what you think,
what you feel,
what you believe.**

**It's about your school,
your church,
your friends,
your family,
yourself.**

**It's about what is important to you in life—
what you do,
what you worry about,
what you enjoy.**

Be honest in giving your answers. Your name will not be attached to the survey, so no one will know what you write. Your answers will be summarized together with the answers of other young people in your church. All of those answers together will provide important clues to the interests, beliefs, problems and hopes of your church's young people. It's important for youth ministry leaders to have those clues so they can do a better job of planning youth ministry for you and your friends.

Do not begin answering questions until you are instructed to do so. As soon as the survey administrator gives the signal to open this booklet to the first page, you may begin. Mark your answers on the answer sheet, not in this booklet.

For each question, decide which answer fits you best, then *circle the corresponding number or letter on the answer sheet*. Mark only one answer for each question. Do not spend a lot of time trying to decide between two answers; it's usually best to mark your first impression and go right on to the next question. There is no "right" or "wrong" answer to any question—so answer each question honestly.

When you have finished, fold your answer sheet in half and put it into the envelope provided by the survey administrator.

Thanks for helping.
Thanks for being *you*.

General Information

1. I am: **F.** Female
           M. Male
2. My grade in school is:
   7   8   9   10   11   12

A. What I Want in Life

Listed below are things that some people want in life. Read through the complete list without making any marks. Then go back and decide how important each one is to you. Your choices are:

> **V.** Very important
> **S.** Somewhat important
> **N.** Not very important

It is _____ to me . . .

3. To be good in music, drama or art.
4. To have a happy family life.
5. To make my parents proud of me.
6. To make my own decisions.
7. To do things that help people.
8. To feel safe and secure in my neighborhood.
9. To feel good about myself.
10. To be popular at school.
11. To have lots of fun and good times.
12. To understand my feelings.
13. To have lots of money.
14. To have God at the center of my life.
15. To have a world without hunger or poverty.
16. To get a good job when I am older.
17. To have things (such as clothes, records and so on) as nice as other kids have.
18. To do something important with my life.
19. To do well in school.
20. To have a world without war.
21. To be really good at sports.
22. To be different in some way from all the other teenagers I know.
23. To have friends I can count on.
24. To do whatever I want to do, when I want to do it.
25. To be part of a church.
26. To have clothes and hair that look good to other kids.

B. What I Worry About

How much do you worry about each of the following statements? Your choices are:

> **V.** Very much
> **S.** Somewhat
> **N.** Very little or not at all

I worry _____ . . .

27. About how my friends treat me.
28. That I might kill myself.
29. That I might not be able to get a good job when I am older.
30. That someone might force me to do sexual things I don't want to do.
31. About how well other teenagers like me.
32. That I might lose my best friend.
33. That one of my parents will hit me so hard that I will be badly hurt.
34. That I may die soon.
35. That a nuclear bomb might be dropped on our country.
36. About all the drugs and drinking I see around me.
37. That one of my parents might die.
38. About all the people who are hungry and poor in our country.
39. That I might get beaten up at school.
40. About whether my body is growing in a normal way.
41. About how much my mother or father drinks.
42. About how I'm doing in school.
43. About my looks.
44. That my friends might get me in trouble.
45. About all the violence in our country.
46. That my parents might get a divorce.
   (Leave this number blank if your parents are already divorced, or if one of your parents is no longer living.)

C. My Family

For each of the following statements, mark the response that best matches your feelings. Your choices are:

> **A.** Strongly agree
> **B.** Agree
> **C.** Not sure
> **D.** Disagree
> **E.** Strongly disagree

I wish my parents (or guardians) would . . .

47. Give me more freedom.
48. Spend more time with me.
49. Yell at me less often.
50. Talk with me more about their views on important issues such as sex and drugs.
51. Be more interested in the things I care about.
52. Give me more responsibility.
53. Say "I love you" more often.
54. Trust me more.

Mark the appropriate response to the following statements and questions.

55. There is a lot of love in my family.
   A. Very true
   B. Somewhat true
   C. Not true

56. How often does your family do projects *together* to help other people (such as collecting food for the hungry or helping a neighbor)?
   A. At least once a month
   B. Once in a while
   C. Never

57. How often does your family talk together about God, the Bible or other religious things?
   A. Every day
   B. At least two or three times a week
   C. At least once a week
   D. At least once or twice a month
   E. Never

58. How often do you hear your mother talk about her religious faith?
   A. Every day
   B. At least two or three times a week
   C. At least once a week
   D. At least once or twice a month
   E. Never

59. How often do you hear your father talk about his religious faith?
   A. Every day
   B. At least two or three times a week
   C. At least once a week
   D. At least once or twice a month
   E. Never

D. How I Feel About Myself

Tell how true each of the following statements is for you. Your options are:

> V. Very true
> S. Somewhat true
> N. Not true

60. On the whole, I like myself.
61. I spend a lot of time thinking about who I am.
62. No one really understands me.
63. I believe life has a purpose.
64. I feel good about my body.

E. My Future

For questions 65 to 70, indicate how likely it is that each statement will come true. Choose one of these answers for each question:

> E. Excellent chance
> G. Good chance
> F. Fair chance
> P. Poor chance
> N. No chance

I believe there is a(n) _____ *that . . .*

65. I will someday be married and have children.
66. I will go to college.

67. I will be very happy 10 years from now.
68. I will be active in church when I am 40.
69. I myself or someone close to me might get AIDS.
70. The world will be destroyed by a nuclear war sometime in the next 10 years.

F. My Friends

71. How many close friends (not relatives) do you have?
   A. None
   B. One or two
   C. Three to five
   D. Six to nine
   E. Ten or more

72. I wish I could be better at making friends.
   A. Strongly agree
   B. Agree
   C. Not sure
   D. Disagree
   E. Strongly disagree

73. I wish I could be better at being a friend to others.
   A. Strongly agree
   B. Agree
   C. Not sure
   D. Disagree
   E. Strongly disagree

74. Some of my best friends belong to this church.
   T. True
   F. False

75. How often do you feel lonely?
   A. Every day
   B. Quite often, but not every day
   C. Once in a while
   D. Never

76. How often do your friends try to get you to do things you know are wrong?
   A. Very often
   B. Often
   C. Sometimes
   D. Once in a while
   E. Never

77. Which of the following choices best describes your parents' feelings toward your friends?
   A. My parents like all of my friends.
   B. My parents like most of my friends, except for one or two.
   C. My parents like about half of my friends, and half they don't.
   D. My parents don't like most of my friends, but one or two are okay.
   E. My parents don't like any of my friends.

G. Where I'd Go for Help

If you were in the following situations, to whom would you most likely turn for help or advice? For each situation, choose one of these answers:

> A. A parent or guardian
> B. A friend my own age
> C. An adult friend or relative
> D. A minister or youth worker
> E. Nobody

78. If I were having trouble in school, I would turn to _____.

79. If I were wondering how to handle my feelings, I would turn to _____.

80. If some of my friends started using alcohol or other drugs, I would turn to _____.

81. If I had questions about sex, I would turn to _____.

82. If I were feeling guilty about something I had done, I would turn to _____.

83. If I were deciding what to do with my life, I would turn to _____.

H. My Christian Faith

84. Overall, how important is religion in your life?
    V. Very important
    S. Somewhat important
    N. Not important

85. Compared to a year ago, would you say your faith is now more important, less important or about the same?
    M. More important
    L. Less important
    S. About the same

86. I am sure God loves me just as I am.
    T. True
    ?. Don't know
    F. False

87. Which of the following statements comes closest to your view of God?
    A. I know for sure that God exists.
    B. I am mostly sure that God exists.
    C. I'm not sure if God exists.
    D. I don't think there is a God.
    E. I am sure there is no such thing as God.

88. Which of the following statements is closest to your view of Jesus?
    A. Jesus is the Son of God who died on the cross and rose again.
    B. Jesus is the Son of God, but I doubt that he actually rose from the dead.
    C. Jesus was a great man who lived long ago, but I don't think he was the Son of God.
    D. Jesus never existed; his life is just a story people made up.

89. My religious beliefs greatly influence how I act at school and with my friends.
    M. Most of the time
    S. Some of the time
    R. Rarely or never

90. I believe God will stop loving me if I do a lot of wrong things.
    T. True
    ?. Not sure
    F. False

What do you think God wants you to do with your life? For each of the following actions, choose one of these responses:

> T. True
> ?. Not sure
> F. False

God wants me . . .

91. To pray.

92. To worship.

93. To read the Bible.

94. To help get rid of hunger, poverty and war.

95. To tell other people about Jesus.

96. To spend time helping other people.

I. What I Do

Please answer the following questions as honestly as you can. Remember, no one will ever find out how you answered.

Choose one of the following answers for questions 97 to 107:

> A. None
> B. Once or twice
> C. Three to five times
> D. Six to nine times
> E. Ten times or more

97. In the past twelve months, how many times have you been to a party where people your age were drinking alcohol?

98. During the past twelve months, how many times have you taken something from a store without paying for it?

99. During the past twelve months, how many times have you cheated on a test at school?

100. During the past twelve months, how many times have you intentionally damaged or destroyed property (for example, broken windows or furniture, put paint on walls or signs, or scratched or dented a car)?

101. During the past twelve months, how many times have you lied to one of your parents?

102. During the past twelve months, how many times have you hit or beat up another kid?

103. During the past twelve months, how many times have you drunk alcohol while you were alone or with friends your own age? (Do not include communion wine.)

104. During the past month, how many times have you drunk alcohol while you were alone or with friends your own age? (Do not include communion wine.)

105. How many times have you used marijuana (grass, pot) or hashish (hash, hash oil) in your lifetime?

106. How many times in the past two weeks have you had five or more drinks in a row? (A "drink" is a glass of wine, a bottle or can of beer, a shot of liquor or a mixed drink.)

107. How many times in your lifetime have you tried cocaine or crack?

108. In the past month, how much time did you spend helping people outside your family with special needs (for example, collecting food for hungry people, mowing lawns for people who can't do it themselves, or spending time with sick or disabled people)? Don't count work for which you were paid.
   A. None
   B. One or two hours
   C. Three to five hours
   D. Six to ten hours
   E. Eleven hours or more

109. How much television do you watch on an average school day? Don't count weekends.
   A. None
   B. One hour or less
   C. About two hours
   D. About three or four hours
   E. Five hours or more

J. School

110. How much time do you usually spend on homework each week?
   A. None
   B. One hour or less
   C. Between one and three hours
   D. Between three and five hours
   E. Between five and ten hours
   F. More than ten hours

111. I enjoy school.
   M. Most of the time
   S. Sometimes
   N. Rarely or never

112. I try to do the best I can at school.
   M. Most of the time
   S. Sometimes
   N. Rarely or never

113. How often, if ever, do you get in trouble at school?
   M. Most of the time
   S. Sometimes
   N. Never

114. During the past four weeks, how many school days have you skipped or "cut"?
   A. None
   B. One day
   C. Two days
   D. Three days or more

K. Right and Wrong

In your opinion, are each of the actions in questions 115 to 120 right or wrong? Here are the possible responses:

> R. Morally right
> ?. Not sure
> W. Morally wrong

115. Sexual intercourse between two unmarried 16-year-olds who love each other.

116. People trying to keep a minority family from moving into a neighborhood.

117. Cheating on a test at school.

118. Lying to one's parents.

119. Sixteen-year-olds drinking a couple of beers at a party.

120. Stealing a shirt from a store.

L. Male-Female Relationships

121. How many times in the past twelve months have you been out on a date (such as going to a party or movie with one person of the opposite sex)?
   A. None
   B. One or two times
   C. Three to five times
   D. Six to nine times
   E. Ten to nineteen times
   F. Twenty times or more

122. In the past twelve months, how many times have you kissed someone about your age who is of the opposite sex?
   A. None
   B. One or two times
   C. Three to five times
   D. Six to nine times
   E. Ten to nineteen times
   F. Twenty times or more

123. Is it difficult for you to talk with other kids of the opposite sex?
   Y. Yes
   N. No

124. Are you in love right now with someone about your age who is of the opposite sex?
   Y. Yes
   N. No

125. Do you like to do things with teenagers of the opposite sex?
   A. Usually
   B. Sometimes
   C. Never

126. How often do you think about sex?
   A. Very often
   B. Sometimes
   C. Never

127. Have you ever had sexual intercourse ("gone all the way" or "made love")?
- **A.** Never
- **B.** Yes, one time
- **C.** Yes, two to five times
- **D.** Yes, six times or more
- **E.** I don't know what sexual intercourse is.

M. My Church

128. How many adults in your church do you think know you well?
- **A.** None
- **B.** One or two
- **C.** Three to five
- **D.** Six to nine
- **E.** Ten or more

129. How much does your church help you answer important questions about your life?
- **V.** Very much
- **S.** Some
- **L.** A little
- **N.** Not at all

130. If you had an important question about life, how many adults in your church would you feel comfortable going to for help? Don't count your parents or other relatives.
- **A.** None
- **B.** One or two
- **C.** Three to five
- **D.** Six to nine
- **E.** Ten or more

131. How important is church to you?
- **A.** Very important
- **B.** Somewhat important
- **C.** Not important

132. Would you recommend your church to a friend who doesn't belong to another church?
- **Y.** Yes
- **?.** Not sure
- **N.** No

N. My Feelings About My Church

For questions 133 to 138, circle the number that best describes the main "feeling" you get from your church. For example, if you believe that most people in your church think teenagers are important, but some don't, you might circle a 6 or 7 for question 133.

In my church . . .

133.	Kids are important	9 8 7 6 5 4 3 2 1	Kids aren't important
134.	I have many church friends.	9 8 7 6 5 4 3 2 1	I have no church friends.
135.	I learn a lot.	9 8 7 6 5 4 3 2 1	I don't learn anything.
136.	Questions are invited.	9 8 7 6 5 4 3 2 1	Questions aren't welcome.
137.	It's exciting.	9 8 7 6 5 4 3 2 1	It's boring.
138.	Everyone cares about me.	9 8 7 6 5 4 3 2 1	Nobody cares about me.

O. What I Want From My Church

When you think about what you want from your church, how important are each of the following to you? Your choices are:

> **5.** Extremely important
> **4.** Important
> **3.** Somewhat important
> **2.** Slightly important
> **1.** Not important

It is _____ to me . . .

139. To learn about the Bible.
140. To learn what it means to be a Christian.
141. To learn what is special about me.
142. To help my religious faith grow.
143. To make good friends.
144. To get to know adults who care about me.
145. To have opportunities to help other people.
146. To learn more about how I can make decisions about what is right and wrong.
147. To learn about sex and sexual values.
148. To learn about alcohol and other drugs, and what my values about them should be.
149. To have lots of fun and good times.
150. To learn what a Christian should do about big issues such as poverty and war.

P. How Well My Church Is Doing

Rate how well your church does in each of the areas listed in questions 151 to 162. Your choices are:

> **5.** Excellent
> **4.** Good
> **3.** Okay
> **2.** Fair
> **1.** Poor

How well does your church . . .

151. Help you learn about the Bible?
152. Help you learn what it means to be a Christian?
153. Help you learn what's special about you?
154. Help your religious faith grow?
155. Help you make friends?
156. Help you get to know adults who care about you?
157. Help you to help other people?
158. Help you learn about what is right or wrong?
159. Help you learn about sex and sexual values?
160. Help you learn about alcohol and other drugs, and what your values about them should be?
161. Provide lots of fun and good times?
162. Help you learn what a Christian should do about big issues such as poverty and war?

YOUTH SURVEY

Directions

**This survey isn't about what you know.
It's about who you are—
what you think,
what you feel,
what you believe.**

**It's about your school,
your church,
your friends,
your family,
yourself.**

**It's about what is important to you in life—
what you do,
what you worry about,
what you enjoy.**

Be honest in giving your answers. Your name will not be attached to the survey, so no one will know what you write. Your answers will be summarized together with the answers of other young people in your church. All of those answers together will provide important clues to the interests, beliefs, problems and hopes of your church's young people. It's important for youth ministry leaders to have those clues so they can do a better job of planning youth ministry for you and your friends.

Do not begin answering questions until you are instructed to do so. As soon as the survey administrator gives the signal to open this booklet to the first page, you may begin. Mark your answers on the answer sheet, not in this booklet.

For each question, decide which answer fits you best, then *circle the corresponding number or letter on the answer sheet*. Mark only one answer for each question. Do not spend a lot of time trying to decide between two answers; it's usually best to mark your first impression and go right on to the next question. There is no "right" or "wrong" answer to any question—so answer each question honestly.

When you have finished, fold your answer sheet in half and put it into the envelope provided by the survey administrator.

**Thanks for helping.
Thanks for being *you*.**

General Information

1. I am: F. Female
           M. Male

2. My grade in school is:
           7   8   9   10   11   12

A. What I Want in Life

Listed below are things that some people want in life. Read through the complete list without making any marks. Then go back and decide how important each one is to you. Your choices are:

> V. Very important
> S. Somewhat important
> N. Not very important

It is _____ to me . . .

3. To be good in music, drama or art.
4. To have a happy family life.
5. To make my parents proud of me.
6. To make my own decisions.
7. To do things that help people.
8. To feel safe and secure in my neighborhood.
9. To feel good about myself.
10. To be popular at school.
11. To have lots of fun and good times.
12. To understand my feelings.
13. To have lots of money.
14. To have God at the center of my life.
15. To have a world without hunger or poverty.
16. To get a good job when I am older.
17. To have things (such as clothes, records and so on) as nice as other kids have.
18. To do something important with my life.
19. To do well in school.
20. To have a world without war.
21. To be really good at sports.
22. To be different in some way from all the other teenagers I know.
23. To have friends I can count on.
24. To do whatever I want to do, when I want to do it.
25. To be part of a church.
26. To have clothes and hair that look good to other kids.

B. What I Worry About

How much do you worry about each of the following statements? Your choices are:

> V. Very much
> S. Somewhat
> N. Very little or not at all

I worry _____ . . .

27. About how my friends treat me.
28. That I might kill myself.
29. That I might not be able to get a good job when I am older.
30. That someone might force me to do sexual things I don't want to do.
31. About how well other teenagers like me.
32. That I might lose my best friend.
33. That one of my parents will hit me so hard that I will be badly hurt.
34. That I may die soon.
35. That a nuclear bomb might be dropped on our country.
36. About all the drugs and drinking I see around me.
37. That one of my parents might die.
38. About all the people who are hungry and poor in our country.
39. That I might get beaten up at school.
40. About whether my body is growing in a normal way.
41. About how much my mother or father drinks.
42. About how I'm doing in school.
43. About my looks.
44. That my friends might get me in trouble.
45. About all the violence in our country.
46. That my parents might get a divorce.
    (Leave this number blank if your parents are already divorced, or if one of your parents is no longer living.)

C. My Family

For each of the following statements, mark the response that best matches your feelings. Your choices are:

> A. Strongly agree
> B. Agree
> C. Not sure
> D. Disagree
> E. Strongly disagree

I wish my parents (or guardians) would . . .

47. Give me more freedom.
48. Spend more time with me.
49. Yell at me less often.
50. Talk with me more about their views on important issues such as sex and drugs.
51. Be more interested in the things I care about.
52. Give me more responsibility.
53. Say "I love you" more often.
54. Trust me more.

Mark the appropriate response to the following statements and questions.

55. There is a lot of love in my family.
    A. Very true
    B. Somewhat true
    C. Not true

56. How often does your family do projects *together* to help other people (such as collecting food for the hungry or helping a neighbor)?
   A. At least once a month
   B. Once in a while
   C. Never

57. How often does your family talk together about God, the Bible or other religious things?
   A. Every day
   B. At least two or three times a week
   C. At least once a week
   D. At least once or twice a month
   E. Never

58. How often do you hear your mother talk about her religious faith?
   A. Every day
   B. At least two or three times a week
   C. At least once a week
   D. At least once or twice a month
   E. Never

59. How often do you hear your father talk about his religious faith?
   A. Every day
   B. At least two or three times a week
   C. At least once a week
   D. At least once or twice a month
   E. Never

D. How I Feel About Myself

Tell how true each of the following statements is for you. Your options are:

> V. Very true
> S. Somewhat true
> N. Not true

60. On the whole, I like myself.
61. I spend a lot of time thinking about who I am.
62. No one really understands me.
63. I believe life has a purpose.
64. I feel good about my body.

E. My Future

For questions 65 to 70, indicate how likely it is that each statement will come true. Choose one of these answers for each question:

> E. Excellent chance
> G. Good chance
> F. Fair chance
> P. Poor chance
> N. No chance

I believe there is a(n) _____ that . . .
65. I will someday be married and have children.
66. I will go to college.

67. I will be very happy 10 years from now.
68. I will be active in church when I am 40.
69. I myself or someone close to me might get AIDS.
70. The world will be destroyed by a nuclear war sometime in the next 10 years.

F. My Friends

71. How many close friends (not relatives) do you have?
   A. None
   B. One or two
   C. Three to five
   D. Six to nine
   E. Ten or more

72. I wish I could be better at making friends.
   A. Strongly agree
   B. Agree
   C. Not sure
   D. Disagree
   E. Strongly disagree

73. I wish I could be better at being a friend to others.
   A. Strongly agree
   B. Agree
   C. Not sure
   D. Disagree
   E. Strongly disagree

74. Some of my best friends belong to this church.
   T. True
   F. False

75. How often do you feel lonely?
   A. Every day
   B. Quite often, but not every day
   C. Once in a while
   D. Never

76. How often do your friends try to get you to do things you know are wrong?
   A. Very often
   B. Often
   C. Sometimes
   D. Once in a while
   E. Never

77. Which of the following choices best describes your parents' feelings toward your friends?
   A. My parents like all of my friends.
   B. My parents like most of my friends, except for one or two.
   C. My parents like about half of my friends, and half they don't.
   D. My parents don't like most of my friends, but one or two are okay.
   E. My parents don't like any of my friends.

G. Where I'd Go for Help

If you were in the following situations, to whom would you most likely turn for help or advice? For each situation, choose one of these answers:

> **A.** A parent or guardian
> **B.** A friend my own age
> **C.** An adult friend or relative
> **D.** A minister or youth worker
> **E.** Nobody

78. If I were having trouble in school, I would turn to _____.

79. If I were wondering how to handle my feelings, I would turn to _____.

80. If some of my friends started using alcohol or other drugs, I would turn to _____.

81. If I had questions about sex, I would turn to _____.

82. If I were feeling guilty about something I had done, I would turn to _____.

83. If I were deciding what to do with my life, I would turn to _____.

H. My Christian Faith

84. Overall, how important is religion in your life?
    V. Very important
    S. Somewhat important
    N. Not important

85. Compared to a year ago, would you say your faith is now more important, less important or about the same?
    M. More important
    L. Less important
    S. About the same

86. I am sure God loves me just as I am.
    T. True
    ?. Don't know
    F. False

87. Which of the following statements comes closest to your view of God?
    A. I know for sure that God exists.
    B. I am mostly sure that God exists.
    C. I'm not sure if God exists.
    D. I don't think there is a God.
    E. I am sure there is no such thing as God.

88. Which of the following statements is closest to your view of Jesus?
    A. Jesus is the Son of God who died on the cross and rose again.
    B. Jesus is the Son of God, but I doubt that he actually rose from the dead.
    C. Jesus was a great man who lived long ago, but I don't think he was the Son of God.
    D. Jesus never existed; his life is just a story people made up.

89. My religious beliefs greatly influence how I act at school and with my friends.
    M. Most of the time
    S. Some of the time
    R. Rarely or never

90. I believe God will stop loving me if I do a lot of wrong things.
    T. True
    ?. Not sure
    F. False

What do you think God wants you to do with your life? For each of the following actions, choose one of these responses:

> **T.** True
> **?.** Not sure
> **F.** False

God wants me . . .
91. To pray.
92. To worship.
93. To read the Bible.
94. To help get rid of hunger, poverty and war.
95. To tell other people about Jesus.
96. To spend time helping other people.

I. What I Do

Please answer the following questions as honestly as you can. Remember, no one will ever find out how you answered.

Choose one of the following answers for questions 97 to 107:

> **A.** None
> **B.** Once or twice
> **C.** Three to five times
> **D.** Six to nine times
> **E.** Ten times or more

97. In the past twelve months, how many times have you been to a party where people your age were drinking alcohol?

98. During the past twelve months, how many times have you taken something from a store without paying for it?

99. During the past twelve months, how many times have you cheated on a test at school?

100. During the past twelve months, how many times have you intentionally damaged or destroyed property (for example, broken windows or furniture, put paint on walls or signs, or scratched or dented a car)?

101. During the past twelve months, how many times have you lied to one of your parents?

102. During the past twelve months, how many times have you hit or beat up another kid?

103. During the past twelve months, how many times have you drunk alcohol while you were alone or with friends your own age? (Do not include communion wine.)

104. During the past month, how many times have you drunk alcohol while you were alone or with friends your own age? (Do not include communion wine.)

105. How many times have you used marijuana (grass, pot) or hashish (hash, hash oil) in your lifetime?

106. How many times in the past two weeks have you had five or more drinks in a row? (A "drink" is a glass of wine, a bottle or can of beer, a shot of liquor or a mixed drink.)

107. How many times in your lifetime have you tried cocaine or crack?

108. In the past month, how much time did you spend helping people outside your family with special needs (for example, collecting food for hungry people, mowing lawns for people who can't do it themselves, or spending time with sick or disabled people)? Don't count work for which you were paid.
   A. None
   B. One or two hours
   C. Three to five hours
   D. Six to ten hours
   E. Eleven hours or more

109. How much television do you watch on an average school day? Don't count weekends.
   A. None
   B. One hour or less
   C. About two hours
   D. About three or four hours
   E. Five hours or more

J. School

110. How much time do you usually spend on homework each week?
   A. None
   B. One hour or less
   C. Between one and three hours
   D. Between three and five hours
   E. Between five and ten hours
   F. More than ten hours

111. I enjoy school.
   M. Most of the time
   S. Sometimes
   N. Rarely or never

112. I try to do the best I can at school.
   M. Most of the time
   S. Sometimes
   N. Rarely or never

113. How often, if ever, do you get in trouble at school?
   M. Most of the time
   S. Sometimes
   N. Never

114. During the past four weeks, how many school days have you skipped or "cut"?
   A. None
   B. One day
   C. Two days
   D. Three days or more

K. Right and Wrong

In your opinion, are each of the actions in questions 115 to 120 right or wrong? Here are the possible responses:

> R. Morally right
> ?. Not sure
> W. Morally wrong

115. Sexual intercourse between two unmarried 16-year-olds who love each other.

116. People trying to keep a minority family from moving into a neighborhood.

117. Cheating on a test at school.

118. Lying to one's parents.

119. Sixteen-year-olds drinking a couple of beers at a party.

120. Stealing a shirt from a store.

L. Male-Female Relationships

121. How many times in the past twelve months have you been out on a date (such as going to a party or movie with one person of the opposite sex)?
   A. None
   B. One or two times
   C. Three to five times
   D. Six to nine times
   E. Ten to nineteen times
   F. Twenty times or more

122. In the past twelve months, how many times have you kissed someone about your age who is of the opposite sex?
   A. None
   B. One or two times
   C. Three to five times
   D. Six to nine times
   E. Ten to nineteen times
   F. Twenty times or more

123. Is it difficult for you to talk with other kids of the opposite sex?
   Y. Yes
   N. No

124. Are you in love right now with someone about your age who is of the opposite sex?
   Y. Yes
   N. No

125. Do you like to do things with teenagers of the opposite sex?
   A. Usually
   B. Sometimes
   C. Never

126. How often do you think about sex?
   A. Very often
   B. Sometimes
   C. Never

127. Have you ever had sexual intercourse ("gone all the way" or "made love")?
- **A.** Never
- **B.** Yes, one time
- **C.** Yes, two to five times
- **D.** Yes, six times or more
- **E.** I don't know what sexual intercourse is.

M. My Church

128. How many adults in your church do you think know you well?
- **A.** None
- **B.** One or two
- **C.** Three to five
- **D.** Six to nine
- **E.** Ten or more

129. How much does your church help you answer important questions about your life?
- **V.** Very much
- **S.** Some
- **L.** A little
- **N.** Not at all

130. If you had an important question about life, how many adults in your church would you feel comfortable going to for help? Don't count your parents or other relatives.
- **A.** None
- **B.** One or two
- **C.** Three to five
- **D.** Six to nine
- **E.** Ten or more

131. How important is church to you?
- **A.** Very important
- **B.** Somewhat important
- **C.** Not important

132. Would you recommend your church to a friend who doesn't belong to another church?
- **Y.** Yes
- **?.** Not sure
- **N.** No

N. My Feelings About My Church

For questions 133 to 138, circle the number that best describes the main "feeling" you get from your church. For example, if you believe that most people in your church think teenagers are important, but some don't, you might circle a 6 or 7 for question 133.

In my church . . .

133.	Kids are important	9 8 7 6 5 4 3 2 1	Kids aren't important
134.	I have many church friends.	9 8 7 6 5 4 3 2 1	I have no church friends.
135.	I learn a lot.	9 8 7 6 5 4 3 2 1	I don't learn anything.
136.	Questions are invited.	9 8 7 6 5 4 3 2 1	Questions aren't welcome.
137.	It's exciting.	9 8 7 6 5 4 3 2 1	It's boring.
138.	Everyone cares about me.	9 8 7 6 5 4 3 2 1	Nobody cares about me.

O. What I Want From My Church

When you think about what you want from your church, how important are each of the following to you? Your choices are:

> **5.** Extremely important
> **4.** Important
> **3.** Somewhat important
> **2.** Slightly important
> **1.** Not important

It is _____ to me . . .

139. To learn about the Bible.
140. To learn what it means to be a Christian.
141. To learn what is special about me.
142. To help my religious faith grow.
143. To make good friends.
144. To get to know adults who care about me.
145. To have opportunities to help other people.
146. To learn more about how I can make decisions about what is right and wrong.
147. To learn about sex and sexual values.
148. To learn about alcohol and other drugs, and what my values about them should be.
149. To have lots of fun and good times.
150. To learn what a Christian should do about big issues such as poverty and war.

P. How Well My Church Is Doing

Rate how well your church does in each of the areas listed in questions 151 to 162. Your choices are:

> **5.** Excellent
> **4.** Good
> **3.** Okay
> **2.** Fair
> **1.** Poor

How well does your church . . .

151. Help you learn about the Bible?
152. Help you learn what it means to be a Christian?
153. Help you learn what's special about you?
154. Help your religious faith grow?
155. Help you make friends?
156. Help you get to know adults who care about you?
157. Help you to help other people?
158. Help you learn about what is right or wrong?
159. Help you learn about sex and sexual values?
160. Help you learn about alcohol and other drugs, and what your values about them should be?
161. Provide lots of fun and good times?
162. Help you learn what a Christian should do about big issues such as poverty and war?

YOUTH SURVEY

Directions

**This survey isn't about what you know.
It's about who you are—
what you think,
what you feel,
what you believe.**

**It's about your school,
your church,
your friends,
your family,
yourself.**

**It's about what is important to you in life—
what you do,
what you worry about,
what you enjoy.**

Be honest in giving your answers. Your name will not be attached to the survey, so no one will know what you write. Your answers will be summarized together with the answers of other young people in your church. All of those answers together will provide important clues to the interests, beliefs, problems and hopes of your church's young people. It's important for youth ministry leaders to have those clues so they can do a better job of planning youth ministry for you and your friends.

Do not begin answering questions until you are instructed to do so. As soon as the survey administrator gives the signal to open this booklet to the first page, you may begin. Mark your answers on the answer sheet, not in this booklet.

For each question, decide which answer fits you best, then *circle the corresponding number or letter on the answer sheet*. Mark only one answer for each question. Do not spend a lot of time trying to decide between two answers; it's usually best to mark your first impression and go right on to the next question. There is no "right" or "wrong" answer to any question—so answer each question honestly.

When you have finished, fold your answer sheet in half and put it into the envelope provided by the survey administrator.

**Thanks for helping.
Thanks for being *you*.**

General Information

1. I am: **F.** Female
          M. Male
2. My grade in school is:
   7 8 9 10 11 12

A. What I Want in Life

Listed below are things that some people want in life. Read through the complete list without making any marks. Then go back and decide how important each one is to you. Your choices are:

> **V.** Very important
> **S.** Somewhat important
> **N.** Not very important

It is _____ to me . . .

3. To be good in music, drama or art.
4. To have a happy family life.
5. To make my parents proud of me.
6. To make my own decisions.
7. To do things that help people.
8. To feel safe and secure in my neighborhood.
9. To feel good about myself.
10. To be popular at school.
11. To have lots of fun and good times.
12. To understand my feelings.
13. To have lots of money.
14. To have God at the center of my life.
15. To have a world without hunger or poverty.
16. To get a good job when I am older.
17. To have things (such as clothes, records and so on) as nice as other kids have.
18. To do something important with my life.
19. To do well in school.
20. To have a world without war.
21. To be really good at sports.
22. To be different in some way from all the other teenagers I know.
23. To have friends I can count on.
24. To do whatever I want to do, when I want to do it.
25. To be part of a church.
26. To have clothes and hair that look good to other kids.

B. What I Worry About

How much do you worry about each of the following statements? Your choices are:

> **V.** Very much
> **S.** Somewhat
> **N.** Very little or not at all

I worry _____ . . .

27. About how my friends treat me.

28. That I might kill myself.
29. That I might not be able to get a good job when I am older.
30. That someone might force me to do sexual things I don't want to do.
31. About how well other teenagers like me.
32. That I might lose my best friend.
33. That one of my parents will hit me so hard that I will be badly hurt.
34. That I may die soon.
35. That a nuclear bomb might be dropped on our country.
36. About all the drugs and drinking I see around me.
37. That one of my parents might die.
38. About all the people who are hungry and poor in our country.
39. That I might get beaten up at school.
40. About whether my body is growing in a normal way.
41. About how much my mother or father drinks.
42. About how I'm doing in school.
43. About my looks.
44. That my friends might get me in trouble.
45. About all the violence in our country.
46. That my parents might get a divorce.
   (Leave this number blank if your parents are already divorced, or if one of your parents is no longer living.)

C. My Family

For each of the following statements, mark the response that best matches your feelings. Your choices are:

> **A.** Strongly agree
> **B.** Agree
> **C.** Not sure
> **D.** Disagree
> **E.** Strongly disagree

I wish my parents (or guardians) would . . .

47. Give me more freedom.
48. Spend more time with me.
49. Yell at me less often.
50. Talk with me more about their views on important issues such as sex and drugs.
51. Be more interested in the things I care about.
52. Give me more responsibility.
53. Say ''I love you'' more often.
54. Trust me more.

Mark the appropriate response to the following statements and questions.

55. There is a lot of love in my family.
   A. Very true
   B. Somewhat true
   C. Not true

56. How often does your family do projects *together* to help other people (such as collecting food for the hungry or helping a neighbor)?
  - **A.** At least once a month
  - **B.** Once in a while
  - **C.** Never

57. How often does your family talk together about God, the Bible or other religious things?
  - **A.** Every day
  - **B.** At least two or three times a week
  - **C.** At least once a week
  - **D.** At least once or twice a month
  - **E.** Never

58. How often do you hear your mother talk about her religious faith?
  - **A.** Every day
  - **B.** At least two or three times a week
  - **C.** At least once a week
  - **D.** At least once or twice a month
  - **E.** Never

59. How often do you hear your father talk about his religious faith?
  - **A.** Every day
  - **B.** At least two or three times a week
  - **C.** At least once a week
  - **D.** At least once or twice a month
  - **E.** Never

D. How I Feel About Myself

Tell how true each of the following statements is for you. Your options are:

> **V.** Very true
> **S.** Somewhat true
> **N.** Not true

60. On the whole, I like myself.
61. I spend a lot of time thinking about who I am.
62. No one really understands me.
63. I believe life has a purpose.
64. I feel good about my body.

E. My Future

For questions 65 to 70, indicate how likely it is that each statement will come true. Choose one of these answers for each question:

> **E.** Excellent chance
> **G.** Good chance
> **F.** Fair chance
> **P.** Poor chance
> **N.** No chance

I believe there is a(n) _____ that . . .
65. I will someday be married and have children.
66. I will go to college.

67. I will be very happy 10 years from now.
68. I will be active in church when I am 40.
69. I myself or someone close to me might get AIDS.
70. The world will be destroyed by a nuclear war sometime in the next 10 years.

F. My Friends

71. How many close friends (not relatives) do you have?
  - **A.** None
  - **B.** One or two
  - **C.** Three to five
  - **D.** Six to nine
  - **E.** Ten or more

72. I wish I could be better at making friends.
  - **A.** Strongly agree
  - **B.** Agree
  - **C.** Not sure
  - **D.** Disagree
  - **E.** Strongly disagree

73. I wish I could be better at being a friend to others.
  - **A.** Strongly agree
  - **B.** Agree
  - **C.** Not sure
  - **D.** Disagree
  - **E.** Strongly disagree

74. Some of my best friends belong to this church.
  - **T.** True
  - **F.** False

75. How often do you feel lonely?
  - **A.** Every day
  - **B.** Quite often, but not every day
  - **C.** Once in a while
  - **D.** Never

76. How often do your friends try to get you to do things you know are wrong?
  - **A.** Very often
  - **B.** Often
  - **C.** Sometimes
  - **D.** Once in a while
  - **E.** Never

77. Which of the following choices best describes your parents' feelings toward your friends?
  - **A.** My parents like all of my friends.
  - **B.** My parents like most of my friends, except for one or two.
  - **C.** My parents like about half of my friends, and half they don't.
  - **D.** My parents don't like most of my friends, but one or two are okay.
  - **E.** My parents don't like any of my friends.

G. Where I'd Go for Help

If you were in the following situations, to whom would you most likely turn for help or advice? For each situation, choose one of these answers:

> A. A parent or guardian
> B. A friend my own age
> C. An adult friend or relative
> D. A minister or youth worker
> E. Nobody

78. If I were having trouble in school, I would turn to _____.

79. If I were wondering how to handle my feelings, I would turn to _____.

80. If some of my friends started using alcohol or other drugs, I would turn to _____.

81. If I had questions about sex, I would turn to _____.

82. If I were feeling guilty about something I had done, I would turn to _____.

83. If I were deciding what to do with my life, I would turn to _____.

H. My Christian Faith

84. Overall, how important is religion in your life?
    V. Very important
    S. Somewhat important
    N. Not important

85. Compared to a year ago, would you say your faith is now more important, less important or about the same?
    M. More important
    L. Less important
    S. About the same

86. I am sure God loves me just as I am.
    T. True
    ?. Don't know
    F. False

87. Which of the following statements comes closest to your view of God?
    A. I know for sure that God exists.
    B. I am mostly sure that God exists.
    C. I'm not sure if God exists.
    D. I don't think there is a God.
    E. I am sure there is no such thing as God.

88. Which of the following statements is closest to your view of Jesus?
    A. Jesus is the Son of God who died on the cross and rose again.
    B. Jesus is the Son of God, but I doubt that he actually rose from the dead.
    C. Jesus was a great man who lived long ago, but I don't think he was the Son of God.
    D. Jesus never existed; his life is just a story people made up.

89. My religious beliefs greatly influence how I act at school and with my friends.
    M. Most of the time
    S. Some of the time
    R. Rarely or never

90. I believe God will stop loving me if I do a lot of wrong things.
    T. True
    ?. Not sure
    F. False

What do you think God wants you to do with your life? For each of the following actions, choose one of these responses:

> T. True
> ?. Not sure
> F. False

God wants me . . .

91. To pray.
92. To worship.
93. To read the Bible.
94. To help get rid of hunger, poverty and war.
95. To tell other people about Jesus.
96. To spend time helping other people.

I. What I Do

Please answer the following questions as honestly as you can. Remember, no one will ever find out how you answered.

Choose one of the following answers for questions 97 to 107:

> A. None
> B. Once or twice
> C. Three to five times
> D. Six to nine times
> E. Ten times or more

97. In the past twelve months, how many times have you been to a party where people your age were drinking alcohol?

98. During the past twelve months, how many times have you taken something from a store without paying for it?

99. During the past twelve months, how many times have you cheated on a test at school?

100. During the past twelve months, how many times have you intentionally damaged or destroyed property (for example, broken windows or furniture, put paint on walls or signs, or scratched or dented a car)?

101. During the past twelve months, how many times have you lied to one of your parents?

102. During the past twelve months, how many times have you hit or beat up another kid?

103. During the past twelve months, how many times have you drunk alcohol while you were alone or with friends your own age? (Do not include communion wine.)

104. During the past month, how many times have you drunk alcohol while you were alone or with friends your own age? (Do not include communion wine.)

105. How many times have you used marijuana (grass, pot) or hashish (hash, hash oil) in your lifetime?

106. How many times in the past two weeks have you had five or more drinks in a row? (A "drink" is a glass of wine, a bottle or can of beer, a shot of liquor or a mixed drink.)

107. How many times in your lifetime have you tried cocaine or crack?

108. In the past month, how much time did you spend helping people outside your family with special needs (for example, collecting food for hungry people, mowing lawns for people who can't do it themselves, or spending time with sick or disabled people)? Don't count work for which you were paid.
   A. None
   B. One or two hours
   C. Three to five hours
   D. Six to ten hours
   E. Eleven hours or more

109. How much television do you watch on an average school day? Don't count weekends.
   A. None
   B. One hour or less
   C. About two hours
   D. About three or four hours
   E. Five hours or more

J. School

110. How much time do you usually spend on homework each week?
   A. None
   B. One hour or less
   C. Between one and three hours
   D. Between three and five hours
   E. Between five and ten hours
   F. More than ten hours

111. I enjoy school.
   M. Most of the time
   S. Sometimes
   N. Rarely or never

112. I try to do the best I can at school.
   M. Most of the time
   S. Sometimes
   N. Rarely or never

113. How often, if ever, do you get in trouble at school?
   M. Most of the time
   S. Sometimes
   N. Never

114. During the past four weeks, how many school days have you skipped or "cut"?
   A. None
   B. One day
   C. Two days
   D. Three days or more

K. Right and Wrong

In your opinion, are each of the actions in questions 115 to 120 right or wrong? Here are the possible responses:

   R. Morally right
   ?. Not sure
   W. Morally wrong

115. Sexual intercourse between two unmarried 16-year-olds who love each other.

116. People trying to keep a minority family from moving into a neighborhood.

117. Cheating on a test at school.

118. Lying to one's parents.

119. Sixteen-year-olds drinking a couple of beers at a party.

120. Stealing a shirt from a store.

L. Male-Female Relationships

121. How many times in the past twelve months have you been out on a date (such as going to a party or movie with one person of the opposite sex)?
   A. None
   B. One or two times
   C. Three to five times
   D. Six to nine times
   E. Ten to nineteen times
   F. Twenty times or more

122. In the past twelve months, how many times have you kissed someone about your age who is of the opposite sex?
   A. None
   B. One or two times
   C. Three to five times
   D. Six to nine times
   E. Ten to nineteen times
   F. Twenty times or more

123. Is it difficult for you to talk with other kids of the opposite sex?
   Y. Yes
   N. No

124. Are you in love right now with someone about your age who is of the opposite sex?
   Y. Yes
   N. No

125. Do you like to do things with teenagers of the opposite sex?
   A. Usually
   B. Sometimes
   C. Never

126. How often do you think about sex?
   A. Very often
   B. Sometimes
   C. Never

127. Have you ever had sexual intercourse ("gone all the way" or "made love")?
- **A.** Never
- **B.** Yes, one time
- **C.** Yes, two to five times
- **D.** Yes, six times or more
- **E.** I don't know what sexual intercourse is.

M. My Church

128. How many adults in your church do you think know you well?
- **A.** None
- **B.** One or two
- **C.** Three to five
- **D.** Six to nine
- **E.** Ten or more

129. How much does your church help you answer important questions about your life?
- **V.** Very much
- **S.** Some
- **L.** A little
- **N.** Not at all

130. If you had an important question about life, how many adults in your church would you feel comfortable going to for help? Don't count your parents or other relatives.
- **A.** None
- **B.** One or two
- **C.** Three to five
- **D.** Six to nine
- **E.** Ten or more

131. How important is church to you?
- **A.** Very important
- **B.** Somewhat important
- **C.** Not important

132. Would you recommend your church to a friend who doesn't belong to another church?
- **Y.** Yes
- **?.** Not sure
- **N.** No

N. My Feelings About My Church

For questions 133 to 138, circle the number that best describes the main "feeling" you get from your church. For example, if you believe that most people in your church think teenagers are important, but some don't, you might circle a 6 or 7 for question 133.

In my church . . .

133. Kids are important	9 8 7 6 5 4 3 2 1	Kids aren't important
134. I have many church friends.	9 8 7 6 5 4 3 2 1	I have no church friends.
135. I learn a lot.	9 8 7 6 5 4 3 2 1	I don't learn anything.
136. Questions are invited.	9 8 7 6 5 4 3 2 1	Questions aren't welcome.
137. It's exciting.	9 8 7 6 5 4 3 2 1	It's boring.
138. Everyone cares about me.	9 8 7 6 5 4 3 2 1	Nobody cares about me.

O. What I Want From My Church

When you think about what you want from your church, how important are each of the following to you? Your choices are:

> **5.** Extremely important
> **4.** Important
> **3.** Somewhat important
> **2.** Slightly important
> **1.** Not important

It is _____ to me . . .
- **139.** To learn about the Bible.
- **140.** To learn what it means to be a Christian.
- **141.** To learn what is special about me.
- **142.** To help my religious faith grow.
- **143.** To make good friends.
- **144.** To get to know adults who care about me.
- **145.** To have opportunities to help other people.
- **146.** To learn more about how I can make decisions about what is right and wrong.
- **147.** To learn about sex and sexual values.
- **148.** To learn about alcohol and other drugs, and what my values about them should be.
- **149.** To have lots of fun and good times.
- **150.** To learn what a Christian should do about big issues such as poverty and war.

P. How Well My Church Is Doing

Rate how well your church does in each of the areas listed in questions 151 to 162. Your choices are:

> **5.** Excellent
> **4.** Good
> **3.** Okay
> **2.** Fair
> **1.** Poor

How well does your church . . .
- **151.** Help you learn about the Bible?
- **152.** Help you learn what it means to be a Christian?
- **153.** Help you learn what's special about you?
- **154.** Help your religious faith grow?
- **155.** Help you make friends?
- **156.** Help you get to know adults who care about you?
- **157.** Help you to help other people?
- **158.** Help you learn about what is right or wrong?
- **159.** Help you learn about sex and sexual values?
- **160.** Help you learn about alcohol and other drugs, and what your values about them should be?
- **161.** Provide lots of fun and good times?
- **162.** Help you learn what a Christian should do about big issues such as poverty and war?

YOUTH SURVEY

Directions

**This survey isn't about what you know.
It's about who you are—
what you think,
what you feel,
what you believe.**

**It's about your school,
your church,
your friends,
your family,
yourself.**

**It's about what is important to you in life—
what you do,
what you worry about,
what you enjoy.**

Be honest in giving your answers. Your name will not be attached to the survey, so no one will know what you write. Your answers will be summarized together with the answers of other young people in your church. All of those answers together will provide important clues to the interests, beliefs, problems and hopes of your church's young people. It's important for youth ministry leaders to have those clues so they can do a better job of planning youth ministry for you and your friends.

Do not begin answering questions until you are instructed to do so. As soon as the survey administrator gives the signal to open this booklet to the first page, you may begin. Mark your answers on the answer sheet, not in this booklet.

For each question, decide which answer fits you best, then *circle the corresponding number or letter on the answer sheet*. Mark only one answer for each question. Do not spend a lot of time trying to decide between two answers; it's usually best to mark your first impression and go right on to the next question. There is no "right" or "wrong" answer to any question—so answer each question honestly.

When you have finished, fold your answer sheet in half and put it into the envelope provided by the survey administrator.

**Thanks for helping.
Thanks for being *you*.**

General Information

1. I am: **F.** Female
          M. Male
2. My grade in school is:
          7   8   9   10   11   12

A. What I Want in Life

Listed below are things that some people want in life. Read through the complete list without making any marks. Then go back and decide how important each one is to you. Your choices are:

> **V.** Very important
> **S.** Somewhat important
> **N.** Not very important

It is _____ to me . . .
3. To be good in music, drama or art.
4. To have a happy family life.
5. To make my parents proud of me.
6. To make my own decisions.
7. To do things that help people.
8. To feel safe and secure in my neighborhood.
9. To feel good about myself.
10. To be popular at school.
11. To have lots of fun and good times.
12. To understand my feelings.
13. To have lots of money.
14. To have God at the center of my life.
15. To have a world without hunger or poverty.
16. To get a good job when I am older.
17. To have things (such as clothes, records and so on) as nice as other kids have.
18. To do something important with my life.
19. To do well in school.
20. To have a world without war.
21. To be really good at sports.
22. To be different in some way from all the other teenagers I know.
23. To have friends I can count on.
24. To do whatever I want to do, when I want to do it.
25. To be part of a church.
26. To have clothes and hair that look good to other kids.

B. What I Worry About

How much do you worry about each of the following statements? Your choices are:

> **V.** Very much
> **S.** Somewhat
> **N.** Very little or not at all

I worry _____ . . .
27. About how my friends treat me.
28. That I might kill myself.
29. That I might not be able to get a good job when I am older.
30. That someone might force me to do sexual things I don't want to do.
31. About how well other teenagers like me.
32. That I might lose my best friend.
33. That one of my parents will hit me so hard that I will be badly hurt.
34. That I may die soon.
35. That a nuclear bomb might be dropped on our country.
36. About all the drugs and drinking I see around me.
37. That one of my parents might die.
38. About all the people who are hungry and poor in our country.
39. That I might get beaten up at school.
40. About whether my body is growing in a normal way.
41. About how much my mother or father drinks.
42. About how I'm doing in school.
43. About my looks.
44. That my friends might get me in trouble.
45. About all the violence in our country.
46. That my parents might get a divorce.
    (Leave this number blank if your parents are already divorced, or if one of your parents is no longer living.)

C. My Family

For each of the following statements, mark the response that best matches your feelings. Your choices are:

> **A.** Strongly agree
> **B.** Agree
> **C.** Not sure
> **D.** Disagree
> **E.** Strongly disagree

I wish my parents (or guardians) would . . .
47. Give me more freedom.
48. Spend more time with me.
49. Yell at me less often.
50. Talk with me more about their views on important issues such as sex and drugs.
51. Be more interested in the things I care about.
52. Give me more responsibility.
53. Say "I love you" more often.
54. Trust me more.

Mark the appropriate response to the following statements and questions.

55. There is a lot of love in my family.
    A. Very true
    B. Somewhat true
    C. Not true

56. How often does your family do projects *together* to help other people (such as collecting food for the hungry or helping a neighbor)?
   A. At least once a month
   B. Once in a while
   C. Never

57. How often does your family talk together about God, the Bible or other religious things?
   A. Every day
   B. At least two or three times a week
   C. At least once a week
   D. At least once or twice a month
   E. Never

58. How often do you hear your mother talk about her religious faith?
   A. Every day
   B. At least two or three times a week
   C. At least once a week
   D. At least once or twice a month
   E. Never

59. How often do you hear your father talk about his religious faith?
   A. Every day
   B. At least two or three times a week
   C. At least once a week
   D. At least once or twice a month
   E. Never

D. How I Feel About Myself

Tell how true each of the following statements is for you. Your options are:

> V. Very true
> S. Somewhat true
> N. Not true

60. On the whole, I like myself.
61. I spend a lot of time thinking about who I am.
62. No one really understands me.
63. I believe life has a purpose.
64. I feel good about my body.

E. My Future

For questions 65 to 70, indicate how likely it is that each statement will come true. Choose one of these answers for each question:

> E. Excellent chance
> G. Good chance
> F. Fair chance
> P. Poor chance
> N. No chance

I believe there is a(n) _____ that . . .
   65. I will someday be married and have children.
   66. I will go to college.

67. I will be very happy 10 years from now.
68. I will be active in church when I am 40.
69. I myself or someone close to me might get AIDS.
70. The world will be destroyed by a nuclear war sometime in the next 10 years.

F. My Friends

71. How many close friends (not relatives) do you have?
   A. None
   B. One or two
   C. Three to five
   D. Six to nine
   E. Ten or more

72. I wish I could be better at making friends.
   A. Strongly agree
   B. Agree
   C. Not sure
   D. Disagree
   E. Strongly disagree

73. I wish I could be better at being a friend to others.
   A. Strongly agree
   B. Agree
   C. Not sure
   D. Disagree
   E. Strongly disagree

74. Some of my best friends belong to this church.
   T. True
   F. False

75. How often do you feel lonely?
   A. Every day
   B. Quite often, but not every day
   C. Once in a while
   D. Never

76. How often do your friends try to get you to do things you know are wrong?
   A. Very often
   B. Often
   C. Sometimes
   D. Once in a while
   E. Never

77. Which of the following choices best describes your parents' feelings toward your friends?
   A. My parents like all of my friends.
   B. My parents like most of my friends, except for one or two.
   C. My parents like about half of my friends, and half they don't.
   D. My parents don't like most of my friends, but one or two are okay.
   E. My parents don't like any of my friends.

G. Where I'd Go for Help

If you were in the following situations, to whom would you most likely turn for help or advice? For each situation, choose one of these answers:

> **A.** A parent or guardian
> **B.** A friend my own age
> **C.** An adult friend or relative
> **D.** A minister or youth worker
> **E.** Nobody

78. If I were having trouble in school, I would turn to _____.

79. If I were wondering how to handle my feelings, I would turn to _____.

80. If some of my friends started using alcohol or other drugs, I would turn to _____.

81. If I had questions about sex, I would turn to _____.

82. If I were feeling guilty about something I had done, I would turn to _____.

83. If I were deciding what to do with my life, I would turn to _____.

H. My Christian Faith

84. Overall, how important is religion in your life?
    V. Very important
    S. Somewhat important
    N. Not important

85. Compared to a year ago, would you say your faith is now more important, less important or about the same?
    M. More important
    L. Less important
    S. About the same

86. I am sure God loves me just as I am.
    T. True
    ?. Don't know
    F. False

87. Which of the following statements comes closest to your view of God?
    A. I know for sure that God exists.
    B. I am mostly sure that God exists.
    C. I'm not sure if God exists.
    D. I don't think there is a God.
    E. I am sure there is no such thing as God.

88. Which of the following statements is closest to your view of Jesus?
    A. Jesus is the Son of God who died on the cross and rose again.
    B. Jesus is the Son of God, but I doubt that he actually rose from the dead.
    C. Jesus was a great man who lived long ago, but I don't think he was the Son of God.
    D. Jesus never existed; his life is just a story people made up.

89. My religious beliefs greatly influence how I act at school and with my friends.
    M. Most of the time
    S. Some of the time
    R. Rarely or never

90. I believe God will stop loving me if I do a lot of wrong things.
    T. True
    ?. Not sure
    F. False

What do you think God wants you to do with your life? For each of the following actions, choose one of these responses:

> **T.** True
> **?.** Not sure
> **F.** False

God wants me . . .

91. To pray.
92. To worship.
93. To read the Bible.
94. To help get rid of hunger, poverty and war.
95. To tell other people about Jesus.
96. To spend time helping other people.

I. What I Do

Please answer the following questions as honestly as you can. Remember, no one will ever find out how you answered.

Choose one of the following answers for questions 97 to 107:

> **A.** None
> **B.** Once or twice
> **C.** Three to five times
> **D.** Six to nine times
> **E.** Ten times or more

97. In the past twelve months, how many times have you been to a party where people your age were drinking alcohol?

98. During the past twelve months, how many times have you taken something from a store without paying for it?

99. During the past twelve months, how many times have you cheated on a test at school?

100. During the past twelve months, how many times have you intentionally damaged or destroyed property (for example, broken windows or furniture, put paint on walls or signs, or scratched or dented a car)?

101. During the past twelve months, how many times have you lied to one of your parents?

102. During the past twelve months, how many times have you hit or beat up another kid?

103. During the past twelve months, how many times have you drunk alcohol while you were alone or with friends your own age? (Do not include communion wine.)

104. During the past month, how many times have you drunk alcohol while you were alone or with friends your own age? (Do not include communion wine.)

105. How many times have you used marijuana (grass, pot) or hashish (hash, hash oil) in your lifetime?

106. How many times in the past two weeks have you had five or more drinks in a row? (A "drink" is a glass of wine, a bottle or can of beer, a shot of liquor or a mixed drink.)

107. How many times in your lifetime have you tried cocaine or crack?

108. In the past month, how much time did you spend helping people outside your family with special needs (for example, collecting food for hungry people, mowing lawns for people who can't do it themselves, or spending time with sick or disabled people)? Don't count work for which you were paid.
    A. None
    B. One or two hours
    C. Three to five hours
    D. Six to ten hours
    E. Eleven hours or more

109. How much television do you watch on an average school day? Don't count weekends.
    A. None
    B. One hour or less
    C. About two hours
    D. About three or four hours
    E. Five hours or more

J. School

110. How much time do you usually spend on homework each week?
    A. None
    B. One hour or less
    C. Between one and three hours
    D. Between three and five hours
    E. Between five and ten hours
    F. More than ten hours

111. I enjoy school.
    M. Most of the time
    S. Sometimes
    N. Rarely or never

112. I try to do the best I can at school.
    M. Most of the time
    S. Sometimes
    N. Rarely or never

113. How often, if ever, do you get in trouble at school?
    M. Most of the time
    S. Sometimes
    N. Never

114. During the past four weeks, how many school days have you skipped or "cut"?
    A. None
    B. One day
    C. Two days
    D. Three days or more

K. Right and Wrong

In your opinion, are each of the actions in questions 115 to 120 right or wrong? Here are the possible responses:

R. Morally right
?. Not sure
W. Morally wrong

115. Sexual intercourse between two unmarried 16-year-olds who love each other.

116. People trying to keep a minority family from moving into a neighborhood.

117. Cheating on a test at school.

118. Lying to one's parents.

119. Sixteen-year-olds drinking a couple of beers at a party.

120. Stealing a shirt from a store.

L. Male-Female Relationships

121. How many times in the past twelve months have you been out on a date (such as going to a party or movie with one person of the opposite sex)?
    A. None
    B. One or two times
    C. Three to five times
    D. Six to nine times
    E. Ten to nineteen times
    F. Twenty times or more

122. In the past twelve months, how many times have you kissed someone about your age who is of the opposite sex?
    A. None
    B. One or two times
    C. Three to five times
    D. Six to nine times
    E. Ten to nineteen times
    F. Twenty times or more

123. Is it difficult for you to talk with other kids of the opposite sex?
    Y. Yes
    N. No

124. Are you in love right now with someone about your age who is of the opposite sex?
    Y. Yes
    N. No

125. Do you like to do things with teenagers of the opposite sex?
    A. Usually
    B. Sometimes
    C. Never

126. How often do you think about sex?
    A. Very often
    B. Sometimes
    C. Never

127. Have you ever had sexual intercourse ("gone all the way" or "made love")?
A. Never
B. Yes, one time
C. Yes, two to five times
D. Yes, six times or more
E. I don't know what sexual intercourse is.

M. My Church

128. How many adults in your church do you think know you well?
A. None
B. One or two
C. Three to five
D. Six to nine
E. Ten or more

129. How much does your church help you answer important questions about your life?
V. Very much
S. Some
L. A little
N. Not at all

130. If you had an important question about life, how many adults in your church would you feel comfortable going to for help? Don't count your parents or other relatives.
A. None
B. One or two
C. Three to five
D. Six to nine
E. Ten or more

131. How important is church to you?
A. Very important
B. Somewhat important
C. Not important

132. Would you recommend your church to a friend who doesn't belong to another church?
Y. Yes
?. Not sure
N. No

N. My Feelings About My Church

For questions 133 to 138, circle the number that best describes the main "feeling" you get from your church. For example, if you believe that most people in your church think teenagers are important, but some don't, you might circle a 6 or 7 for question 133.

In my church . . .

133.	Kids are important	9 8 7 6 5 4 3 2 1	Kids aren't important
134.	I have many church friends.	9 8 7 6 5 4 3 2 1	I have no church friends.
135.	I learn a lot.	9 8 7 6 5 4 3 2 1	I don't learn anything.
136.	Questions are invited.	9 8 7 6 5 4 3 2 1	Questions aren't welcome.
137.	It's exciting.	9 8 7 6 5 4 3 2 1	It's boring.
138.	Everyone cares about me.	9 8 7 6 5 4 3 2 1	Nobody cares about me.

O. What I Want From My Church

When you think about what you want from your church, how important are each of the following to you? Your choices are:

> 5. Extremely important
> 4. Important
> 3. Somewhat important
> 2. Slightly important
> 1. Not important

It is _____ to me . . .

139. To learn about the Bible.
140. To learn what it means to be a Christian.
141. To learn what is special about me.
142. To help my religious faith grow.
143. To make good friends.
144. To get to know adults who care about me.
145. To have opportunities to help other people.
146. To learn more about how I can make decisions about what is right and wrong.
147. To learn about sex and sexual values.
148. To learn about alcohol and other drugs, and what my values about them should be.
149. To have lots of fun and good times.
150. To learn what a Christian should do about big issues such as poverty and war.

P. How Well My Church Is Doing

Rate how well your church does in each of the areas listed in questions 151 to 162. Your choices are:

> 5. Excellent
> 4. Good
> 3. Okay
> 2. Fair
> 1. Poor

How well does your church . . .

151. Help you learn about the Bible?
152. Help you learn what it means to be a Christian?
153. Help you learn what's special about you?
154. Help your religious faith grow?
155. Help you make friends?
156. Help you get to know adults who care about you?
157. Help you to help other people?
158. Help you learn about what is right or wrong?
159. Help you learn about sex and sexual values?
160. Help you learn about alcohol and other drugs, and what your values about them should be?
161. Provide lots of fun and good times?
162. Help you learn what a Christian should do about big issues such as poverty and war?

YOUTH SURVEY

Directions

**This survey isn't about what you know.
It's about who you are—
what you think,
what you feel,
what you believe.**

**It's about your school,
your church,
your friends,
your family,
yourself.**

**It's about what is important to you in life—
what you do,
what you worry about,
what you enjoy.**

Be honest in giving your answers. Your name will not be attached to the survey, so no one will know what you write. Your answers will be summarized together with the answers of other young people in your church. All of those answers together will provide important clues to the interests, beliefs, problems and hopes of your church's young people. It's important for youth ministry leaders to have those clues so they can do a better job of planning youth ministry for you and your friends.

Do not begin answering questions until you are instructed to do so. As soon as the survey administrator gives the signal to open this booklet to the first page, you may begin. Mark your answers on the answer sheet, not in this booklet.

For each question, decide which answer fits you best, then *circle the corresponding number or letter on the answer sheet*. Mark only one answer for each question. Do not spend a lot of time trying to decide between two answers; it's usually best to mark your first impression and go right on to the next question. There is no "right" or "wrong" answer to any question—so answer each question honestly.

When you have finished, fold your answer sheet in half and put it into the envelope provided by the survey administrator.

**Thanks for helping.
Thanks for being *you*.**

General Information

1. I am: **F.** Female
                M. Male

2. My grade in school is:
        7   8   9   10   11   12

A. What I Want in Life

Listed below are things that some people want in life. Read through the complete list without making any marks. Then go back and decide how important each one is to you. Your choices are:

> **V.** Very important
> **S.** Somewhat important
> **N.** Not very important

It is _____ to me . . .

3. To be good in music, drama or art.
4. To have a happy family life.
5. To make my parents proud of me.
6. To make my own decisions.
7. To do things that help people.
8. To feel safe and secure in my neighborhood.
9. To feel good about myself.
10. To be popular at school.
11. To have lots of fun and good times.
12. To understand my feelings.
13. To have lots of money.
14. To have God at the center of my life.
15. To have a world without hunger or poverty.
16. To get a good job when I am older.
17. To have things (such as clothes, records and so on) as nice as other kids have.
18. To do something important with my life.
19. To do well in school.
20. To have a world without war.
21. To be really good at sports.
22. To be different in some way from all the other teenagers I know.
23. To have friends I can count on.
24. To do whatever I want to do, when I want to do it.
25. To be part of a church.
26. To have clothes and hair that look good to other kids.

B. What I Worry About

How much do you worry about each of the following statements? Your choices are:

> **V.** Very much
> **S.** Somewhat
> **N.** Very little or not at all

I worry _____ . . .
27. About how my friends treat me.

28. That I might kill myself.
29. That I might not be able to get a good job when I am older.
30. That someone might force me to do sexual things I don't want to do.
31. About how well other teenagers like me.
32. That I might lose my best friend.
33. That one of my parents will hit me so hard that I will be badly hurt.
34. That I may die soon.
35. That a nuclear bomb might be dropped on our country.
36. About all the drugs and drinking I see around me.
37. That one of my parents might die.
38. About all the people who are hungry and poor in our country.
39. That I might get beaten up at school.
40. About whether my body is growing in a normal way.
41. About how much my mother or father drinks.
42. About how I'm doing in school.
43. About my looks.
44. That my friends might get me in trouble.
45. About all the violence in our country.
46. That my parents might get a divorce.

> **(Leave this number blank if your parents are already divorced, or if one of your parents is no longer living.)**

C. My Family

For each of the following statements, mark the response that best matches your feelings. Your choices are:

> **A.** Strongly agree
> **B.** Agree
> **C.** Not sure
> **D.** Disagree
> **E.** Strongly disagree

I wish my parents (or guardians) would . . .
47. Give me more freedom.
48. Spend more time with me.
49. Yell at me less often.
50. Talk with me more about their views on important issues such as sex and drugs.
51. Be more interested in the things I care about.
52. Give me more responsibility.
53. Say "I love you" more often.
54. Trust me more.

Mark the appropriate response to the following statements and questions.

55. There is a lot of love in my family.
    A. Very true
    B. Somewhat true
    C. Not true

56. How often does your family do projects *together* to help other people (such as collecting food for the hungry or helping a neighbor)?
    A. At least once a month
    B. Once in a while
    C. Never

57. How often does your family talk together about God, the Bible or other religious things?
    A. Every day
    B. At least two or three times a week
    C. At least once a week
    D. At least once or twice a month
    E. Never

58. How often do you hear your mother talk about her religious faith?
    A. Every day
    B. At least two or three times a week
    C. At least once a week
    D. At least once or twice a month
    E. Never

59. How often do you hear your father talk about his religious faith?
    A. Every day
    B. At least two or three times a week
    C. At least once a week
    D. At least once or twice a month
    E. Never

D. How I Feel About Myself

Tell how true each of the following statements is for you. Your options are:

> V. Very true
> S. Somewhat true
> N. Not true

60. On the whole, I like myself.
61. I spend a lot of time thinking about who I am.
62. No one really understands me.
63. I believe life has a purpose.
64. I feel good about my body.

E. My Future

For questions 65 to 70, indicate how likely it is that each statement will come true. Choose one of these answers for each question:

> E. Excellent chance
> G. Good chance
> F. Fair chance
> P. Poor chance
> N. No chance

I believe there is a(n) _____ that . . .

65. I will someday be married and have children.
66. I will go to college.

67. I will be very happy 10 years from now.
68. I will be active in church when I am 40.
69. I myself or someone close to me might get AIDS.
70. The world will be destroyed by a nuclear war sometime in the next 10 years.

F. My Friends

71. How many close friends (not relatives) do you have?
    A. None
    B. One or two
    C. Three to five
    D. Six to nine
    E. Ten or more

72. I wish I could be better at making friends.
    A. Strongly agree
    B. Agree
    C. Not sure
    D. Disagree
    E. Strongly disagree

73. I wish I could be better at being a friend to others.
    A. Strongly agree
    B. Agree
    C. Not sure
    D. Disagree
    E. Strongly disagree

74. Some of my best friends belong to this church.
    T. True
    F. False

75. How often do you feel lonely?
    A. Every day
    B. Quite often, but not every day
    C. Once in a while
    D. Never

76. How often do your friends try to get you to do things you know are wrong?
    A. Very often
    B. Often
    C. Sometimes
    D. Once in a while
    E. Never

77. Which of the following choices best describes your parents' feelings toward your friends?
    A. My parents like all of my friends.
    B. My parents like most of my friends, except for one or two.
    C. My parents like about half of my friends, and half they don't.
    D. My parents don't like most of my friends, but one or two are okay.
    E. My parents don't like any of my friends.

G. Where I'd Go for Help

If you were in the following situations, to whom would you most likely turn for help or advice? For each situation, choose one of these answers:

> A. A parent or guardian
> B. A friend my own age
> C. An adult friend or relative
> D. A minister or youth worker
> E. Nobody

78. If I were having trouble in school, I would turn to _____.

79. If I were wondering how to handle my feelings, I would turn to _____.

80. If some of my friends started using alcohol or other drugs, I would turn to _____.

81. If I had questions about sex, I would turn to _____.

82. If I were feeling guilty about something I had done, I would turn to _____.

83. If I were deciding what to do with my life, I would turn to _____.

H. My Christian Faith

84. Overall, how important is religion in your life?
    V. Very important
    S. Somewhat important
    N. Not important

85. Compared to a year ago, would you say your faith is now more important, less important or about the same?
    M. More important
    L. Less important
    S. About the same

86. I am sure God loves me just as I am.
    T. True
    ?. Don't know
    F. False

87. Which of the following statements comes closest to your view of God?
    A. I know for sure that God exists.
    B. I am mostly sure that God exists.
    C. I'm not sure if God exists.
    D. I don't think there is a God.
    E. I am sure there is no such thing as God.

88. Which of the following statements is closest to your view of Jesus?
    A. Jesus is the Son of God who died on the cross and rose again.
    B. Jesus is the Son of God, but I doubt that he actually rose from the dead.
    C. Jesus was a great man who lived long ago, but I don't think he was the Son of God.
    D. Jesus never existed; his life is just a story people made up.

89. My religious beliefs greatly influence how I act at school and with my friends.
    M. Most of the time
    S. Some of the time
    R. Rarely or never

90. I believe God will stop loving me if I do a lot of wrong things.
    T. True
    ?. Not sure
    F. False

What do you think God wants you to do with your life? For each of the following actions, choose one of these responses:

> T. True
> ?. Not sure
> F. False

God wants me . . .

91. To pray.
92. To worship.
93. To read the Bible.
94. To help get rid of hunger, poverty and war.
95. To tell other people about Jesus.
96. To spend time helping other people.

I. What I Do

Please answer the following questions as honestly as you can. Remember, no one will ever find out how you answered.

Choose one of the following answers for questions 97 to 107:

> A. None
> B. Once or twice
> C. Three to five times
> D. Six to nine times
> E. Ten times or more

97. In the past twelve months, how many times have you been to a party where people your age were drinking alcohol?

98. During the past twelve months, how many times have you taken something from a store without paying for it?

99. During the past twelve months, how many times have you cheated on a test at school?

100. During the past twelve months, how many times have you intentionally damaged or destroyed property (for example, broken windows or furniture, put paint on walls or signs, or scratched or dented a car)?

101. During the past twelve months, how many times have you lied to one of your parents?

102. During the past twelve months, how many times have you hit or beat up another kid?

103. During the past twelve months, how many times have you drunk alcohol while you were alone or with friends your own age? (Do not include communion wine.)

104. During the past month, how many times have you drunk alcohol while you were alone or with friends your own age? (Do not include communion wine.)

105. How many times have you used marijuana (grass, pot) or hashish (hash, hash oil) in your lifetime?

106. How many times in the past two weeks have you had five or more drinks in a row? (A ''drink'' is a glass of wine, a bottle or can of beer, a shot of liquor or a mixed drink.)

107. How many times in your lifetime have you tried cocaine or crack?

108. In the past month, how much time did you spend helping people outside your family with special needs (for example, collecting food for hungry people, mowing lawns for people who can't do it themselves, or spending time with sick or disabled people)? Don't count work for which you were paid.
   A. None
   B. One or two hours
   C. Three to five hours
   D. Six to ten hours
   E. Eleven hours or more

109. How much television do you watch on an average school day? Don't count weekends.
   A. None
   B. One hour or less
   C. About two hours
   D. About three or four hours
   E. Five hours or more

J. School

110. How much time do you usually spend on homework each week?
   A. None
   B. One hour or less
   C. Between one and three hours
   D. Between three and five hours
   E. Between five and ten hours
   F. More than ten hours

111. I enjoy school.
   M. Most of the time
   S. Sometimes
   N. Rarely or never

112. I try to do the best I can at school.
   M. Most of the time
   S. Sometimes
   N. Rarely or never

113. How often, if ever, do you get in trouble at school?
   M. Most of the time
   S. Sometimes
   N. Never

114. During the past four weeks, how many school days have you skipped or ''cut''?
   A. None
   B. One day
   C. Two days
   D. Three days or more

K. Right and Wrong

In your opinion, are each of the actions in questions 115 to 120 right or wrong? Here are the possible responses:

> R. Morally right
> ?. Not sure
> W. Morally wrong

115. Sexual intercourse between two unmarried 16-year-olds who love each other.

116. People trying to keep a minority family from moving into a neighborhood.

117. Cheating on a test at school.

118. Lying to one's parents.

119. Sixteen-year-olds drinking a couple of beers at a party.

120. Stealing a shirt from a store.

L. Male-Female Relationships

121. How many times in the past twelve months have you been out on a date (such as going to a party or movie with one person of the opposite sex)?
   A. None
   B. One or two times
   C. Three to five times
   D. Six to nine times
   E. Ten to nineteen times
   F. Twenty times or more

122. In the past twelve months, how many times have you kissed someone about your age who is of the opposite sex?
   A. None
   B. One or two times
   C. Three to five times
   D. Six to nine times
   E. Ten to nineteen times
   F. Twenty times or more

123. Is it difficult for you to talk with other kids of the opposite sex?
   Y. Yes
   N. No

124. Are you in love right now with someone about your age who is of the opposite sex?
   Y. Yes
   N. No

125. Do you like to do things with teenagers of the opposite sex?
   A. Usually
   B. Sometimes
   C. Never

126. How often do you think about sex?
   A. Very often
   B. Sometimes
   C. Never

127. Have you ever had sexual intercourse ("gone all the way" or "made love")?
   A. Never
   B. Yes, one time
   C. Yes, two to five times
   D. Yes, six times or more
   E. I don't know what sexual intercourse is.

M. My Church

128. How many adults in your church do you think know you well?
   A. None
   B. One or two
   C. Three to five
   D. Six to nine
   E. Ten or more

129. How much does your church help you answer important questions about your life?
   V. Very much
   S. Some
   L. A little
   N. Not at all

130. If you had an important question about life, how many adults in your church would you feel comfortable going to for help? Don't count your parents or other relatives.
   A. None
   B. One or two
   C. Three to five
   D. Six to nine
   E. Ten or more

131. How important is church to you?
   A. Very important
   B. Somewhat important
   C. Not important

132. Would you recommend your church to a friend who doesn't belong to another church?
   Y. Yes
   ?. Not sure
   N. No

N. My Feelings About My Church

For questions 133 to 138, circle the number that best describes the main "feeling" you get from your church. For example, if you believe that most people in your church think teenagers are important, but some don't, you might circle a 6 or 7 for question 133.

In my church . . .

133. Kids are important   9 8 7 6 5 4 3 2 1   Kids aren't important
134. I have many church friends.   9 8 7 6 5 4 3 2 1   I have no church friends.
135. I learn a lot.   9 8 7 6 5 4 3 2 1   I don't learn anything.
136. Questions are invited.   9 8 7 6 5 4 3 2 1   Questions aren't welcome.
137. It's exciting.   9 8 7 6 5 4 3 2 1   It's boring.
138. Everyone cares about me.   9 8 7 6 5 4 3 2 1   Nobody cares about me.

O. What I Want From My Church

When you think about what you want from your church, how important are each of the following to you? Your choices are:

> 5. Extremely important
> 4. Important
> 3. Somewhat important
> 2. Slightly important
> 1. Not important

It is _____ to me . . .

139. To learn about the Bible.
140. To learn what it means to be a Christian.
141. To learn what is special about me.
142. To help my religious faith grow.
143. To make good friends.
144. To get to know adults who care about me.
145. To have opportunities to help other people.
146. To learn more about how I can make decisions about what is right and wrong.
147. To learn about sex and sexual values.
148. To learn about alcohol and other drugs, and what my values about them should be.
149. To have lots of fun and good times.
150. To learn what a Christian should do about big issues such as poverty and war.

P. How Well My Church Is Doing

Rate how well your church does in each of the areas listed in questions 151 to 162. Your choices are:

> 5. Excellent
> 4. Good
> 3. Okay
> 2. Fair
> 1. Poor

How well does your church . . .

151. Help you learn about the Bible?
152. Help you learn what it means to be a Christian?
153. Help you learn what's special about you?
154. Help your religious faith grow?
155. Help you make friends?
156. Help you get to know adults who care about you?
157. Help you to help other people?
158. Help you learn about what is right or wrong?
159. Help you learn about sex and sexual values?
160. Help you learn about alcohol and other drugs, and what your values about them should be?
161. Provide lots of fun and good times?
162. Help you learn what a Christian should do about big issues such as poverty and war?

Determining Needs in Your Youth Ministry

YOUTH SURVEY

Directions

**This survey isn't about what you know.
It's about who you are—
what you think,
what you feel,
what you believe.**

**It's about your school,
your church,
your friends,
your family,
yourself.**

**It's about what is important to you in life—
what you do,
what you worry about,
what you enjoy.**

Be honest in giving your answers. Your name will not be attached to the survey, so no one will know what you write. Your answers will be summarized together with the answers of other young people in your church. All of those answers together will provide important clues to the interests, beliefs, problems and hopes of your church's young people. It's important for youth ministry leaders to have those clues so they can do a better job of planning youth ministry for you and your friends.

Do not begin answering questions until you are instructed to do so. As soon as the survey administrator gives the signal to open this booklet to the first page, you may begin. Mark your answers on the answer sheet, not in this booklet.

For each question, decide which answer fits you best, then *circle the corresponding number or letter on the answer sheet*. Mark only one answer for each question. Do not spend a lot of time trying to decide between two answers; it's usually best to mark your first impression and go right on to the next question. There is no "right" or "wrong" answer to any question—so answer each question honestly.

When you have finished, fold your answer sheet in half and put it into the envelope provided by the survey administrator.

**Thanks for helping.
Thanks for being *you*.**

General Information

1. I am: **F.** Female
            M. Male
2. My grade in school is:
            7   8   9   10   11   12

A. What I Want in Life

Listed below are things that some people want in life. Read through the complete list without making any marks. Then go back and decide how important each one is to you. Your choices are:

> **V.** Very important
> **S.** Somewhat important
> **N.** Not very important

It is _____ to me . . .
3. To be good in music, drama or art.
4. To have a happy family life.
5. To make my parents proud of me.
6. To make my own decisions.
7. To do things that help people.
8. To feel safe and secure in my neighborhood.
9. To feel good about myself.
10. To be popular at school.
11. To have lots of fun and good times.
12. To understand my feelings.
13. To have lots of money.
14. To have God at the center of my life.
15. To have a world without hunger or poverty.
16. To get a good job when I am older.
17. To have things (such as clothes, records and so on) as nice as other kids have.
18. To do something important with my life.
19. To do well in school.
20. To have a world without war.
21. To be really good at sports.
22. To be different in some way from all the other teenagers I know.
23. To have friends I can count on.
24. To do whatever I want to do, when I want to do it.
25. To be part of a church.
26. To have clothes and hair that look good to other kids.

B. What I Worry About

How much do you worry about each of the following statements? Your choices are:

> **V.** Very much
> **S.** Somewhat
> **N.** Very little or not at all

I worry _____ . . .
27. About how my friends treat me.

28. That I might kill myself.
29. That I might not be able to get a good job when I am older.
30. That someone might force me to do sexual things I don't want to do.
31. About how well other teenagers like me.
32. That I might lose my best friend.
33. That one of my parents will hit me so hard that I will be badly hurt.
34. That I may die soon.
35. That a nuclear bomb might be dropped on our country.
36. About all the drugs and drinking I see around me.
37. That one of my parents might die.
38. About all the people who are hungry and poor in our country.
39. That I might get beaten up at school.
40. About whether my body is growing in a normal way.
41. About how much my mother or father drinks.
42. About how I'm doing in school.
43. About my looks.
44. That my friends might get me in trouble.
45. About all the violence in our country.
46. That my parents might get a divorce.
    (Leave this number blank if your parents are already divorced, or if one of your parents is no longer living.)

C. My Family

For each of the following statements, mark the response that best matches your feelings. Your choices are:

> **A.** Strongly agree
> **B.** Agree
> **C.** Not sure
> **D.** Disagree
> **E.** Strongly disagree

I wish my parents (or guardians) would . . .
47. Give me more freedom.
48. Spend more time with me.
49. Yell at me less often.
50. Talk with me more about their views on important issues such as sex and drugs.
51. Be more interested in the things I care about.
52. Give me more responsibility.
53. Say "I love you" more often.
54. Trust me more.

Mark the appropriate response to the following statements and questions.

55. There is a lot of love in my family.
    A. Very true
    B. Somewhat true
    C. Not true

56. How often does your family do projects *together* to help other people (such as collecting food for the hungry or helping a neighbor)?
   A. At least once a month
   B. Once in a while
   C. Never

57. How often does your family talk together about God, the Bible or other religious things?
   A. Every day
   B. At least two or three times a week
   C. At least once a week
   D. At least once or twice a month
   E. Never

58. How often do you hear your mother talk about her religious faith?
   A. Every day
   B. At least two or three times a week
   C. At least once a week
   D. At least once or twice a month
   E. Never

59. How often do you hear your father talk about his religious faith?
   A. Every day
   B. At least two or three times a week
   C. At least once a week
   D. At least once or twice a month
   E. Never

D. How I Feel About Myself

Tell how true each of the following statements is for you. Your options are:

V. Very true
S. Somewhat true
N. Not true

60. On the whole, I like myself.
61. I spend a lot of time thinking about who I am.
62. No one really understands me.
63. I believe life has a purpose.
64. I feel good about my body.

E. My Future

For questions 65 to 70, indicate how likely it is that each statement will come true. Choose one of these answers for each question:

E. Excellent chance
G. Good chance
F. Fair chance
P. Poor chance
N. No chance

I believe there is a(n) _____ that . . .
65. I will someday be married and have children.
66. I will go to college.

67. I will be very happy 10 years from now.
68. I will be active in church when I am 40.
69. I myself or someone close to me might get AIDS.
70. The world will be destroyed by a nuclear war sometime in the next 10 years.

F. My Friends

71. How many close friends (not relatives) do you have?
   A. None
   B. One or two
   C. Three to five
   D. Six to nine
   E. Ten or more

72. I wish I could be better at making friends.
   A. Strongly agree
   B. Agree
   C. Not sure
   D. Disagree
   E. Strongly disagree

73. I wish I could be better at being a friend to others.
   A. Strongly agree
   B. Agree
   C. Not sure
   D. Disagree
   E. Strongly disagree

74. Some of my best friends belong to this church.
   T. True
   F. False

75. How often do you feel lonely?
   A. Every day
   B. Quite often, but not every day
   C. Once in a while
   D. Never

76. How often do your friends try to get you to do things you know are wrong?
   A. Very often
   B. Often
   C. Sometimes
   D. Once in a while
   E. Never

77. Which of the following choices best describes your parents' feelings toward your friends?
   A. My parents like all of my friends.
   B. My parents like most of my friends, except for one or two.
   C. My parents like about half of my friends, and half they don't.
   D. My parents don't like most of my friends, but one or two are okay.
   E. My parents don't like any of my friends.

G. Where I'd Go for Help

If you were in the following situations, to whom would you most likely turn for help or advice? For each situation, choose one of these answers:

> A. A parent or guardian
> B. A friend my own age
> C. An adult friend or relative
> D. A minister or youth worker
> E. Nobody

78. If I were having trouble in school, I would turn to _____.

79. If I were wondering how to handle my feelings, I would turn to _____.

80. If some of my friends started using alcohol or other drugs, I would turn to _____.

81. If I had questions about sex, I would turn to _____.

82. If I were feeling guilty about something I had done, I would turn to _____.

83. If I were deciding what to do with my life, I would turn to _____.

H. My Christian Faith

84. Overall, how important is religion in your life?
   V. Very important
   S. Somewhat important
   N. Not important

85. Compared to a year ago, would you say your faith is now more important, less important or about the same?
   M. More important
   L. Less important
   S. About the same

86. I am sure God loves me just as I am.
   T. True
   ?. Don't know
   F. False

87. Which of the following statements comes closest to your view of God?
   A. I know for sure that God exists.
   B. I am mostly sure that God exists.
   C. I'm not sure if God exists.
   D. I don't think there is a God.
   E. I am sure there is no such thing as God.

88. Which of the following statements is closest to your view of Jesus?
   A. Jesus is the Son of God who died on the cross and rose again.
   B. Jesus is the Son of God, but I doubt that he actually rose from the dead.
   C. Jesus was a great man who lived long ago, but I don't think he was the Son of God.
   D. Jesus never existed; his life is just a story people made up.

89. My religious beliefs greatly influence how I act at school and with my friends.
   M. Most of the time
   S. Some of the time
   R. Rarely or never

90. I believe God will stop loving me if I do a lot of wrong things.
   T. True
   ?. Not sure
   F. False

What do you think God wants you to do with your life? For each of the following actions, choose one of these responses:

> T. True
> ?. Not sure
> F. False

God wants me . . .
91. To pray.
92. To worship.
93. To read the Bible.
94. To help get rid of hunger, poverty and war.
95. To tell other people about Jesus.
96. To spend time helping other people.

I. What I Do

Please answer the following questions as honestly as you can. Remember, no one will ever find out how you answered.

Choose one of the following answers for questions 97 to 107:

> A. None
> B. Once or twice
> C. Three to five times
> D. Six to nine times
> E. Ten times or more

97. In the past twelve months, how many times have you been to a party where people your age were drinking alcohol?

98. During the past twelve months, how many times have you taken something from a store without paying for it?

99. During the past twelve months, how many times have you cheated on a test at school?

100. During the past twelve months, how many times have you intentionally damaged or destroyed property (for example, broken windows or furniture, put paint on walls or signs, or scratched or dented a car)?

101. During the past twelve months, how many times have you lied to one of your parents?

102. During the past twelve months, how many times have you hit or beat up another kid?

103. During the past twelve months, how many times have you drunk alcohol while you were alone or with friends your own age? (Do not include communion wine.)

104. During the past month, how many times have you drunk alcohol while you were alone or with friends your own age? (Do not include communion wine.)

105. How many times have you used marijuana (grass, pot) or hashish (hash, hash oil) in your lifetime?

106. How many times in the past two weeks have you had five or more drinks in a row? (A "drink" is a glass of wine, a bottle or can of beer, a shot of liquor or a mixed drink.)

107. How many times in your lifetime have you tried cocaine or crack?

108. In the past month, how much time did you spend helping people outside your family with special needs (for example, collecting food for hungry people, mowing lawns for people who can't do it themselves, or spending time with sick or disabled people)? Don't count work for which you were paid.
    A. None
    B. One or two hours
    C. Three to five hours
    D. Six to ten hours
    E. Eleven hours or more

109. How much television do you watch on an average school day? Don't count weekends.
    A. None
    B. One hour or less
    C. About two hours
    D. About three or four hours
    E. Five hours or more

J. School

110. How much time do you usually spend on homework each week?
    A. None
    B. One hour or less
    C. Between one and three hours
    D. Between three and five hours
    E. Between five and ten hours
    F. More than ten hours

111. I enjoy school.
    M. Most of the time
    S. Sometimes
    N. Rarely or never

112. I try to do the best I can at school.
    M. Most of the time
    S. Sometimes
    N. Rarely or never

113. How often, if ever, do you get in trouble at school?
    M. Most of the time
    S. Sometimes
    N. Never

114. During the past four weeks, how many school days have you skipped or "cut"?
    A. None
    B. One day
    C. Two days
    D. Three days or more

K. Right and Wrong

In your opinion, are each of the actions in questions 115 to 120 right or wrong? Here are the possible responses:

> R. Morally right
> ?. Not sure
> W. Morally wrong

115. Sexual intercourse between two unmarried 16-year-olds who love each other.

116. People trying to keep a minority family from moving into a neighborhood.

117. Cheating on a test at school.

118. Lying to one's parents.

119. Sixteen-year-olds drinking a couple of beers at a party.

120. Stealing a shirt from a store.

L. Male-Female Relationships

121. How many times in the past twelve months have you been out on a date (such as going to a party or movie with one person of the opposite sex)?
    A. None
    B. One or two times
    C. Three to five times
    D. Six to nine times
    E. Ten to nineteen times
    F. Twenty times or more

122. In the past twelve months, how many times have you kissed someone about your age who is of the opposite sex?
    A. None
    B. One or two times
    C. Three to five times
    D. Six to nine times
    E. Ten to nineteen times
    F. Twenty times or more

123. Is it difficult for you to talk with other kids of the opposite sex?
    Y. Yes
    N. No

124. Are you in love right now with someone about your age who is of the opposite sex?
    Y. Yes
    N. No

125. Do you like to do things with teenagers of the opposite sex?
    A. Usually
    B. Sometimes
    C. Never

126. How often do you think about sex?
    A. Very often
    B. Sometimes
    C. Never

127. Have you ever had sexual intercourse ("gone all the way" or "made love")?
- A. Never
- B. Yes, one time
- C. Yes, two to five times
- D. Yes, six times or more
- E. I don't know what sexual intercourse is.

M. My Church

128. How many adults in your church do you think know you well?
- A. None
- B. One or two
- C. Three to five
- D. Six to nine
- E. Ten or more

129. How much does your church help you answer important questions about your life?
- V. Very much
- S. Some
- L. A little
- N. Not at all

130. If you had an important question about life, how many adults in your church would you feel comfortable going to for help? Don't count your parents or other relatives.
- A. None
- B. One or two
- C. Three to five
- D. Six to nine
- E. Ten or more

131. How important is church to you?
- A. Very important
- B. Somewhat important
- C. Not important

132. Would you recommend your church to a friend who doesn't belong to another church?
- Y. Yes
- ?. Not sure
- N. No

N. My Feelings About My Church

For questions 133 to 138, circle the number that best describes the main "feeling" you get from your church. For example, if you believe that most people in your church think teenagers are important, but some don't, you might circle a 6 or 7 for question 133.

In my church . . .

133.	Kids are important	9 8 7 6 5 4 3 2 1	Kids aren't important
134.	I have many church friends.	9 8 7 6 5 4 3 2 1	I have no church friends.
135.	I learn a lot.	9 8 7 6 5 4 3 2 1	I don't learn anything.
136.	Questions are invited.	9 8 7 6 5 4 3 2 1	Questions aren't welcome.
137.	It's exciting.	9 8 7 6 5 4 3 2 1	It's boring.
138.	Everyone cares about me.	9 8 7 6 5 4 3 2 1	Nobody cares about me.

O. What I Want From My Church

When you think about what you want from your church, how important are each of the following to you? Your choices are:

5. Extremely important
4. Important
3. Somewhat important
2. Slightly important
1. Not important

It is _____ to me . . .

139. To learn about the Bible.
140. To learn what it means to be a Christian.
141. To learn what is special about me.
142. To help my religious faith grow.
143. To make good friends.
144. To get to know adults who care about me.
145. To have opportunities to help other people.
146. To learn more about how I can make decisions about what is right and wrong.
147. To learn about sex and sexual values.
148. To learn about alcohol and other drugs, and what my values about them should be.
149. To have lots of fun and good times.
150. To learn what a Christian should do about big issues such as poverty and war.

P. How Well My Church Is Doing

Rate how well your church does in each of the areas listed in questions 151 to 162. Your choices are:

5. Excellent
4. Good
3. Okay
2. Fair
1. Poor

How well does your church . . .

151. Help you learn about the Bible?
152. Help you learn what it means to be a Christian?
153. Help you learn what's special about you?
154. Help your religious faith grow?
155. Help you make friends?
156. Help you get to know adults who care about you?
157. Help you to help other people?
158. Help you learn about what is right or wrong?
159. Help you learn about sex and sexual values?
160. Help you learn about alcohol and other drugs, and what your values about them should be?
161. Provide lots of fun and good times?
162. Help you learn what a Christian should do about big issues such as poverty and war?

YOUTH SURVEY

Directions

**This survey isn't about what you know.
It's about who you are—
what you think,
what you feel,
what you believe.**

**It's about your school,
your church,
your friends,
your family,
yourself.**

**It's about what is important to you in life—
what you do,
what you worry about,
what you enjoy.**

Be honest in giving your answers. Your name will not be attached to the survey, so no one will know what you write. Your answers will be summarized together with the answers of other young people in your church. All of those answers together will provide important clues to the interests, beliefs, problems and hopes of your church's young people. It's important for youth ministry leaders to have those clues so they can do a better job of planning youth ministry for you and your friends.

Do not begin answering questions until you are instructed to do so. As soon as the survey administrator gives the signal to open this booklet to the first page, you may begin. Mark your answers on the answer sheet, not in this booklet.

For each question, decide which answer fits you best, then *circle the corresponding number or letter on the answer sheet*. Mark only one answer for each question. Do not spend a lot of time trying to decide between two answers; it's usually best to mark your first impression and go right on to the next question. There is no "right" or "wrong" answer to any question—so answer each question honestly.

When you have finished, fold your answer sheet in half and put it into the envelope provided by the survey administrator.

Thanks for helping.
Thanks for being *you*.

General Information

1. I am: **F.** Female
M. Male

2. My grade in school is:
7 8 9 10 11 12

A. What I Want in Life

Listed below are things that some people want in life. Read through the complete list without making any marks. Then go back and decide how important each one is to you. Your choices are:

> **V.** Very important
> **S.** Somewhat important
> **N.** Not very important

It is _____ to me . . .

3. To be good in music, drama or art.
4. To have a happy family life.
5. To make my parents proud of me.
6. To make my own decisions.
7. To do things that help people.
8. To feel safe and secure in my neighborhood.
9. To feel good about myself.
10. To be popular at school.
11. To have lots of fun and good times.
12. To understand my feelings.
13. To have lots of money.
14. To have God at the center of my life.
15. To have a world without hunger or poverty.
16. To get a good job when I am older.
17. To have things (such as clothes, records and so on) as nice as other kids have.
18. To do something important with my life.
19. To do well in school.
20. To have a world without war.
21. To be really good at sports.
22. To be different in some way from all the other teenagers I know.
23. To have friends I can count on.
24. To do whatever I want to do, when I want to do it.
25. To be part of a church.
26. To have clothes and hair that look good to other kids.

B. What I Worry About

How much do you worry about each of the following statements? Your choices are:

> **V.** Very much
> **S.** Somewhat
> **N.** Very little or not at all

I worry _____ . . .
27. About how my friends treat me.

28. That I might kill myself.
29. That I might not be able to get a good job when I am older.
30. That someone might force me to do sexual things I don't want to do.
31. About how well other teenagers like me.
32. That I might lose my best friend.
33. That one of my parents will hit me so hard that I will be badly hurt.
34. That I may die soon.
35. That a nuclear bomb might be dropped on our country.
36. About all the drugs and drinking I see around me.
37. That one of my parents might die.
38. About all the people who are hungry and poor in our country.
39. That I might get beaten up at school.
40. About whether my body is growing in a normal way.
41. About how much my mother or father drinks.
42. About how I'm doing in school.
43. About my looks.
44. That my friends might get me in trouble.
45. About all the violence in our country.
46. That my parents might get a divorce.

(Leave this number blank if your parents are already divorced, or if one of your parents is no longer living.)

C. My Family

For each of the following statements, mark the response that best matches your feelings. Your choices are:

> **A.** Strongly agree
> **B.** Agree
> **C.** Not sure
> **D.** Disagree
> **E.** Strongly disagree

I wish my parents (or guardians) would . . .
47. Give me more freedom.
48. Spend more time with me.
49. Yell at me less often.
50. Talk with me more about their views on important issues such as sex and drugs.
51. Be more interested in the things I care about.
52. Give me more responsibility.
53. Say "I love you" more often.
54. Trust me more.

Mark the appropriate response to the following statements and questions.

55. There is a lot of love in my family.
   A. Very true
   B. Somewhat true
   C. Not true

56. How often does your family do projects *together* to help other people (such as collecting food for the hungry or helping a neighbor)?
   A. At least once a month
   B. Once in a while
   C. Never

57. How often does your family talk together about God, the Bible or other religious things?
   A. Every day
   B. At least two or three times a week
   C. At least once a week
   D. At least once or twice a month
   E. Never

58. How often do you hear your mother talk about her religious faith?
   A. Every day
   B. At least two or three times a week
   C. At least once a week
   D. At least once or twice a month
   E. Never

59. How often do you hear your father talk about his religious faith?
   A. Every day
   B. At least two or three times a week
   C. At least once a week
   D. At least once or twice a month
   E. Never

D. How I Feel About Myself

Tell how true each of the following statements is for you. Your options are:

> V. Very true
> S. Somewhat true
> N. Not true

60. On the whole, I like myself.
61. I spend a lot of time thinking about who I am.
62. No one really understands me.
63. I believe life has a purpose.
64. I feel good about my body.

E. My Future

For questions 65 to 70, indicate how likely it is that each statement will come true. Choose one of these answers for each question:

> E. Excellent chance
> G. Good chance
> F. Fair chance
> P. Poor chance
> N. No chance

I believe there is a(n) _____ that . . .

65. I will someday be married and have children.
66. I will go to college.

67. I will be very happy 10 years from now.
68. I will be active in church when I am 40.
69. I myself or someone close to me might get AIDS.
70. The world will be destroyed by a nuclear war sometime in the next 10 years.

F. My Friends

71. How many close friends (not relatives) do you have?
   A. None
   B. One or two
   C. Three to five
   D. Six to nine
   E. Ten or more

72. I wish I could be better at making friends.
   A. Strongly agree
   B. Agree
   C. Not sure
   D. Disagree
   E. Strongly disagree

73. I wish I could be better at being a friend to others.
   A. Strongly agree
   B. Agree
   C. Not sure
   D. Disagree
   E. Strongly disagree

74. Some of my best friends belong to this church.
   T. True
   F. False

75. How often do you feel lonely?
   A. Every day
   B. Quite often, but not every day
   C. Once in a while
   D. Never

76. How often do your friends try to get you to do things you know are wrong?
   A. Very often
   B. Often
   C. Sometimes
   D. Once in a while
   E. Never

77. Which of the following choices best describes your parents' feelings toward your friends?
   A. My parents like all of my friends.
   B. My parents like most of my friends, except for one or two.
   C. My parents like about half of my friends, and half they don't.
   D. My parents don't like most of my friends, but one or two are okay.
   E. My parents don't like any of my friends.

G. Where I'd Go for Help

If you were in the following situations, to whom would you most likely turn for help or advice? For each situation, choose one of these answers:

> **A.** A parent or guardian
> **B.** A friend my own age
> **C.** An adult friend or relative
> **D.** A minister or youth worker
> **E.** Nobody

78. If I were having trouble in school, I would turn to _____.
79. If I were wondering how to handle my feelings, I would turn to _____.
80. If some of my friends started using alcohol or other drugs, I would turn to _____.
81. If I had questions about sex, I would turn to _____.
82. If I were feeling guilty about something I had done, I would turn to _____.
83. If I were deciding what to do with my life, I would turn to _____.

H. My Christian Faith

84. Overall, how important is religion in your life?
    V. Very important
    S. Somewhat important
    N. Not important

85. Compared to a year ago, would you say your faith is now more important, less important or about the same?
    M. More important
    L. Less important
    S. About the same

86. I am sure God loves me just as I am.
    T. True
    ?. Don't know
    F. False

87. Which of the following statements comes closest to your view of God?
    A. I know for sure that God exists.
    B. I am mostly sure that God exists.
    C. I'm not sure if God exists.
    D. I don't think there is a God.
    E. I am sure there is no such thing as God.

88. Which of the following statements is closest to your view of Jesus?
    A. Jesus is the Son of God who died on the cross and rose again.
    B. Jesus is the Son of God, but I doubt that he actually rose from the dead.
    C. Jesus was a great man who lived long ago, but I don't think he was the Son of God.
    D. Jesus never existed; his life is just a story people made up.

89. My religious beliefs greatly influence how I act at school and with my friends.
    M. Most of the time
    S. Some of the time
    R. Rarely or never

90. I believe God will stop loving me if I do a lot of wrong things.
    T. True
    ?. Not sure
    F. False

What do you think God wants you to do with your life? For each of the following actions, choose one of these responses:

> **T.** True
> **?.** Not sure
> **F.** False

God wants me . . .
91. To pray.
92. To worship.
93. To read the Bible.
94. To help get rid of hunger, poverty and war.
95. To tell other people about Jesus.
96. To spend time helping other people.

I. What I Do

Please answer the following questions as honestly as you can. Remember, no one will ever find out how you answered.
Choose one of the following answers for questions 97 to 107:

> **A.** None
> **B.** Once or twice
> **C.** Three to five times
> **D.** Six to nine times
> **E.** Ten times or more

97. In the past twelve months, how many times have you been to a party where people your age were drinking alcohol?
98. During the past twelve months, how many times have you taken something from a store without paying for it?
99. During the past twelve months, how many times have you cheated on a test at school?
100. During the past twelve months, how many times have you intentionally damaged or destroyed property (for example, broken windows or furniture, put paint on walls or signs, or scratched or dented a car)?
101. During the past twelve months, how many times have you lied to one of your parents?
102. During the past twelve months, how many times have you hit or beat up another kid?
103. During the past twelve months, how many times have you drunk alcohol while you were alone or with friends your own age? (Do not include communion wine.)

104. During the past month, how many times have you drunk alcohol while you were alone or with friends your own age? (Do not include communion wine.)

105. How many times have you used marijuana (grass, pot) or hashish (hash, hash oil) in your lifetime?

106. How many times in the past two weeks have you had five or more drinks in a row? (A "drink" is a glass of wine, a bottle or can of beer, a shot of liquor or a mixed drink.)

107. How many times in your lifetime have you tried cocaine or crack?

108. In the past month, how much time did you spend helping people outside your family with special needs (for example, collecting food for hungry people, mowing lawns for people who can't do it themselves, or spending time with sick or disabled people)? Don't count work for which you were paid.
    A. None
    B. One or two hours
    C. Three to five hours
    D. Six to ten hours
    E. Eleven hours or more

109. How much television do you watch on an average school day? Don't count weekends.
    A. None
    B. One hour or less
    C. About two hours
    D. About three or four hours
    E. Five hours or more

J. School

110. How much time do you usually spend on homework each week?
    A. None
    B. One hour or less
    C. Between one and three hours
    D. Between three and five hours
    E. Between five and ten hours
    F. More than ten hours

111. I enjoy school.
    M. Most of the time
    S. Sometimes
    N. Rarely or never

112. I try to do the best I can at school.
    M. Most of the time
    S. Sometimes
    N. Rarely or never

113. How often, if ever, do you get in trouble at school?
    M. Most of the time
    S. Sometimes
    N. Never

114. During the past four weeks, how many school days have you skipped or "cut"?
    A. None
    B. One day
    C. Two days
    D. Three days or more

K. Right and Wrong

In your opinion, are each of the actions in questions 115 to 120 right or wrong? Here are the possible responses:

> R. Morally right
> ?. Not sure
> W. Morally wrong

115. Sexual intercourse between two unmarried 16-year-olds who love each other.

116. People trying to keep a minority family from moving into a neighborhood.

117. Cheating on a test at school.

118. Lying to one's parents.

119. Sixteen-year-olds drinking a couple of beers at a party.

120. Stealing a shirt from a store.

L. Male-Female Relationships

121. How many times in the past twelve months have you been out on a date (such as going to a party or movie with one person of the opposite sex)?
    A. None
    B. One or two times
    C. Three to five times
    D. Six to nine times
    E. Ten to nineteen times
    F. Twenty times or more

122. In the past twelve months, how many times have you kissed someone about your age who is of the opposite sex?
    A. None
    B. One or two times
    C. Three to five times
    D. Six to nine times
    E. Ten to nineteen times
    F. Twenty times or more

123. Is it difficult for you to talk with other kids of the opposite sex?
    Y. Yes
    N. No

124. Are you in love right now with someone about your age who is of the opposite sex?
    Y. Yes
    N. No

125. Do you like to do things with teenagers of the opposite sex?
    A. Usually
    B. Sometimes
    C. Never

126. How often do you think about sex?
    A. Very often
    B. Sometimes
    C. Never

127. Have you ever had sexual intercourse ("gone all the way" or "made love")?
A. Never
B. Yes, one time
C. Yes, two to five times
D. Yes, six times or more
E. I don't know what sexual intercourse is.

M. My Church

128. How many adults in your church do you think know you well?
A. None
B. One or two
C. Three to five
D. Six to nine
E. Ten or more

129. How much does your church help you answer important questions about your life?
V. Very much
S. Some
L. A little
N. Not at all

130. If you had an important question about life, how many adults in your church would you feel comfortable going to for help? Don't count your parents or other relatives.
A. None
B. One or two
C. Three to five
D. Six to nine
E. Ten or more

131. How important is church to you?
A. Very important
B. Somewhat important
C. Not important

132. Would you recommend your church to a friend who doesn't belong to another church?
Y. Yes
?. Not sure
N. No

N. My Feelings About My Church

For questions 133 to 138, circle the number that best describes the main "feeling" you get from your church. For example, if you believe that most people in your church think teenagers are important, but some don't, you might circle a 6 or 7 for question 133.

In my church . . .

133.	Kids are important	9 8 7 6 5 4 3 2 1	Kids aren't important
134.	I have many church friends.	9 8 7 6 5 4 3 2 1	I have no church friends.
135.	I learn a lot.	9 8 7 6 5 4 3 2 1	I don't learn anything.
136.	Questions are invited.	9 8 7 6 5 4 3 2 1	Questions aren't welcome.
137.	It's exciting.	9 8 7 6 5 4 3 2 1	It's boring.
138.	Everyone cares about me.	9 8 7 6 5 4 3 2 1	Nobody cares about me.

O. What I Want From My Church

When you think about what you want from your church, how important are each of the following to you? Your choices are:

5. Extremely important
4. Important
3. Somewhat important
2. Slightly important
1. Not important

It is _____ to me . . .
139. To learn about the Bible.
140. To learn what it means to be a Christian.
141. To learn what is special about me.
142. To help my religious faith grow.
143. To make good friends.
144. To get to know adults who care about me.
145. To have opportunities to help other people.
146. To learn more about how I can make decisions about what is right and wrong.
147. To learn about sex and sexual values.
148. To learn about alcohol and other drugs, and what my values about them should be.
149. To have lots of fun and good times.
150. To learn what a Christian should do about big issues such as poverty and war.

P. How Well My Church Is Doing

Rate how well your church does in each of the areas listed in questions 151 to 162. Your choices are:

5. Excellent
4. Good
3. Okay
2. Fair
1. Poor

How well does your church . . .
151. Help you learn about the Bible?
152. Help you learn what it means to be a Christian?
153. Help you learn what's special about you?
154. Help your religious faith grow?
155. Help you make friends?
156. Help you get to know adults who care about you?
157. Help you to help other people?
158. Help you learn about what is right or wrong?
159. Help you learn about sex and sexual values?
160. Help you learn about alcohol and other drugs, and what your values about them should be?
161. Provide lots of fun and good times?
162. Help you learn what a Christian should do about big issues such as poverty and war?

YOUTH SURVEY

Directions

**This survey isn't about what you know.
It's about who you are—
what you think,
what you feel,
what you believe.**

**It's about your school,
your church,
your friends,
your family,
yourself.**

**It's about what is important to you in life—
what you do,
what you worry about,
what you enjoy.**

Be honest in giving your answers. Your name will not be attached to the survey, so no one will know what you write. Your answers will be summarized together with the answers of other young people in your church. All of those answers together will provide important clues to the interests, beliefs, problems and hopes of your church's young people. It's important for youth ministry leaders to have those clues so they can do a better job of planning youth ministry for you and your friends.

Do not begin answering questions until you are instructed to do so. As soon as the survey administrator gives the signal to open this booklet to the first page, you may begin. Mark your answers on the answer sheet, not in this booklet.

For each question, decide which answer fits you best, then *circle the corresponding number or letter on the answer sheet*. Mark only one answer for each question. Do not spend a lot of time trying to decide between two answers; it's usually best to mark your first impression and go right on to the next question. There is no "right" or "wrong" answer to any question—so answer each question honestly.

When you have finished, fold your answer sheet in half and put it into the envelope provided by the survey administrator.

**Thanks for helping.
Thanks for being *you*.**

General Information

1. I am: **F.** Female
            M. Male

2. My grade in school is:
   7   8   9   10   11   12

A. What I Want in Life

Listed below are things that some people want in life. Read through the complete list without making any marks. Then go back and decide how important each one is to you. Your choices are:

> **V.** Very important
> **S.** Somewhat important
> **N.** Not very important

It is _____ to me . . .

3. To be good in music, drama or art.
4. To have a happy family life.
5. To make my parents proud of me.
6. To make my own decisions.
7. To do things that help people.
8. To feel safe and secure in my neighborhood.
9. To feel good about myself.
10. To be popular at school.
11. To have lots of fun and good times.
12. To understand my feelings.
13. To have lots of money.
14. To have God at the center of my life.
15. To have a world without hunger or poverty.
16. To get a good job when I am older.
17. To have things (such as clothes, records and so on) as nice as other kids have.
18. To do something important with my life.
19. To do well in school.
20. To have a world without war.
21. To be really good at sports.
22. To be different in some way from all the other teenagers I know.
23. To have friends I can count on.
24. To do whatever I want to do, when I want to do it.
25. To be part of a church.
26. To have clothes and hair that look good to other kids.

B. What I Worry About

How much do you worry about each of the following statements? Your choices are:

> **V.** Very much
> **S.** Somewhat
> **N.** Very little or not at all

I worry _____ . . .

27. About how my friends treat me.

28. That I might kill myself.
29. That I might not be able to get a good job when I am older.
30. That someone might force me to do sexual things I don't want to do.
31. About how well other teenagers like me.
32. That I might lose my best friend.
33. That one of my parents will hit me so hard that I will be badly hurt.
34. That I may die soon.
35. That a nuclear bomb might be dropped on our country.
36. About all the drugs and drinking I see around me.
37. That one of my parents might die.
38. About all the people who are hungry and poor in our country.
39. That I might get beaten up at school.
40. About whether my body is growing in a normal way.
41. About how much my mother or father drinks.
42. About how I'm doing in school.
43. About my looks.
44. That my friends might get me in trouble.
45. About all the violence in our country.
46. That my parents might get a divorce.

   (Leave this number blank if your parents are already divorced, or if one of your parents is no longer living.)

C. My Family

For each of the following statements, mark the response that best matches your feelings. Your choices are:

> **A.** Strongly agree
> **B.** Agree
> **C.** Not sure
> **D.** Disagree
> **E.** Strongly disagree

I wish my parents (or guardians) would . . .

47. Give me more freedom.
48. Spend more time with me.
49. Yell at me less often.
50. Talk with me more about their views on important issues such as sex and drugs.
51. Be more interested in the things I care about.
52. Give me more responsibility.
53. Say "I love you" more often.
54. Trust me more.

Mark the appropriate response to the following statements and questions.

55. There is a lot of love in my family.
    A. Very true
    B. Somewhat true
    C. Not true

56. How often does your family do projects *together* to help other people (such as collecting food for the hungry or helping a neighbor)?
   A. At least once a month
   B. Once in a while
   C. Never

57. How often does your family talk together about God, the Bible or other religious things?
   A. Every day
   B. At least two or three times a week
   C. At least once a week
   D. At least once or twice a month
   E. Never

58. How often do you hear your mother talk about her religious faith?
   A. Every day
   B. At least two or three times a week
   C. At least once a week
   D. At least once or twice a month
   E. Never

59. How often do you hear your father talk about his religious faith?
   A. Every day
   B. At least two or three times a week
   C. At least once a week
   D. At least once or twice a month
   E. Never

D. How I Feel About Myself

Tell how true each of the following statements is for you. Your options are:

> V. Very true
> S. Somewhat true
> N. Not true

60. On the whole, I like myself.
61. I spend a lot of time thinking about who I am.
62. No one really understands me.
63. I believe life has a purpose.
64. I feel good about my body.

E. My Future

For questions 65 to 70, indicate how likely it is that each statement will come true. Choose one of these answers for each question:

> E. Excellent chance
> G. Good chance
> F. Fair chance
> P. Poor chance
> N. No chance

I believe there is a(n) _____ that . . .

65. I will someday be married and have children.
66. I will go to college.

67. I will be very happy 10 years from now.
68. I will be active in church when I am 40.
69. I myself or someone close to me might get AIDS.
70. The world will be destroyed by a nuclear war sometime in the next 10 years.

F. My Friends

71. How many close friends (not relatives) do you have?
   A. None
   B. One or two
   C. Three to five
   D. Six to nine
   E. Ten or more

72. I wish I could be better at making friends.
   A. Strongly agree
   B. Agree
   C. Not sure
   D. Disagree
   E. Strongly disagree

73. I wish I could be better at being a friend to others.
   A. Strongly agree
   B. Agree
   C. Not sure
   D. Disagree
   E. Strongly disagree

74. Some of my best friends belong to this church.
   T. True
   F. False

75. How often do you feel lonely?
   A. Every day
   B. Quite often, but not every day
   C. Once in a while
   D. Never

76. How often do your friends try to get you to do things you know are wrong?
   A. Very often
   B. Often
   C. Sometimes
   D. Once in a while
   E. Never

77. Which of the following choices best describes your parents' feelings toward your friends?
   A. My parents like all of my friends.
   B. My parents like most of my friends, except for one or two.
   C. My parents like about half of my friends, and half they don't.
   D. My parents don't like most of my friends, but one or two are okay.
   E. My parents don't like any of my friends.

G. Where I'd Go for Help

If you were in the following situations, to whom would you most likely turn for help or advice? For each situation, choose one of these answers:

> **A.** A parent or guardian
> **B.** A friend my own age
> **C.** An adult friend or relative
> **D.** A minister or youth worker
> **E.** Nobody

78. If I were having trouble in school, I would turn to _____.

79. If I were wondering how to handle my feelings, I would turn to _____.

80. If some of my friends started using alcohol or other drugs, I would turn to _____.

81. If I had questions about sex, I would turn to _____.

82. If I were feeling guilty about something I had done, I would turn to _____.

83. If I were deciding what to do with my life, I would turn to _____.

H. My Christian Faith

84. Overall, how important is religion in your life?
    V. Very important
    S. Somewhat important
    N. Not important

85. Compared to a year ago, would you say your faith is now more important, less important or about the same?
    M. More important
    L. Less important
    S. About the same

86. I am sure God loves me just as I am.
    T. True
    ?. Don't know
    F. False

87. Which of the following statements comes closest to your view of God?
    A. I know for sure that God exists.
    B. I am mostly sure that God exists.
    C. I'm not sure if God exists.
    D. I don't think there is a God.
    E. I am sure there is no such thing as God.

88. Which of the following statements is closest to your view of Jesus?
    A. Jesus is the Son of God who died on the cross and rose again.
    B. Jesus is the Son of God, but I doubt that he actually rose from the dead.
    C. Jesus was a great man who lived long ago, but I don't think he was the Son of God.
    D. Jesus never existed; his life is just a story people made up.

89. My religious beliefs greatly influence how I act at school and with my friends.
    M. Most of the time
    S. Some of the time
    R. Rarely or never

90. I believe God will stop loving me if I do a lot of wrong things.
    T. True
    ?. Not sure
    F. False

What do you think God wants you to do with your life? For each of the following actions, choose one of these responses:

> **T.** True
> **?.** Not sure
> **F.** False

God wants me . . .

91. To pray.
92. To worship.
93. To read the Bible.
94. To help get rid of hunger, poverty and war.
95. To tell other people about Jesus.
96. To spend time helping other people.

I. What I Do

Please answer the following questions as honestly as you can. Remember, no one will ever find out how you answered.

Choose one of the following answers for questions 97 to 107:

> **A.** None
> **B.** Once or twice
> **C.** Three to five times
> **D.** Six to nine times
> **E.** Ten times or more

97. In the past twelve months, how many times have you been to a party where people your age were drinking alcohol?

98. During the past twelve months, how many times have you taken something from a store without paying for it?

99. During the past twelve months, how many times have you cheated on a test at school?

100. During the past twelve months, how many times have you intentionally damaged or destroyed property (for example, broken windows or furniture, put paint on walls or signs, or scratched or dented a car)?

101. During the past twelve months, how many times have you lied to one of your parents?

102. During the past twelve months, how many times have you hit or beat up another kid?

103. During the past twelve months, how many times have you drunk alcohol while you were alone or with friends your own age? (Do not include communion wine.)

104. During the past month, how many times have you drunk alcohol while you were alone or with friends your own age? (Do not include communion wine.)

105. How many times have you used marijuana (grass, pot) or hashish (hash, hash oil) in your lifetime?

106. How many times in the past two weeks have you had five or more drinks in a row? (A "drink" is a glass of wine, a bottle or can of beer, a shot of liquor or a mixed drink.)

107. How many times in your lifetime have you tried cocaine or crack?

108. In the past month, how much time did you spend helping people outside your family with special needs (for example, collecting food for hungry people, mowing lawns for people who can't do it themselves, or spending time with sick or disabled people)? Don't count work for which you were paid.
   A. None
   B. One or two hours
   C. Three to five hours
   D. Six to ten hours
   E. Eleven hours or more

109. How much television do you watch on an average school day? Don't count weekends.
   A. None
   B. One hour or less
   C. About two hours
   D. About three or four hours
   E. Five hours or more

J. School

110. How much time do you usually spend on homework each week?
   A. None
   B. One hour or less
   C. Between one and three hours
   D. Between three and five hours
   E. Between five and ten hours
   F. More than ten hours

111. I enjoy school.
   M. Most of the time
   S. Sometimes
   N. Rarely or never

112. I try to do the best I can at school.
   M. Most of the time
   S. Sometimes
   N. Rarely or never

113. How often, if ever, do you get in trouble at school?
   M. Most of the time
   S. Sometimes
   N. Never

114. During the past four weeks, how many school days have you skipped or "cut"?
   A. None
   B. One day
   C. Two days
   D. Three days or more

K. Right and Wrong

In your opinion, are each of the actions in questions 115 to 120 right or wrong? Here are the possible responses:

> R. Morally right
> ?. Not sure
> W. Morally wrong

115. Sexual intercourse between two unmarried 16-year-olds who love each other.

116. People trying to keep a minority family from moving into a neighborhood.

117. Cheating on a test at school.

118. Lying to one's parents.

119. Sixteen-year-olds drinking a couple of beers at a party.

120. Stealing a shirt from a store.

L. Male-Female Relationships

121. How many times in the past twelve months have you been out on a date (such as going to a party or movie with one person of the opposite sex)?
   A. None
   B. One or two times
   C. Three to five times
   D. Six to nine times
   E. Ten to nineteen times
   F. Twenty times or more

122. In the past twelve months, how many times have you kissed someone about your age who is of the opposite sex?
   A. None
   B. One or two times
   C. Three to five times
   D. Six to nine times
   E. Ten to nineteen times
   F. Twenty times or more

123. Is it difficult for you to talk with other kids of the opposite sex?
   Y. Yes
   N. No

124. Are you in love right now with someone about your age who is of the opposite sex?
   Y. Yes
   N. No

125. Do you like to do things with teenagers of the opposite sex?
   A. Usually
   B. Sometimes
   C. Never

126. How often do you think about sex?
   A. Very often
   B. Sometimes
   C. Never

127. Have you ever had sexual intercourse ("gone all the way" or "made love")?
  A. Never
  B. Yes, one time
  C. Yes, two to five times
  D. Yes, six times or more
  E. I don't know what sexual intercourse is.

M. My Church

128. How many adults in your church do you think know you well?
  A. None
  B. One or two
  C. Three to five
  D. Six to nine
  E. Ten or more

129. How much does your church help you answer important questions about your life?
  V. Very much
  S. Some
  L. A little
  N. Not at all

130. If you had an important question about life, how many adults in your church would you feel comfortable going to for help? Don't count your parents or other relatives.
  A. None
  B. One or two
  C. Three to five
  D. Six to nine
  E. Ten or more

131. How important is church to you?
  A. Very important
  B. Somewhat important
  C. Not important

132. Would you recommend your church to a friend who doesn't belong to another church?
  Y. Yes
  ?. Not sure
  N. No

N. My Feelings About My Church

For questions 133 to 138, circle the number that best describes the main "feeling" you get from your church. For example, if you believe that most people in your church think teenagers are important, but some don't, you might circle a 6 or 7 for question 133.

In my church . . .

133.	Kids are important	9 8 7 6 5 4 3 2 1	Kids aren't important
134.	I have many church friends.	9 8 7 6 5 4 3 2 1	I have no church friends.
135.	I learn a lot.	9 8 7 6 5 4 3 2 1	I don't learn anything.
136.	Questions are invited.	9 8 7 6 5 4 3 2 1	Questions aren't welcome.
137.	It's exciting.	9 8 7 6 5 4 3 2 1	It's boring.
138.	Everyone cares about me.	9 8 7 6 5 4 3 2 1	Nobody cares about me.

O. What I Want From My Church

When you think about what you want from your church, how important are each of the following to you? Your choices are:

| 5. Extremely important |
| 4. Important |
| 3. Somewhat important |
| 2. Slightly important |
| 1. Not important |

It is _____ to me . . .
139. To learn about the Bible.
140. To learn what it means to be a Christian.
141. To learn what is special about me.
142. To help my religious faith grow.
143. To make good friends.
144. To get to know adults who care about me.
145. To have opportunities to help other people.
146. To learn more about how I can make decisions about what is right and wrong.
147. To learn about sex and sexual values.
148. To learn about alcohol and other drugs, and what my values about them should be.
149. To have lots of fun and good times.
150. To learn what a Christian should do about big issues such as poverty and war.

P. How Well My Church Is Doing

Rate how well your church does in each of the areas listed in questions 151 to 162. Your choices are:

| 5. Excellent |
| 4. Good |
| 3. Okay |
| 2. Fair |
| 1. Poor |

How well does your church . . .
151. Help you learn about the Bible?
152. Help you learn what it means to be a Christian?
153. Help you learn what's special about you?
154. Help your religious faith grow?
155. Help you make friends?
156. Help you get to know adults who care about you?
157. Help you to help other people?
158. Help you learn about what is right or wrong?
159. Help you learn about sex and sexual values?
160. Help you learn about alcohol and other drugs, and what your values about them should be?
161. Provide lots of fun and good times?
162. Help you learn what a Christian should do about big issues such as poverty and war?

ANSWER SHEET
Circle the answer you want to give.

General Information
1. F M
2. 7 8
   9 10
   11 12

A. What I Want in Life
3. V S N
4. V S N
5. V S N
6. V S N
7. V S N
8. V S N
9. V S N
10. V S N
11. V S N
12. V S N
13. V S N
14. V S N
15. V S N
16. V S N
17. V S N
18. V S N
19. V S N
20. V S N
21. V S N
22. V S N
23. V S N
24. V S N
25. V S N
26. V S N

B. What I Worry About
27. V S N
28. V S N
29. V S N
30. V S N
31. V S N
32. V S N
33. V S N
34. V S N
35. V S N
36. V S N
37. V S N
38. V S N
39. V S N
40. V S N
41. V S N
42. V S N
43. V S N
44. V S N
45. V S N
46. V S N

C. My Family
47. A B C D E
48. A B C D E
49. A B C D E
50. A B C D E
51. A B C D E
52. A B C D E
53. A B C D E
54. A B C D E
55. A B C
56. A B C
57. A B C D E
58. A B C D E
59. A B C D E

D. How I Feel About Myself
60. V S N
61. V S N
62. V S N
63. V S N
64. V S N

E. My Future
65. E G F P N
66. E G F P N
67. E G F P N
68. E G F P N
69. E G F P N
70. E G F P N

F. My Friends
71. A B C D E
72. A B C D E
73. A B C D E
74. T F
75. A B C D
76. A B C D E
77. A B C D E

G. Where I'd Go for Help
78. A B C D E
79. A B C D E
80. A B C D E
81. A B C D E
82. A B C D E
83. A B C D E

H. My Christian Faith
84. V S N
85. M L S
86. T ? F
87. A B C D E
88. A B C D
89. M S R
90. T ? F
91. T ? F
92. T ? F
93. T ? F
94. T ? F
95. T ? F
96. T ? F

I. What I Do
97. A B C D E
98. A B C D E
99. A B C D E
100. A B C D E
101. A B C D E
102. A B C D E
103. A B C D E
104. A B C D E
105. A B C D E
106. A B C D E
107. A B C D E
108. A B C D E
109. A B C D E

J. School
110. A B C D E F
111. M S N
112. M S N
113. M S N
114. A B C D

K. Right and Wrong
115. R ? W
116. R ? W
117. R ? W
118. R ? W
119. R ? W
120. R ? W

L. Male-Female Relationships
121. A B C D E F
122. A B C D E F
123. Y N
124. Y N
125. A B C
126. A B C
127. A B C D E

M. My Church
128. A B C D E
129. V S L N
130. A B C D E
131. A B C
132. Y ? N

N. My Feelings About My Church
133. 9 8 7 6 5 4 3 2 1
134. 9 8 7 6 5 4 3 2 1
135. 9 8 7 6 5 4 3 2 1
136. 9 8 7 6 5 4 3 2 1
137. 9 8 7 6 5 4 3 2 1
138. 9 8 7 6 5 4 3 2 1

O. What I Want From My Church
139. 5 4 3 2 1
140. 5 4 3 2 1
141. 5 4 3 2 1
142. 5 4 3 2 1
143. 5 4 3 2 1
144. 5 4 3 2 1
145. 5 4 3 2 1
146. 5 4 3 2 1
147. 5 4 3 2 1
148. 5 4 3 2 1
149. 5 4 3 2 1
150. 5 4 3 2 1

P. How Well My Church Is Doing
151. 5 4 3 2 1
152. 5 4 3 2 1
153. 5 4 3 2 1
154. 5 4 3 2 1
155. 5 4 3 2 1
156. 5 4 3 2 1
157. 5 4 3 2 1
158. 5 4 3 2 1
159. 5 4 3 2 1
160. 5 4 3 2 1
161. 5 4 3 2 1
162. 5 4 3 2 1

ANSWER SHEET
Circle the answer you want to give.

General Information
1. F   M
2. 7   8
   9   10
   11   12

A. What I Want in Life
3. V   S   N
4. V   S   N
5. V   S   N
6. V   S   N
7. V   S   N
8. V   S   N
9. V   S   N
10. V   S   N
11. V   S   N
12. V   S   N
13. V   S   N
14. V   S   N
15. V   S   N
16. V   S   N
17. V   S   N
18. V   S   N
19. V   S   N
20. V   S   N
21. V   S   N
22. V   S   N
23. V   S   N
24. V   S   N
25. V   S   N
26. V   S   N

B. What I Worry About
27. V   S   N
28. V   S   N
29. V   S   N
30. V   S   N
31. V   S   N
32. V   S   N
33. V   S   N
34. V   S   N
35. V   S   N
36. V   S   N
37. V   S   N
38. V   S   N
39. V   S   N
40. V   S   N
41. V   S   N
42. V   S   N
43. V   S   N
44. V   S   N
45. V   S   N
46. V   S   N

C. My Family
47. A   B   C   D   E
48. A   B   C   D   E
49. A   B   C   D   E
50. A   B   C   D   E
51. A   B   C   D   E
52. A   B   C   D   E
53. A   B   C   D   E
54. A   B   C   D   E
55. A   B   C
56. A   B   C
57. A   B   C   D   E
58. A   B   C   D   E
59. A   B   C   D   E

D. How I Feel About Myself
60. V   S   N
61. V   S   N
62. V   S   N
63. V   S   N
64. V   S   N

E. My Future
65. E   G   F   P   N
66. E   G   F   P   N
67. E   G   F   P   N
68. E   G   F   P   N
69. E   G   F   P   N
70. E   G   F   P   N

F. My Friends
71. A   B   C   D   E
72. A   B   C   D   E
73. A   B   C   D   E
74. T   F
75. A   B   C   D
76. A   B   C   D   E
77. A   B   C   D   E

G. Where I'd Go for Help
78. A   B   C   D   E
79. A   B   C   D   E
80. A   B   C   D   E
81. A   B   C   D   E
82. A   B   C   D   E
83. A   B   C   D   E

H. My Christian Faith
84. V   S   N
85. M   L   S
86. T   ?   F
87. A   B   C   D   E
88. A   B   C   D
89. M   S   R
90. T   ?   F
91. T   ?   F
92. T   ?   F
93. T   ?   F
94. T   ?   F
95. T   ?   F
96. T   ?   F

I. What I Do
97. A   B   C   D   E
98. A   B   C   D   E
99. A   B   C   D   E
100. A   B   C   D   E
101. A   B   C   D   E
102. A   B   C   D   E
103. A   B   C   D   E
104. A   B   C   D   E
105. A   B   C   D   E
106. A   B   C   D   E
107. A   B   C   D   E
108. A   B   C   D   E
109. A   B   C   D   E

J. School
110. A   B   C   D   E   F
111. M   S   N
112. M   S   N
113. M   S   N
114. A   B   C   D

K. Right and Wrong
115. R   ?   W
116. R   ?   W
117. R   ?   W
118. R   ?   W
119. R   ?   W
120. R   ?   W

L. Male-Female Relationships
121. A   B   C   D   E   F
122. A   B   C   D   E   F
123. Y   N
124. Y   N
125. A   B   C
126. A   B   C
127. A   B   C   D   E

M. My Church
128. A   B   C   D   E
129. V   S   L   N
130. A   B   C   D   E
131. A   B   C
132. Y   ?   N

N. My Feelings About My Church
133. 9 8 7 6 5 4 3 2 1
134. 9 8 7 6 5 4 3 2 1
135. 9 8 7 6 5 4 3 2 1
136. 9 8 7 6 5 4 3 2 1
137. 9 8 7 6 5 4 3 2 1
138. 9 8 7 6 5 4 3 2 1

O. What I Want From My Church
139. 5   4   3   2   1
140. 5   4   3   2   1
141. 5   4   3   2   1
142. 5   4   3   2   1
143. 5   4   3   2   1
144. 5   4   3   2   1
145. 5   4   3   2   1
146. 5   4   3   2   1
147. 5   4   3   2   1
148. 5   4   3   2   1
149. 5   4   3   2   1
150. 5   4   3   2   1

P. How Well My Church Is Doing
151. 5   4   3   2   1
152. 5   4   3   2   1
153. 5   4   3   2   1
154. 5   4   3   2   1
155. 5   4   3   2   1
156. 5   4   3   2   1
157. 5   4   3   2   1
158. 5   4   3   2   1
159. 5   4   3   2   1
160. 5   4   3   2   1
161. 5   4   3   2   1
162. 5   4   3   2   1

ANSWER SHEET
Circle the answer you want to give.

General Information
1. F M
2. 7 8
   9 10
   11 12

A. What I Want in Life
3. V S N
4. V S N
5. V S N
6. V S N
7. V S N
8. V S N
9. V S N
10. V S N
11. V S N
12. V S N
13. V S N
14. V S N
15. V S N
16. V S N
17. V S N
18. V S N
19. V S N
20. V S N
21. V S N
22. V S N
23. V S N
24. V S N
25. V S N
26. V S N

B. What I Worry About
27. V S N
28. V S N
29. V S N
30. V S N
31. V S N
32. V S N
33. V S N
34. V S N
35. V S N
36. V S N
37. V S N
38. V S N
39. V S N
40. V S N
41. V S N
42. V S N
43. V S N
44. V S N
45. V S N
46. V S N

C. My Family
47. A B C D E
48. A B C D E
49. A B C D E
50. A B C D E
51. A B C D E
52. A B C D E
53. A B C D E
54. A B C D E
55. A B C
56. A B C
57. A B C D E
58. A B C D E
59. A B C D E

D. How I Feel About Myself
60. V S N
61. V S N
62. V S N
63. V S N
64. V S N

E. My Future
65. E G F P N
66. E G F P N
67. E G F P N
68. E G F P N
69. E G F P N
70. E G F P N

F. My Friends
71. A B C D E
72. A B C D E
73. A B C D E
74. T F
75. A B C D
76. A B C D E
77. A B C D E

G. Where I'd Go for Help
78. A B C D E
79. A B C D E
80. A B C D E
81. A B C D E
82. A B C D E
83. A B C D E

H. My Christian Faith
84. V S N
85. M L S
86. T ? F
87. A B C D E
88. A B C D
89. M S R
90. T ? F
91. T ? F
92. T ? F
93. T ? F
94. T ? F
95. T ? F
96. T ? F

I. What I Do
97. A B C D E
98. A B C D E
99. A B C D E
100. A B C D E
101. A B C D E
102. A B C D E
103. A B C D E
104. A B C D E
105. A B C D E
106. A B C D E
107. A B C D E
108. A B C D E
109. A B C D E

J. School
110. A B C D E F
111. M S N
112. M S N
113. M S N
114. A B C D

K. Right and Wrong
115. R ? W
116. R ? W
117. R ? W
118. R ? W
119. R ? W
120. R ? W

L. Male-Female Relationships
121. A B C D E F
122. A B C D E F
123. Y N
124. Y N
125. A B C
126. A B C
127. A B C D E

M. My Church
128. A B C D E
129. V S L N
130. A B C D E
131. A B C
132. Y ? N

N. My Feelings About My Church
133. 9 8 7 6 5 4 3 2 1
134. 9 8 7 6 5 4 3 2 1
135. 9 8 7 6 5 4 3 2 1
136. 9 8 7 6 5 4 3 2 1
137. 9 8 7 6 5 4 3 2 1
138. 9 8 7 6 5 4 3 2 1

O. What I Want From My Church
139. 5 4 3 2 1
140. 5 4 3 2 1
141. 5 4 3 2 1
142. 5 4 3 2 1
143. 5 4 3 2 1
144. 5 4 3 2 1
145. 5 4 3 2 1
146. 5 4 3 2 1
147. 5 4 3 2 1
148. 5 4 3 2 1
149. 5 4 3 2 1
150. 5 4 3 2 1

P. How Well My Church Is Doing
151. 5 4 3 2 1
152. 5 4 3 2 1
153. 5 4 3 2 1
154. 5 4 3 2 1
155. 5 4 3 2 1
156. 5 4 3 2 1
157. 5 4 3 2 1
158. 5 4 3 2 1
159. 5 4 3 2 1
160. 5 4 3 2 1
161. 5 4 3 2 1
162. 5 4 3 2 1

ANSWER SHEET

Circle the answer you want to give.

General Information
1. F M
2. 7 8
   9 10
   11 12

A. What I Want in Life
3. V S N
4. V S N
5. V S N
6. V S N
7. V S N
8. V S N
9. V S N
10. V S N
11. V S N
12. V S N
13. V S N
14. V S N
15. V S N
16. V S N
17. V S N
18. V S N
19. V S N
20. V S N
21. V S N
22. V S N
23. V S N
24. V S N
25. V S N
26. V S N

B. What I Worry About
27. V S N
28. V S N
29. V S N
30. V S N
31. V S N
32. V S N
33. V S N
34. V S N
35. V S N
36. V S N
37. V S N
38. V S N
39. V S N
40. V S N
41. V S N
42. V S N
43. V S N
44. V S N
45. V S N
46. V S N

C. My Family
47. A B C D E
48. A B C D E
49. A B C D E
50. A B C D E
51. A B C D E
52. A B C D E
53. A B C D E
54. A B C D E
55. A B C
56. A B C
57. A B C D E
58. A B C D E
59. A B C D E

D. How I Feel About Myself
60. V S N
61. V S N
62. V S N
63. V S N
64. V S N

E. My Future
65. E G F P N
66. E G F P N
67. E G F P N
68. E G F P N
69. E G F P N
70. E G F P N

F. My Friends
71. A B C D E
72. A B C D E
73. A B C D E
74. T F
75. A B C D
76. A B C D E
77. A B C D E

G. Where I'd Go for Help
78. A B C D E
79. A B C D E
80. A B C D E
81. A B C D E
82. A B C D E
83. A B C D E

H. My Christian Faith
84. V S N
85. M L S
86. T ? F
87. A B C D E
88. A B C D
89. M S R
90. T ? F
91. T ? F
92. T ? F
93. T ? F
94. T ? F
95. T ? F
96. T ? F

I. What I Do
97. A B C D E
98. A B C D E
99. A B C D E
100. A B C D E
101. A B C D E
102. A B C D E
103. A B C D E
104. A B C D E
105. A B C D E
106. A B C D E
107. A B C D E
108. A B C D E
109. A B C D E

J. School
110. A B C D E F
111. M S N
112. M S N
113. M S N
114. A B C D

K. Right and Wrong
115. R ? W
116. R ? W
117. R ? W
118. R ? W
119. R ? W
120. R ? W

L. Male-Female Relationships
121. A B C D E F
122. A B C D E F
123. Y N
124. Y N
125. A B C
126. A B C
127. A B C D E

M. My Church
128. A B C D E
129. V S L N
130. A B C D E
131. A B C
132. Y ? N

N. My Feelings About My Church
133. 9 8 7 6 5 4 3 2 1
134. 9 8 7 6 5 4 3 2 1
135. 9 8 7 6 5 4 3 2 1
136. 9 8 7 6 5 4 3 2 1
137. 9 8 7 6 5 4 3 2 1
138. 9 8 7 6 5 4 3 2 1

O. What I Want From My Church
139. 5 4 3 2 1
140. 5 4 3 2 1
141. 5 4 3 2 1
142. 5 4 3 2 1
143. 5 4 3 2 1
144. 5 4 3 2 1
145. 5 4 3 2 1
146. 5 4 3 2 1
147. 5 4 3 2 1
148. 5 4 3 2 1
149. 5 4 3 2 1
150. 5 4 3 2 1

P. How Well My Church Is Doing
151. 5 4 3 2 1
152. 5 4 3 2 1
153. 5 4 3 2 1
154. 5 4 3 2 1
155. 5 4 3 2 1
156. 5 4 3 2 1
157. 5 4 3 2 1
158. 5 4 3 2 1
159. 5 4 3 2 1
160. 5 4 3 2 1
161. 5 4 3 2 1
162. 5 4 3 2 1

ANSWER SHEET

Circle the answer you want to give.

General Information

1. F   M
2. 7   8
   9   10
   11 12

A. What I Want in Life

3. V   S   N
4. V   S   N
5. V   S   N
6. V   S   N
7. V   S   N
8. V   S   N
9. V   S   N
10. V   S   N
11. V   S   N
12. V   S   N
13. V   S   N
14. V   S   N
15. V   S   N
16. V   S   N
17. V   S   N
18. V   S   N
19. V   S   N
20. V   S   N
21. V   S   N
22. V   S   N
23. V   S   N
24. V   S   N
25. V   S   N
26. V   S   N

B. What I Worry About

27. V   S   N
28. V   S   N
29. V   S   N
30. V   S   N
31. V   S   N
32. V   S   N
33. V   S   N
34. V   S   N
35. V   S   N
36. V   S   N
37. V   S   N
38. V   S   N
39. V   S   N
40. V   S   N
41. V   S   N
42. V   S   N
43. V   S   N
44. V   S   N
45. V   S   N
46. V   S   N

C. My Family

47. A   B   C   D   E
48. A   B   C   D   E
49. A   B   C   D   E
50. A   B   C   D   E
51. A   B   C   D   E
52. A   B   C   D   E
53. A   B   C   D   E
54. A   B   C   D   E
55. A   B   C
56. A   B   C
57. A   B   C   D   E
58. A   B   C   D   E
59. A   B   C   D   E

D. How I Feel About Myself

60. V   S   N
61. V   S   N
62. V   S   N
63. V   S   N
64. V   S   N

E. My Future

65. E   G   F   P   N
66. E   G   F   P   N
67. E   G   F   P   N
68. E   G   F   P   N
69. E   G   F   P   N
70. E   G   F   P   N

F. My Friends

71. A   B   C   D   E
72. A   B   C   D   E
73. A   B   C   D   E
74. T   F
75. A   B   C   D
76. A   B   C   D   E
77. A   B   C   D   E

G. Where I'd Go for Help

78. A   B   C   D   E
79. A   B   C   D   E
80. A   B   C   D   E
81. A   B   C   D   E
82. A   B   C   D   E
83. A   B   C   D   E

H. My Christian Faith

84. V   S   N
85. M   L   S
86. T   ?   F
87. A   B   C   D   E
88. A   B   C   D
89. M   S   R
90. T   ?   F
91. T   ?   F
92. T   ?   F
93. T   ?   F
94. T   ?   F
95. T   ?   F
96. T   ?   F

I. What I Do

97. A   B   C   D   E
98. A   B   C   D   E
99. A   B   C   D   E
100. A   B   C   D   E
101. A   B   C   D   E
102. A   B   C   D   E
103. A   B   C   D   E
104. A   B   C   D   E
105. A   B   C   D   E
106. A   B   C   D   E
107. A   B   C   D   E
108. A   B   C   D   E
109. A   B   C   D   E

J. School

110. A   B   C   D   E   F
111. M   S   N
112. M   S   N
113. M   S   N
114. A   B   C   D

K. Right and Wrong

115. R   ?   W
116. R   ?   W
117. R   ?   W
118. R   ?   W
119. R   ?   W
120. R   ?   W

L. Male-Female Relationships

121. A   B   C   D   E   F
122. A   B   C   D   E   F
123. Y   N
124. Y   N
125. A   B   C
126. A   B   C
127. A   B   C   D   E

M. My Church

128. A   B   C   D   E
129. V   S   L   N
130. A   B   C   D   E
131. A   B   C
132. Y   ?   N

N. My Feelings About My Church

133. 9 8 7 6 5 4 3 2 1
134. 9 8 7 6 5 4 3 2 1
135. 9 8 7 6 5 4 3 2 1
136. 9 8 7 6 5 4 3 2 1
137. 9 8 7 6 5 4 3 2 1
138. 9 8 7 6 5 4 3 2 1

O. What I Want From My Church

139. 5   4   3   2   1
140. 5   4   3   2   1
141. 5   4   3   2   1
142. 5   4   3   2   1
143. 5   4   3   2   1
144. 5   4   3   2   1
145. 5   4   3   2   1
146. 5   4   3   2   1
147. 5   4   3   2   1
148. 5   4   3   2   1
149. 5   4   3   2   1
150. 5   4   3   2   1

P. How Well My Church Is Doing

151. 5   4   3   2   1
152. 5   4   3   2   1
153. 5   4   3   2   1
154. 5   4   3   2   1
155. 5   4   3   2   1
156. 5   4   3   2   1
157. 5   4   3   2   1
158. 5   4   3   2   1
159. 5   4   3   2   1
160. 5   4   3   2   1
161. 5   4   3   2   1
162. 5   4   3   2   1

ANSWER SHEET

Circle the answer you want to give.

General Information

1. F M
2. 7 8
   9 10
   11 12

A. What I Want in Life

3. V S N
4. V S N
5. V S N
6. V S N
7. V S N
8. V S N
9. V S N
10. V S N
11. V S N
12. V S N
13. V S N
14. V S N
15. V S N
16. V S N
17. V S N
18. V S N
19. V S N
20. V S N
21. V S N
22. V S N
23. V S N
24. V S N
25. V S N
26. V S N

B. What I Worry About

27. V S N
28. V S N
29. V S N
30. V S N
31. V S N
32. V S N
33. V S N
34. V S N
35. V S N
36. V S N
37. V S N
38. V S N
39. V S N
40. V S N
41. V S N
42. V S N
43. V S N
44. V S N
45. V S N
46. V S N

C. My Family

47. A B C D E
48. A B C D E
49. A B C D E
50. A B C D E
51. A B C D E
52. A B C D E
53. A B C D E
54. A B C D E
55. A B C
56. A B C
57. A B C D E
58. A B C D E
59. A B C D E

D. How I Feel About Myself

60. V S N
61. V S N
62. V S N
63. V S N
64. V S N

E. My Future

65. E G F P N
66. E G F P N
67. E G F P N
68. E G F P N
69. E G F P N
70. E G F P N

F. My Friends

71. A B C D E
72. A B C D E
73. A B C D E
74. T F
75. A B C D
76. A B C D E
77. A B C D E

G. Where I'd Go for Help

78. A B C D E
79. A B C D E
80. A B C D E
81. A B C D E
82. A B C D E
83. A B C D E

H. My Christian Faith

84. V S N
85. M L S
86. T ? F
87. A B C D E
88. A B C D
89. M S R
90. T ? F
91. T ? F
92. T ? F
93. T ? F
94. T ? F
95. T ? F
96. T ? F

I. What I Do

97. A B C D E
98. A B C D E
99. A B C D E
100. A B C D E
101. A B C D E
102. A B C D E
103. A B C D E
104. A B C D E
105. A B C D E
106. A B C D E
107. A B C D E
108. A B C D E
109. A B C D E

J. School

110. A B C D E F
111. M S N
112. M S N
113. M S N
114. A B C D

K. Right and Wrong

115. R ? W
116. R ? W
117. R ? W
118. R ? W
119. R ? W
120. R ? W

L. Male-Female Relationships

121. A B C D E F
122. A B C D E F
123. Y N
124. Y N
125. A B C
126. A B C
127. A B C D E

M. My Church

128. A B C D E
129. V S L N
130. A B C D E
131. A B C
132. Y ? N

N. My Feelings About My Church

133. 9 8 7 6 5 4 3 2 1
134. 9 8 7 6 5 4 3 2 1
135. 9 8 7 6 5 4 3 2 1
136. 9 8 7 6 5 4 3 2 1
137. 9 8 7 6 5 4 3 2 1
138. 9 8 7 6 5 4 3 2 1

O. What I Want From My Church

139. 5 4 3 2 1
140. 5 4 3 2 1
141. 5 4 3 2 1
142. 5 4 3 2 1
143. 5 4 3 2 1
144. 5 4 3 2 1
145. 5 4 3 2 1
146. 5 4 3 2 1
147. 5 4 3 2 1
148. 5 4 3 2 1
149. 5 4 3 2 1
150. 5 4 3 2 1

P. How Well My Church Is Doing

151. 5 4 3 2 1
152. 5 4 3 2 1
153. 5 4 3 2 1
154. 5 4 3 2 1
155. 5 4 3 2 1
156. 5 4 3 2 1
157. 5 4 3 2 1
158. 5 4 3 2 1
159. 5 4 3 2 1
160. 5 4 3 2 1
161. 5 4 3 2 1
162. 5 4 3 2 1

ANSWER SHEET

Circle the answer you want to give.

General Information
1. F   M
2. 7   8
   9   10
   11   12

A. What I Want in Life
3. V   S   N
4. V   S   N
5. V   S   N
6. V   S   N
7. V   S   N
8. V   S   N
9. V   S   N
10. V   S   N
11. V   S   N
12. V   S   N
13. V   S   N
14. V   S   N
15. V   S   N
16. V   S   N
17. V   S   N
18. V   S   N
19. V   S   N
20. V   S   N
21. V   S   N
22. V   S   N
23. V   S   N
24. V   S   N
25. V   S   N
26. V   S   N

B. What I Worry About
27. V   S   N
28. V   S   N
29. V   S   N
30. V   S   N
31. V   S   N
32. V   S   N
33. V   S   N
34. V   S   N
35. V   S   N
36. V   S   N
37. V   S   N
38. V   S   N
39. V   S   N
40. V   S   N
41. V   S   N
42. V   S   N
43. V   S   N
44. V   S   N
45. V   S   N
46. V   S   N

C. My Family
47. A   B   C   D   E
48. A   B   C   D   E
49. A   B   C   D   E
50. A   B   C   D   E
51. A   B   C   D   E
52. A   B   C   D   E
53. A   B   C   D   E
54. A   B   C   D   E
55. A   B   C
56. A   B   C
57. A   B   C   D   E
58. A   B   C   D   E
59. A   B   C   D   E

D. How I Feel About Myself
60. V   S   N
61. V   S   N
62. V   S   N
63. V   S   N
64. V   S   N

E. My Future
65. E   G   F   P   N
66. E   G   F   P   N
67. E   G   F   P   N
68. E   G   F   P   N
69. E   G   F   P   N
70. E   G   F   P   N

F. My Friends
71. A   B   C   D   E
72. A   B   C   D   E
73. A   B   C   D   E
74. T   F
75. A   B   C   D
76. A   B   C   D   E
77. A   B   C   D   E

G. Where I'd Go for Help
78. A   B   C   D   E
79. A   B   C   D   E
80. A   B   C   D   E
81. A   B   C   D   E
82. A   B   C   D   E
83. A   B   C   D   E

H. My Christian Faith
84. V   S   N
85. M   L   S
86. T   ?   F
87. A   B   C   D   E
88. A   B   C   D
89. M   S   R
90. T   ?   F
91. T   ?   F
92. T   ?   F
93. T   ?   F
94. T   ?   F
95. T   ?   F
96. T   ?   F

I. What I Do
97. A   B   C   D   E
98. A   B   C   D   E
99. A   B   C   D   E
100. A   B   C   D   E
101. A   B   C   D   E
102. A   B   C   D   E
103. A   B   C   D   E
104. A   B   C   D   E
105. A   B   C   D   E
106. A   B   C   D   E
107. A   B   C   D   E
108. A   B   C   D   E
109. A   B   C   D   E

J. School
110. A   B   C   D   E   F
111. M   S   N
112. M   S   N
113. M   S   N
114. A   B   C   D

K. Right and Wrong
115. R   ?   W
116. R   ?   W
117. R   ?   W
118. R   ?   W
119. R   ?   W
120. R   ?   W

L. Male-Female Relationships
121. A   B   C   D   E   F
122. A   B   C   D   E   F
123. Y   N
124. Y   N
125. A   B   C
126. A   B   C
127. A   B   C   D   E

M. My Church
128. A   B   C   D   E
129. V   S   L   N
130. A   B   C   D   E
131. A   B   C
132. Y   ?   N

N. My Feelings About My Church
133. 9 8 7 6 5 4 3 2 1
134. 9 8 7 6 5 4 3 2 1
135. 9 8 7 6 5 4 3 2 1
136. 9 8 7 6 5 4 3 2 1
137. 9 8 7 6 5 4 3 2 1
138. 9 8 7 6 5 4 3 2 1

O. What I Want From My Church
139. 5   4   3   2   1
140. 5   4   3   2   1
141. 5   4   3   2   1
142. 5   4   3   2   1
143. 5   4   3   2   1
144. 5   4   3   2   1
145. 5   4   3   2   1
146. 5   4   3   2   1
147. 5   4   3   2   1
148. 5   4   3   2   1
149. 5   4   3   2   1
150. 5   4   3   2   1

P. How Well My Church Is Doing
151. 5   4   3   2   1
152. 5   4   3   2   1
153. 5   4   3   2   1
154. 5   4   3   2   1
155. 5   4   3   2   1
156. 5   4   3   2   1
157. 5   4   3   2   1
158. 5   4   3   2   1
159. 5   4   3   2   1
160. 5   4   3   2   1
161. 5   4   3   2   1
162. 5   4   3   2   1

ANSWER SHEET

Circle the answer you want to give.

General Information
1. F M
2. 7 8
    9 10
    11 12

A. What I Want in Life
3. V S N
4. V S N
5. V S N
6. V S N
7. V S N
8. V S N
9. V S N
10. V S N
11. V S N
12. V S N
13. V S N
14. V S N
15. V S N
16. V S N
17. V S N
18. V S N
19. V S N
20. V S N
21. V S N
22. V S N
23. V S N
24. V S N
25. V S N
26. V S N

B. What I Worry About
27. V S N
28. V S N
29. V S N
30. V S N
31. V S N
32. V S N
33. V S N
34. V S N
35. V S N
36. V S N
37. V S N
38. V S N
39. V S N
40. V S N
41. V S N
42. V S N
43. V S N
44. V S N
45. V S N
46. V S N

C. My Family
47. A B C D E
48. A B C D E
49. A B C D E
50. A B C D E
51. A B C D E
52. A B C D E
53. A B C D E
54. A B C D E
55. A B C
56. A B C
57. A B C D E
58. A B C D E
59. A B C D E

D. How I Feel About Myself
60. V S N
61. V S N
62. V S N
63. V S N
64. V S N

E. My Future
65. E G F P N
66. E G F P N
67. E G F P N
68. E G F P N
69. E G F P N
70. E G F P N

F. My Friends
71. A B C D E
72. A B C D E
73. A B C D E
74. T F
75. A B C D
76. A B C D E
77. A B C D E

G. Where I'd Go for Help
78. A B C D E
79. A B C D E
80. A B C D E
81. A B C D E
82. A B C D E
83. A B C D E

H. My Christian Faith
84. V S N
85. M L S
86. T ? F
87. A B C D E
88. A B C D
89. M S R
90. T ? F
91. T ? F
92. T ? F
93. T ? F
94. T ? F
95. T ? F
96. T ? F

I. What I Do
97. A B C D E
98. A B C D E
99. A B C D E
100. A B C D E
101. A B C D E
102. A B C D E
103. A B C D E
104. A B C D E
105. A B C D E
106. A B C D E
107. A B C D E
108. A B C D E
109. A B C D E

J. School
110. A B C D E F
111. M S N
112. M S N
113. M S N
114. A B C D

K. Right and Wrong
115. R ? W
116. R ? W
117. R ? W
118. R ? W
119. R ? W
120. R ? W

L. Male-Female Relationships
121. A B C D E F
122. A B C D E F
123. Y N
124. Y N
125. A B C
126. A B C
127. A B C D E

M. My Church
128. A B C D E
129. V S L N
130. A B C D E
131. A B C
132. Y ? N

N. My Feelings About My Church
133. 9 8 7 6 5 4 3 2 1
134. 9 8 7 6 5 4 3 2 1
135. 9 8 7 6 5 4 3 2 1
136. 9 8 7 6 5 4 3 2 1
137. 9 8 7 6 5 4 3 2 1
138. 9 8 7 6 5 4 3 2 1

O. What I Want From My Church
139. 5 4 3 2 1
140. 5 4 3 2 1
141. 5 4 3 2 1
142. 5 4 3 2 1
143. 5 4 3 2 1
144. 5 4 3 2 1
145. 5 4 3 2 1
146. 5 4 3 2 1
147. 5 4 3 2 1
148. 5 4 3 2 1
149. 5 4 3 2 1
150. 5 4 3 2 1

P. How Well My Church Is Doing
151. 5 4 3 2 1
152. 5 4 3 2 1
153. 5 4 3 2 1
154. 5 4 3 2 1
155. 5 4 3 2 1
156. 5 4 3 2 1
157. 5 4 3 2 1
158. 5 4 3 2 1
159. 5 4 3 2 1
160. 5 4 3 2 1
161. 5 4 3 2 1
162. 5 4 3 2 1

ANSWER SHEET

Circle the answer you want to give.

General Information
1. F   M
2. 7   8
   9   10
   11 12

A. What I Want in Life
3. V   S   N
4. V   S   N
5. V   S   N
6. V   S   N
7. V   S   N
8. V   S   N
9. V   S   N
10. V   S   N
11. V   S   N
12. V   S   N
13. V   S   N
14. V   S   N
15. V   S   N
16. V   S   N
17. V   S   N
18. V   S   N
19. V   S   N
20. V   S   N
21. V   S   N
22. V   S   N
23. V   S   N
24. V   S   N
25. V   S   N
26. V   S   N

B. What I Worry About
27. V   S   N
28. V   S   N
29. V   S   N
30. V   S   N
31. V   S   N
32. V   S   N
33. V   S   N
34. V   S   N
35. V   S   N
36. V   S   N
37. V   S   N
38. V   S   N
39. V   S   N
40. V   S   N
41. V   S   N
42. V   S   N
43. V   S   N
44. V   S   N
45. V   S   N
46. V   S   N

C. My Family
47. A   B   C   D   E
48. A   B   C   D   E
49. A   B   C   D   E
50. A   B   C   D   E
51. A   B   C   D   E
52. A   B   C   D   E
53. A   B   C   D   E
54. A   B   C   D   E
55. A   B   C
56. A   B   C
57. A   B   C   D   E
58. A   B   C   D   E
59. A   B   C   D   E

D. How I Feel About Myself
60. V   S   N
61. V   S   N
62. V   S   N
63. V   S   N
64. V   S   N

E. My Future
65. E   G   F   P   N
66. E   G   F   P   N
67. E   G   F   P   N
68. E   G   F   P   N
69. E   G   F   P   N
70. E   G   F   P   N

F. My Friends
71. A   B   C   D   E
72. A   B   C   D   E
73. A   B   C   D   E
74. T   F
75. A   B   C   D
76. A   B   C   D   E
77. A   B   C   D   E

G. Where I'd Go for Help
78. A   B   C   D   E
79. A   B   C   D   E
80. A   B   C   D   E
81. A   B   C   D   E
82. A   B   C   D   E
83. A   B   C   D   E

H. My Christian Faith
84. V   S   N
85. M   L   S
86. T   ?   F
87. A   B   C   D   E
88. A   B   C   D
89. M   S   R
90. T   ?   F
91. T   ?   F
92. T   ?   F
93. T   ?   F
94. T   ?   F
95. T   ?   F
96. T   ?   F

I. What I Do
97. A   B   C   D   E
98. A   B   C   D   E
99. A   B   C   D   E
100. A   B   C   D   E
101. A   B   C   D   E
102. A   B   C   D   E
103. A   B   C   D   E
104. A   B   C   D   E
105. A   B   C   D   E
106. A   B   C   D   E
107. A   B   C   D   E
108. A   B   C   D   E
109. A   B   C   D   E

J. School
110. A   B   C   D   E   F
111. M   S   N
112. M   S   N
113. M   S   N
114. A   B   C   D

K. Right and Wrong
115. R   ?   W
116. R   ?   W
117. R   ?   W
118. R   ?   W
119. R   ?   W
120. R   ?   W

L. Male-Female Relationships
121. A   B   C   D   E   F
122. A   B   C   D   E   F
123. Y   N
124. Y   N
125. A   B   C
126. A   B   C
127. A   B   C   D   E

M. My Church
128. A   B   C   D   E
129. V   S   L   N
130. A   B   C   D   E
131. A   B   C
132. Y   ?   N

N. My Feelings About My Church
133. 9 8 7 6 5 4 3 2 1
134. 9 8 7 6 5 4 3 2 1
135. 9 8 7 6 5 4 3 2 1
136. 9 8 7 6 5 4 3 2 1
137. 9 8 7 6 5 4 3 2 1
138. 9 8 7 6 5 4 3 2 1

O. What I Want From My Church
139. 5   4   3   2   1
140. 5   4   3   2   1
141. 5   4   3   2   1
142. 5   4   3   2   1
143. 5   4   3   2   1
144. 5   4   3   2   1
145. 5   4   3   2   1
146. 5   4   3   2   1
147. 5   4   3   2   1
148. 5   4   3   2   1
149. 5   4   3   2   1
150. 5   4   3   2   1

P. How Well My Church Is Doing
151. 5   4   3   2   1
152. 5   4   3   2   1
153. 5   4   3   2   1
154. 5   4   3   2   1
155. 5   4   3   2   1
156. 5   4   3   2   1
157. 5   4   3   2   1
158. 5   4   3   2   1
159. 5   4   3   2   1
160. 5   4   3   2   1
161. 5   4   3   2   1
162. 5   4   3   2   1

ANSWER SHEET
Circle the answer you want to give.

General Information
1. F M
2. 7 8
   9 10
   11 12

A. What I Want in Life
3. V S N
4. V S N
5. V S N
6. V S N
7. V S N
8. V S N
9. V S N
10. V S N
11. V S N
12. V S N
13. V S N
14. V S N
15. V S N
16. V S N
17. V S N
18. V S N
19. V S N
20. V S N
21. V S N
22. V S N
23. V S N
24. V S N
25. V S N
26. V S N

B. What I Worry About
27. V S N
28. V S N
29. V S N
30. V S N
31. V S N
32. V S N
33. V S N
34. V S N
35. V S N
36. V S N
37. V S N
38. V S N
39. V S N
40. V S N
41. V S N
42. V S N
43. V S N
44. V S N
45. V S N
46. V S N

C. My Family
47. A B C D E
48. A B C D E
49. A B C D E
50. A B C D E
51. A B C D E
52. A B C D E
53. A B C D E
54. A B C D E
55. A B C
56. A B C
57. A B C D E
58. A B C D E
59. A B C D E

D. How I Feel About Myself
60. V S N
61. V S N
62. V S N
63. V S N
64. V S N

E. My Future
65. E G F P N
66. E G F P N
67. E G F P N
68. E G F P N
69. E G F P N
70. E G F P N

F. My Friends
71. A B C D E
72. A B C D E
73. A B C D E
74. T F
75. A B C D
76. A B C D E
77. A B C D E

G. Where I'd Go for Help
78. A B C D E
79. A B C D E
80. A B C D E
81. A B C D E
82. A B C D E
83. A B C D E

H. My Christian Faith
84. V S N
85. M L S
86. T ? F
87. A B C D E
88. A B C D
89. M S R
90. T ? F
91. T ? F
92. T ? F
93. T ? F
94. T ? F
95. T ? F
96. T ? F

I. What I Do
97. A B C D E
98. A B C D E
99. A B C D E
100. A B C D E
101. A B C D E
102. A B C D E
103. A B C D E
104. A B C D E
105. A B C D E
106. A B C D E
107. A B C D E
108. A B C D E
109. A B C D E

J. School
110. A B C D E F
111. M S N
112. M S N
113. M S N
114. A B C D

K. Right and Wrong
115. R ? W
116. R ? W
117. R ? W
118. R ? W
119. R ? W
120. R ? W

L. Male-Female Relationships
121. A B C D E F
122. A B C D E F
123. Y N
124. Y N
125. A B C
126. A B C
127. A B C D E

M. My Church
128. A B C D E
129. V S L N
130. A B C D E
131. A B C
132. Y ? N

N. My Feelings About My Church
133. 9 8 7 6 5 4 3 2 1
134. 9 8 7 6 5 4 3 2 1
135. 9 8 7 6 5 4 3 2 1
136. 9 8 7 6 5 4 3 2 1
137. 9 8 7 6 5 4 3 2 1
138. 9 8 7 6 5 4 3 2 1

O. What I Want From My Church
139. 5 4 3 2 1
140. 5 4 3 2 1
141. 5 4 3 2 1
142. 5 4 3 2 1
143. 5 4 3 2 1
144. 5 4 3 2 1
145. 5 4 3 2 1
146. 5 4 3 2 1
147. 5 4 3 2 1
148. 5 4 3 2 1
149. 5 4 3 2 1
150. 5 4 3 2 1

P. How Well My Church Is Doing
151. 5 4 3 2 1
152. 5 4 3 2 1
153. 5 4 3 2 1
154. 5 4 3 2 1
155. 5 4 3 2 1
156. 5 4 3 2 1
157. 5 4 3 2 1
158. 5 4 3 2 1
159. 5 4 3 2 1
160. 5 4 3 2 1
161. 5 4 3 2 1
162. 5 4 3 2 1

ANSWER SHEET
Circle the answer you want to give.

General Information
1. F M
2. 7 8
   9 10
   11 12

A. What I Want in Life
3. V S N
4. V S N
5. V S N
6. V S N
7. V S N
8. V S N
9. V S N
10. V S N
11. V S N
12. V S N
13. V S N
14. V S N
15. V S N
16. V S N
17. V S N
18. V S N
19. V S N
20. V S N
21. V S N
22. V S N
23. V S N
24. V S N
25. V S N
26. V S N

B. What I Worry About
27. V S N
28. V S N
29. V S N
30. V S N
31. V S N
32. V S N
33. V S N
34. V S N
35. V S N
36. V S N
37. V S N
38. V S N
39. V S N
40. V S N
41. V S N
42. V S N
43. V S N
44. V S N
45. V S N
46. V S N

C. My Family
47. A B C D E
48. A B C D E
49. A B C D E
50. A B C D E
51. A B C D E
52. A B C D E
53. A B C D E
54. A B C D E
55. A B C
56. A B C
57. A B C D E
58. A B C D E
59. A B C D E

D. How I Feel About Myself
60. V S N
61. V S N
62. V S N
63. V S N
64. V S N

E. My Future
65. E G F P N
66. E G F P N
67. E G F P N
68. E G F P N
69. E G F P N
70. E G F P N

F. My Friends
71. A B C D E
72. A B C D E
73. A B C D E
74. T F
75. A B C D
76. A B C D E
77. A B C D E

G. Where I'd Go for Help
78. A B C D E
79. A B C D E
80. A B C D E
81. A B C D E
82. A B C D E
83. A B C D E

H. My Christian Faith
84. V S N
85. M L S
86. T ? F
87. A B C D E
88. A B C D
89. M S R
90. T ? F
91. T ? F
92. T ? F
93. T ? F
94. T ? F
95. T ? F
96. T ? F

I. What I Do
97. A B C D E
98. A B C D E
99. A B C D E
100. A B C D E
101. A B C D E
102. A B C D E
103. A B C D E
104. A B C D E
105. A B C D E
106. A B C D E
107. A B C D E
108. A B C D E
109. A B C D E

J. School
110. A B C D E F
111. M S N
112. M S N
113. M S N
114. A B C D

K. Right and Wrong
115. R ? W
116. R ? W
117. R ? W
118. R ? W
119. R ? W
120. R ? W

L. Male-Female Relationships
121. A B C D E F
122. A B C D E F
123. Y N
124. Y N
125. A B C
126. A B C
127. A B C D E

M. My Church
128. A B C D E
129. V S L N
130. A B C D E
131. A B C
132. Y ? N

N. My Feelings About My Church
133. 9 8 7 6 5 4 3 2 1
134. 9 8 7 6 5 4 3 2 1
135. 9 8 7 6 5 4 3 2 1
136. 9 8 7 6 5 4 3 2 1
137. 9 8 7 6 5 4 3 2 1
138. 9 8 7 6 5 4 3 2 1

O. What I Want From My Church
139. 5 4 3 2 1
140. 5 4 3 2 1
141. 5 4 3 2 1
142. 5 4 3 2 1
143. 5 4 3 2 1
144. 5 4 3 2 1
145. 5 4 3 2 1
146. 5 4 3 2 1
147. 5 4 3 2 1
148. 5 4 3 2 1
149. 5 4 3 2 1
150. 5 4 3 2 1

P. How Well My Church Is Doing
151. 5 4 3 2 1
152. 5 4 3 2 1
153. 5 4 3 2 1
154. 5 4 3 2 1
155. 5 4 3 2 1
156. 5 4 3 2 1
157. 5 4 3 2 1
158. 5 4 3 2 1
159. 5 4 3 2 1
160. 5 4 3 2 1
161. 5 4 3 2 1
162. 5 4 3 2 1

ANSWER SHEET
Circle the answer you want to give.

General Information
1. F M
2. 7 8
   9 10
   11 12

A. What I Want in Life
3. V S N
4. V S N
5. V S N
6. V S N
7. V S N
8. V S N
9. V S N
10. V S N
11. V S N
12. V S N
13. V S N
14. V S N
15. V S N
16. V S N
17. V S N
18. V S N
19. V S N
20. V S N
21. V S N
22. V S N
23. V S N
24. V S N
25. V S N
26. V S N

B. What I Worry About
27. V S N
28. V S N
29. V S N
30. V S N
31. V S N
32. V S N
33. V S N
34. V S N
35. V S N
36. V S N
37. V S N
38. V S N
39. V S N
40. V S N
41. V S N
42. V S N
43. V S N
44. V S N
45. V S N
46. V S N

C. My Family
47. A B C D E
48. A B C D E
49. A B C D E
50. A B C D E
51. A B C D E
52. A B C D E
53. A B C D E
54. A B C D E
55. A B C
56. A B C
57. A B C D E
58. A B C D E
59. A B C D E

D. How I Feel About Myself
60. V S N
61. V S N
62. V S N
63. V S N
64. V S N

E. My Future
65. E G F P N
66. E G F P N
67. E G F P N
68. E G F P N
69. E G F P N
70. E G F P N

F. My Friends
71. A B C D E
72. A B C D E
73. A B C D E
74. T F
75. A B C D
76. A B C D E
77. A B C D E

G. Where I'd Go for Help
78. A B C D E
79. A B C D E
80. A B C D E
81. A B C D E
82. A B C D E
83. A B C D E

H. My Christian Faith
84. V S N
85. M L S
86. T ? F
87. A B C D E
88. A B C D
89. M S R
90. T ? F
91. T ? F
92. T ? F
93. T ? F
94. T ? F
95. T ? F
96. T ? F

I. What I Do
97. A B C D E
98. A B C D E
99. A B C D E
100. A B C D E
101. A B C D E
102. A B C D E
103. A B C D E
104. A B C D E
105. A B C D E
106. A B C D E
107. A B C D E
108. A B C D E
109. A B C D E

J. School
110. A B C D E F
111. M S N
112. M S N
113. M S N
114. A B C D

K. Right and Wrong
115. R ? W
116. R ? W
117. R ? W
118. R ? W
119. R ? W
120. R ? W

L. Male-Female Relationships
121. A B C D E F
122. A B C D E F
123. Y N
124. Y N
125. A B C
126. A B C
127. A B C D E

M. My Church
128. A B C D E
129. V S L N
130. A B C D E
131. A B C
132. Y ? N

N. My Feelings About My Church
133. 9 8 7 6 5 4 3 2 1
134. 9 8 7 6 5 4 3 2 1
135. 9 8 7 6 5 4 3 2 1
136. 9 8 7 6 5 4 3 2 1
137. 9 8 7 6 5 4 3 2 1
138. 9 8 7 6 5 4 3 2 1

O. What I Want From My Church
139. 5 4 3 2 1
140. 5 4 3 2 1
141. 5 4 3 2 1
142. 5 4 3 2 1
143. 5 4 3 2 1
144. 5 4 3 2 1
145. 5 4 3 2 1
146. 5 4 3 2 1
147. 5 4 3 2 1
148. 5 4 3 2 1
149. 5 4 3 2 1
150. 5 4 3 2 1

P. How Well My Church Is Doing
151. 5 4 3 2 1
152. 5 4 3 2 1
153. 5 4 3 2 1
154. 5 4 3 2 1
155. 5 4 3 2 1
156. 5 4 3 2 1
157. 5 4 3 2 1
158. 5 4 3 2 1
159. 5 4 3 2 1
160. 5 4 3 2 1
161. 5 4 3 2 1
162. 5 4 3 2 1

ANSWER SHEET
Circle the answer you want to give.

General Information
1. F M
2. 7 8
   9 10
   11 12

A. What I Want in Life
3. V S N
4. V S N
5. V S N
6. V S N
7. V S N
8. V S N
9. V S N
10. V S N
11. V S N
12. V S N
13. V S N
14. V S N
15. V S N
16. V S N
17. V S N
18. V S N
19. V S N
20. V S N
21. V S N
22. V S N
23. V S N
24. V S N
25. V S N
26. V S N

B. What I Worry About
27. V S N
28. V S N
29. V S N
30. V S N
31. V S N
32. V S N
33. V S N
34. V S N
35. V S N
36. V S N
37. V S N
38. V S N
39. V S N
40. V S N
41. V S N
42. V S N
43. V S N
44. V S N
45. V S N
46. V S N

C. My Family
47. A B C D E
48. A B C D E
49. A B C D E
50. A B C D E
51. A B C D E
52. A B C D E
53. A B C D E
54. A B C D E
55. A B C
56. A B C
57. A B C D E
58. A B C D E
59. A B C D E

D. How I Feel About Myself
60. V S N
61. V S N
62. V S N
63. V S N
64. V S N

E. My Future
65. E G F P N
66. E G F P N
67. E G F P N
68. E G F P N
69. E G F P N
70. E G F P N

F. My Friends
71. A B C D E
72. A B C D E
73. A B C D E
74. T F
75. A B C D
76. A B C D E
77. A B C D E

G. Where I'd Go for Help
78. A B C D E
79. A B C D E
80. A B C D E
81. A B C D E
82. A B C D E
83. A B C D E

H. My Christian Faith
84. V S N
85. M L S
86. T ? F
87. A B C D E
88. A B C D
89. M S R
90. T ? F
91. T ? F
92. T ? F
93. T ? F
94. T ? F
95. T ? F
96. T ? F

I. What I Do
97. A B C D E
98. A B C D E
99. A B C D E
100. A B C D E
101. A B C D E
102. A B C D E
103. A B C D E
104. A B C D E
105. A B C D E
106. A B C D E
107. A B C D E
108. A B C D E
109. A B C D E

J. School
110. A B C D E F
111. M S N
112. M S N
113. M S N
114. A B C D

K. Right and Wrong
115. R ? W
116. R ? W
117. R ? W
118. R ? W
119. R ? W
120. R ? W

L. Male-Female Relationships
121. A B C D E F
122. A B C D E F
123. Y N
124. Y N
125. A B C
126. A B C
127. A B C D E

M. My Church
128. A B C D E
129. V S L N
130. A B C D E
131. A B C
132. Y ? N

N. My Feelings About My Church
133. 9 8 7 6 5 4 3 2 1
134. 9 8 7 6 5 4 3 2 1
135. 9 8 7 6 5 4 3 2 1
136. 9 8 7 6 5 4 3 2 1
137. 9 8 7 6 5 4 3 2 1
138. 9 8 7 6 5 4 3 2 1

O. What I Want From My Church
139. 5 4 3 2 1
140. 5 4 3 2 1
141. 5 4 3 2 1
142. 5 4 3 2 1
143. 5 4 3 2 1
144. 5 4 3 2 1
145. 5 4 3 2 1
146. 5 4 3 2 1
147. 5 4 3 2 1
148. 5 4 3 2 1
149. 5 4 3 2 1
150. 5 4 3 2 1

P. How Well My Church Is Doing
151. 5 4 3 2 1
152. 5 4 3 2 1
153. 5 4 3 2 1
154. 5 4 3 2 1
155. 5 4 3 2 1
156. 5 4 3 2 1
157. 5 4 3 2 1
158. 5 4 3 2 1
159. 5 4 3 2 1
160. 5 4 3 2 1
161. 5 4 3 2 1
162. 5 4 3 2 1

ANSWER SHEET
Circle the answer you want to give.

General Information
1. F M
2. 7 8
   9 10
   11 12

A. What I Want in Life
3. V S N
4. V S N
5. V S N
6. V S N
7. V S N
8. V S N
9. V S N
10. V S N
11. V S N
12. V S N
13. V S N
14. V S N
15. V S N
16. V S N
17. V S N
18. V S N
19. V S N
20. V S N
21. V S N
22. V S N
23. V S N
24. V S N
25. V S N
26. V S N

B. What I Worry About
27. V S N
28. V S N
29. V S N
30. V S N
31. V S N
32. V S N
33. V S N
34. V S N
35. V S N
36. V S N
37. V S N
38. V S N
39. V S N
40. V S N
41. V S N
42. V S N
43. V S N
44. V S N
45. V S N
46. V S N

C. My Family
47. A B C D E
48. A B C D E
49. A B C D E
50. A B C D E
51. A B C D E
52. A B C D E
53. A B C D E
54. A B C D E
55. A B C
56. A B C
57. A B C D E
58. A B C D E
59. A B C D E

D. How I Feel About Myself
60. V S N
61. V S N
62. V S N
63. V S N
64. V S N

E. My Future
65. E G F P N
66. E G F P N
67. E G F P N
68. E G F P N
69. E G F P N
70. E G F P N

F. My Friends
71. A B C D E
72. A B C D E
73. A B C D E
74. T F
75. A B C D
76. A B C D E
77. A B C D E

G. Where I'd Go for Help
78. A B C D E
79. A B C D E
80. A B C D E
81. A B C D E
82. A B C D E
83. A B C D E

H. My Christian Faith
84. V S N
85. M L S
86. T ? F
87. A B C D E
88. A B C D
89. M S R
90. T ? F
91. T ? F
92. T ? F
93. T ? F
94. T ? F
95. T ? F
96. T ? F

I. What I Do
97. A B C D E
98. A B C D E
99. A B C D E
100. A B C D E
101. A B C D E
102. A B C D E
103. A B C D E
104. A B C D E
105. A B C D E
106. A B C D E
107. A B C D E
108. A B C D E
109. A B C D E

J. School
110. A B C D E F
111. M S N
112. M S N
113. M S N
114. A B C D

K. Right and Wrong
115. R ? W
116. R ? W
117. R ? W
118. R ? W
119. R ? W
120. R ? W

L. Male-Female Relationships
121. A B C D E F
122. A B C D E F
123. Y N
124. Y N
125. A B C
126. A B C
127. A B C D E

M. My Church
128. A B C D E
129. V S L N
130. A B C D E
131. A B C
132. Y ? N

N. My Feelings About My Church
133. 9 8 7 6 5 4 3 2 1
134. 9 8 7 6 5 4 3 2 1
135. 9 8 7 6 5 4 3 2 1
136. 9 8 7 6 5 4 3 2 1
137. 9 8 7 6 5 4 3 2 1
138. 9 8 7 6 5 4 3 2 1

O. What I Want From My Church
139. 5 4 3 2 1
140. 5 4 3 2 1
141. 5 4 3 2 1
142. 5 4 3 2 1
143. 5 4 3 2 1
144. 5 4 3 2 1
145. 5 4 3 2 1
146. 5 4 3 2 1
147. 5 4 3 2 1
148. 5 4 3 2 1
149. 5 4 3 2 1
150. 5 4 3 2 1

P. How Well My Church Is Doing
151. 5 4 3 2 1
152. 5 4 3 2 1
153. 5 4 3 2 1
154. 5 4 3 2 1
155. 5 4 3 2 1
156. 5 4 3 2 1
157. 5 4 3 2 1
158. 5 4 3 2 1
159. 5 4 3 2 1
160. 5 4 3 2 1
161. 5 4 3 2 1
162. 5 4 3 2 1

ANSWER SHEET

Circle the answer you want to give.

General Information

1. F M
2. 7 8
   9 10
   11 12

A. What I Want in Life

3. V S N
4. V S N
5. V S N
6. V S N
7. V S N
8. V S N
9. V S N
10. V S N
11. V S N
12. V S N
13. V S N
14. V S N
15. V S N
16. V S N
17. V S N
18. V S N
19. V S N
20. V S N
21. V S N
22. V S N
23. V S N
24. V S N
25. V S N
26. V S N

B. What I Worry About

27. V S N
28. V S N
29. V S N
30. V S N
31. V S N
32. V S N
33. V S N
34. V S N
35. V S N
36. V S N
37. V S N
38. V S N
39. V S N
40. V S N
41. V S N
42. V S N
43. V S N
44. V S N
45. V S N
46. V S N

C. My Family

47. A B C D E
48. A B C D E
49. A B C D E
50. A B C D E
51. A B C D E
52. A B C D E
53. A B C D E
54. A B C D E
55. A B C
56. A B C
57. A B C D E
58. A B C D E
59. A B C D E

D. How I Feel About Myself

60. V S N
61. V S N
62. V S N
63. V S N
64. V S N

E. My Future

65. E G F P N
66. E G F P N
67. E G F P N
68. E G F P N
69. E G F P N
70. E G F P N

F. My Friends

71. A B C D E
72. A B C D E
73. A B C D E
74. T F
75. A B C D
76. A B C D E
77. A B C D E

G. Where I'd Go for Help

78. A B C D E
79. A B C D E
80. A B C D E
81. A B C D E
82. A B C D E
83. A B C D E

H. My Christian Faith

84. V S N
85. M L S
86. T ? F
87. A B C D E
88. A B C D
89. M S R
90. T ? F
91. T ? F
92. T ? F
93. T ? F
94. T ? F
95. T ? F
96. T ? F

I. What I Do

97. A B C D E
98. A B C D E
99. A B C D E
100. A B C D E
101. A B C D E
102. A B C D E
103. A B C D E
104. A B C D E
105. A B C D E
106. A B C D E
107. A B C D E
108. A B C D E
109. A B C D E

J. School

110. A B C D E F
111. M S N
112. M S N
113. M S N
114. A B C D

K. Right and Wrong

115. R ? W
116. R ? W
117. R ? W
118. R ? W
119. R ? W
120. R ? W

L. Male-Female Relationships

121. A B C D E F
122. A B C D E F
123. Y N
124. Y N
125. A B C
126. A B C
127. A B C D E

M. My Church

128. A B C D E
129. V S L N
130. A B C D
131. A B C
132. Y ? N

N. My Feelings About My Church

133. 9 8 7 6 5 4 3 2 1
134. 9 8 7 6 5 4 3 2 1
135. 9 8 7 6 5 4 3 2 1
136. 9 8 7 6 5 4 3 2 1
137. 9 8 7 6 5 4 3 2 1
138. 9 8 7 6 5 4 3 2 1

O. What I Want From My Church

139. 5 4 3 2 1
140. 5 4 3 2 1
141. 5 4 3 2 1
142. 5 4 3 2 1
143. 5 4 3 2 1
144. 5 4 3 2 1
145. 5 4 3 2 1
146. 5 4 3 2 1
147. 5 4 3 2 1
148. 5 4 3 2 1
149. 5 4 3 2 1
150. 5 4 3 2 1

P. How Well My Church Is Doing

151. 5 4 3 2 1
152. 5 4 3 2 1
153. 5 4 3 2 1
154. 5 4 3 2 1
155. 5 4 3 2 1
156. 5 4 3 2 1
157. 5 4 3 2 1
158. 5 4 3 2 1
159. 5 4 3 2 1
160. 5 4 3 2 1
161. 5 4 3 2 1
162. 5 4 3 2 1

ANSWER SHEET

Circle the answer you want to give.

General Information

1. F M
2. 7 8
   9 10
   11 12

A. What I Want in Life

3. V S N
4. V S N
5. V S N
6. V S N
7. V S N
8. V S N
9. V S N
10. V S N
11. V S N
12. V S N
13. V S N
14. V S N
15. V S N
16. V S N
17. V S N
18. V S N
19. V S N
20. V S N
21. V S N
22. V S N
23. V S N
24. V S N
25. V S N
26. V S N

B. What I Worry About

27. V S N
28. V S N
29. V S N
30. V S N
31. V S N
32. V S N
33. V S N
34. V S N
35. V S N
36. V S N
37. V S N
38. V S N
39. V S N
40. V S N
41. V S N
42. V S N
43. V S N
44. V S N
45. V S N
46. V S N

C. My Family

47. A B C D E
48. A B C D E
49. A B C D E
50. A B C D E
51. A B C D E
52. A B C D E
53. A B C D E
54. A B C D E
55. A B C
56. A B C
57. A B C D E
58. A B C D E
59. A B C D E

D. How I Feel About Myself

60. V S N
61. V S N
62. V S N
63. V S N
64. V S N

E. My Future

65. E G F P N
66. E G F P N
67. E G F P N
68. E G F P N
69. E G F P N
70. E G F P N

F. My Friends

71. A B C D E
72. A B C D E
73. A B C D E
74. T F
75. A B C D
76. A B C D E
77. A B C D E

G. Where I'd Go for Help

78. A B C D E
79. A B C D E
80. A B C D E
81. A B C D E
82. A B C D E
83. A B C D E

H. My Christian Faith

84. V S N
85. M L S
86. T ? F
87. A B C D E
88. A B C D
89. M S R
90. T ? F
91. T ? F
92. T ? F
93. T ? F
94. T ? F
95. T ? F
96. T ? F

I. What I Do

97. A B C D E
98. A B C D E
99. A B C D E
100. A B C D E
101. A B C D E
102. A B C D E
103. A B C D E
104. A B C D E
105. A B C D E
106. A B C D E
107. A B C D E
108. A B C D E
109. A B C D E

J. School

110. A B C D E F
111. M S N
112. M S N
113. M S N
114. A B C D

K. Right and Wrong

115. R ? W
116. R ? W
117. R ? W
118. R ? W
119. R ? W
120. R ? W

L. Male-Female Relationships

121. A B C D E F
122. A B C D E F
123. Y N
124. Y N
125. A B C
126. A B C
127. A B C D E

M. My Church

128. A B C D E
129. V S L N
130. A B C D E
131. A B C
132. Y ? N

N. My Feelings About My Church

133. 9 8 7 6 5 4 3 2 1
134. 9 8 7 6 5 4 3 2 1
135. 9 8 7 6 5 4 3 2 1
136. 9 8 7 6 5 4 3 2 1
137. 9 8 7 6 5 4 3 2 1
138. 9 8 7 6 5 4 3 2 1

O. What I Want From My Church

139. 5 4 3 2 1
140. 5 4 3 2 1
141. 5 4 3 2 1
142. 5 4 3 2 1
143. 5 4 3 2 1
144. 5 4 3 2 1
145. 5 4 3 2 1
146. 5 4 3 2 1
147. 5 4 3 2 1
148. 5 4 3 2 1
149. 5 4 3 2 1
150. 5 4 3 2 1

P. How Well My Church Is Doing

151. 5 4 3 2 1
152. 5 4 3 2 1
153. 5 4 3 2 1
154. 5 4 3 2 1
155. 5 4 3 2 1
156. 5 4 3 2 1
157. 5 4 3 2 1
158. 5 4 3 2 1
159. 5 4 3 2 1
160. 5 4 3 2 1
161. 5 4 3 2 1
162. 5 4 3 2 1

ANSWER SHEET

Circle the answer you want to give.

General Information
1. F M
2. 7 8
   9 10
   11 12

A. What I Want in Life
3. V S N
4. V S N
5. V S N
6. V S N
7. V S N
8. V S N
9. V S N
10. V S N
11. V S N
12. V S N
13. V S N
14. V S N
15. V S N
16. V S N
17. V S N
18. V S N
19. V S N
20. V S N
21. V S N
22. V S N
23. V S N
24. V S N
25. V S N
26. V S N

B. What I Worry About
27. V S N
28. V S N
29. V S N
30. V S N
31. V S N
32. V S N
33. V S N
34. V S N
35. V S N
36. V S N
37. V S N
38. V S N
39. V S N
40. V S N
41. V S N
42. V S N
43. V S N
44. V S N
45. V S N
46. V S N

C. My Family
47. A B C D E
48. A B C D E
49. A B C D E
50. A B C D E
51. A B C D E
52. A B C D E
53. A B C D E
54. A B C D E
55. A B C
56. A B C
57. A B C D E
58. A B C D E
59. A B C D E

D. How I Feel About Myself
60. V S N
61. V S N
62. V S N
63. V S N
64. V S N

E. My Future
65. E G F P N
66. E G F P N
67. E G F P N
68. E G F P N
69. E G F P N
70. E G F P N

F. My Friends
71. A B C D E
72. A B C D E
73. A B C D E
74. T F
75. A B C D
76. A B C D E
77. A B C D E

G. Where I'd Go for Help
78. A B C D E
79. A B C D E
80. A B C D E
81. A B C D E
82. A B C D E
83. A B C D E

H. My Christian Faith
84. V S N
85. M L S
86. T ? F
87. A B C D E
88. A B C D
89. M S R
90. T ? F
91. T ? F
92. T ? F
93. T ? F
94. T ? F
95. T ? F
96. T ? F

I. What I Do
97. A B C D E
98. A B C D E
99. A B C D E
100. A B C D E
101. A B C D E
102. A ⌐ C D E
103. A B C D E
104. A B C D E
105. A B C D E
106. A B C D E
107. A B C D E
108. A B C D E
109. A B C D E

J. School
110. A B C D E F
111. M S N
112. M S N
113. M S N
114. A B C D

K. Right and Wrong
115. R ? W
116. R ? W
117. R ? W
118. R ? W
119. R ? W
120. R ? W

L. Male-Female Relationships
121. A B C D E F
122. A B C D E F
123. Y N
124. Y N
125. A B C
126. A B C
127. A B C D E

M. My Church
128. A B C D E
129. V S L N
130. A B C D E
131. A B C
132. Y ? N

N. My Feelings About My Church
133. 9 8 7 6 5 4 3 2 1
134. 9 8 7 6 5 4 3 2 1
135. 9 8 7 6 5 4 3 2 1
136. 9 8 7 6 5 4 3 2 1
137. 9 8 7 6 5 4 3 2 1
138. 9 8 7 6 5 4 3 2 1

O. What I Want From My Church
139. 5 4 3 2 1
140. 5 4 3 2 1
141. 5 4 3 2 1
142. 5 4 3 2 1
143. 5 4 3 2 1
144. 5 4 3 2 1
145. 5 4 3 2 1
146. 5 4 3 2 1
147. 5 4 3 2 1
148. 5 4 3 2 1
149. 5 4 3 2 1
150. 5 4 3 2 1

P. How Well My Church Is Doing
151. 5 4 3 2 1
152. 5 4 3 2 1
153. 5 4 3 2 1
154. 5 4 3 2 1
155. 5 4 3 2 1
156. 5 4 3 2 1
157. 5 4 3 2 1
158. 5 4 3 2 1
159. 5 4 3 2 1
160. 5 4 3 2 1
161. 5 4 3 2 1
162. 5 4 3 2 1

ANSWER SHEET

Circle the answer you want to give.

General Information
1. F M
2. 7 8
   9 10
   11 12

A. What I Want in Life
3. V S N
4. V S N
5. V S N
6. V S N
7. V S N
8. V S N
9. V S N
10. V S N
11. V S N
12. V S N
13. V S N
14. V S N
15. V S N
16. V S N
17. V S N
18. V S N
19. V S N
20. V S N
21. V S N
22. V S N
23. V S N
24. V S N
25. V S N
26. V S N

B. What I Worry About
27. V S N
28. V S N
29. V S N
30. V S N
31. V S N
32. V S N
33. V S N
34. V S N
35. V S N
36. V S N
37. V S N
38. V S N
39. V S N
40. V S N
41. V S N
42. V S N
43. V S N
44. V S N
45. V S N
46. V S N

C. My Family
47. A B C D E
48. A B C D E
49. A B C D E
50. A B C D E
51. A B C D E
52. A B C D E
53. A B C D E
54. A B C D E
55. A B C
56. A B C
57. A B C D E
58. A B C D E
59. A B C D E

D. How I Feel About Myself
60. V S N
61. V S N
62. V S N
63. V S N
64. V S N

E. My Future
65. E G F P N
66. E G F P N
67. E G F P N
68. E G F P N
69. E G F P N
70. E G F P N

F. My Friends
71. A B C D E
72. A B C D E
73. A B C D E
74. T F
75. A B C D
76. A B C D E
77. A B C D E

G. Where I'd Go for Help
78. A B C D E
79. A B C D E
80. A B C D E
81. A B C D E
82. A B C D E
83. A B C D E

H. My Christian Faith
84. V S N
85. M L S
86. T ? F
87. A B C D E
88. A B C D
89. M S R
90. T ? F
91. T ? F
92. T ? F
93. T ? F
94. T ? F
95. T ? F
96. T ? F

I. What I Do
97. A B C D E
98. A B C D E
99. A B C D E
100. A B C D E
101. A B C D E
102. A B C D E
103. A B C D E
104. A B C D E
105. A B C D E
106. A B C D E
107. A B C D E
108. A B C D E
109. A B C D E

J. School
110. A B C D E F
111. M S N
112. M S N
113. M S N
114. A B C D

K. Right and Wrong
115. R ? W
116. R ? W
117. R ? W
118. R ? W
119. R ? W
120. R ? W

L. Male-Female Relationships
121. A B C D E F
122. A B C D E F
123. Y N
124. Y N
125. A B C
126. A B C
127. A B C D E

M. My Church
128. A B C D E
129. V S L N
130. A B C D E
131. A B C
132. Y ? N

N. My Feelings About My Church
133. 9 8 7 6 5 4 3 2 1
134. 9 8 7 6 5 4 3 2 1
135. 9 8 7 6 5 4 3 2 1
136. 9 8 7 6 5 4 3 2 1
137. 9 8 7 6 5 4 3 2 1
138. 9 8 7 6 5 4 3 2 1

O. What I Want From My Church
139. 5 4 3 2 1
140. 5 4 3 2 1
141. 5 4 3 2 1
142. 5 4 3 2 1
143. 5 4 3 2 1
144. 5 4 3 2 1
145. 5 4 3 2 1
146. 5 4 3 2 1
147. 5 4 3 2 1
148. 5 4 3 2 1
149. 5 4 3 2 1
150. 5 4 3 2 1

P. How Well My Church Is Doing
151. 5 4 3 2 1
152. 5 4 3 2 1
153. 5 4 3 2 1
154. 5 4 3 2 1
155. 5 4 3 2 1
156. 5 4 3 2 1
157. 5 4 3 2 1
158. 5 4 3 2 1
159. 5 4 3 2 1
160. 5 4 3 2 1
161. 5 4 3 2 1
162. 5 4 3 2 1

ANSWER SHEET

Circle the answer you want to give.

General Information

1. F M
2. 7 8
   9 10
   11 12

A. What I Want in Life

3. V S N
4. V S N
5. V S N
6. V S N
7. V S N
8. V S N
9. V S N
10. V S N
11. V S N
12. V S N
13. V S N
14. V S N
15. V S N
16. V S N
17. V S N
18. V S N
19. V S N
20. V S N
21. V S N
22. V S N
23. V S N
24. V S N
25. V S N
26. V S N

B. What I Worry About

27. V S N
28. V S N
29. V S N
30. V S N
31. V S N
32. V S N
33. V S N
34. V S N
35. V S N
36. V S N
37. V S N
38. V S N
39. V S N
40. V S N
41. V S N
42. V S N
43. V S N
44. V S N
45. V S N
46. V S N

C. My Family

47. A B C D E
48. A B C D E
49. A B C D E
50. A B C D E
51. A B C D E
52. A B C D E
53. A B C D E
54. A B C D E
55. A B C
56. A B C
57. A B C D E
58. A B C D E
59. A B C D E

D. How I Feel About Myself

60. V S N
61. V S N
62. V S N
63. V S N
64. V S N

E. My Future

65. E G F P N
66. E G F P N
67. E G F P N
68. E G F P N
69. E G F P N
70. E G F P N

F. My Friends

71. A B C D E
72. A B C D E
73. A B C D E
74. T F
75. A B C D
76. A B C D E
77. A B C D E

G. Where I'd Go for Help

78. A B C D E
79. A B C D E
80. A B C D E
81. A B C D E
82. A B C D E
83. A B C D E

H. My Christian Faith

84. V S N
85. M L S
86. T ? F
87. A B C D E
88. A B C D
89. M S R
90. T ? F
91. T ? F
92. T ? F
93. T ? F
94. T ? F
95. T ? F
96. T ? F

I. What I Do

97. A B C D E
98. A B C D E
99. A B C D E
100. A B C D E
101. A B C D E
102. A B C D E
103. A B C D E
104. A B C D E
105. A B C D E
106. A B C D E
107. A B C D E
108. A B C D E
109. A B C D E

J. School

110. A B C D E F
111. M S N
112. M S N
113. M S N
114. A B C D

K. Right and Wrong

115. R ? W
116. R ? W
117. R ? W
118. R ? W
119. R ? W
120. R ? W

L. Male-Female Relationships

121. A B C D E F
122. A B C D E F
123. Y N
124. Y N
125. A B C
126. A B C
127. A B C D E

M. My Church

128. A B C D E
129. V S L N
130. A B C D E
131. A B C
132. Y ? N

N. My Feelings About My Church

133. 9 8 7 6 5 4 3 2 1
134. 9 8 7 6 5 4 3 2 1
135. 9 8 7 6 5 4 3 2 1
136. 9 8 7 6 5 4 3 2 1
137. 9 8 7 6 5 4 3 2 1
138. 9 8 7 6 5 4 3 2 1

O. What I Want From My Church

139. 5 4 3 2 1
140. 5 4 3 2 1
141. 5 4 3 2 1
142. 5 4 3 2 1
143. 5 4 3 2 1
144. 5 4 3 2 1
145. 5 4 3 2 1
146. 5 4 3 2 1
147. 5 4 3 2 1
148. 5 4 3 2 1
149. 5 4 3 2 1
150. 5 4 3 2 1

P. How Well My Church Is Doing

151. 5 4 3 2 1
152. 5 4 3 2 1
153. 5 4 3 2 1
154. 5 4 3 2 1
155. 5 4 3 2 1
156. 5 4 3 2 1
157. 5 4 3 2 1
158. 5 4 3 2 1
159. 5 4 3 2 1
160. 5 4 3 2 1
161. 5 4 3 2 1
162. 5 4 3 2 1

ANSWER SHEET
Circle the answer you want to give.

General Information
1. F M
2. 7 8
   9 10
   11 12

A. What I Want in Life
3. V S N
4. V S N
5. V S N
6. V S N
7. V S N
8. V S N
9. V S N
10. V S N
11. V S N
12. V S N
13. V S N
14. V S N
15. V S N
16. V S N
17. V S N
18. V S N
19. V S N
20. V S N
21. V S N
22. V S N
23. V S N
24. V S N
25. V S N
26. V S N

B. What I Worry About
27. V S N
28. V S N
29. V S N
30. V S N
31. V S N
32. V S N
33. V S N
34. V S N
35. V S N
36. V S N
37. V S N
38. V S N
39. V S N
40. V S N
41. V S N
42. V S N
43. V S N
44. V S N
45. V S N
46. V S N

C. My Family
47. A B C D E
48. A B C D E
49. A B C D E
50. A B C D E
51. A B C D E
52. A B C D E
53. A B C D E
54. A B C D E
55. A B C
56. A B C
57. A B C D E
58. A B C D E
59. A B C D E

D. How I Feel About Myself
60. V S N
61. V S N
62. V S N
63. V S N
64. V S N

E. My Future
65. E G F P N
66. E G F P N
67. E G F P N
68. E G F P N
69. E G F P N
70. E G F P N

F. My Friends
71. A B C D E
72. A B C D E
73. A B C D E
74. T F
75. A B C D E
76. A B C D E
77. A B C D E

G. Where I'd Go for Help
78. A B C D E
79. A B C D E
80. A B C D E
81. A B C D E
82. A B C D E
83. A B C D E

H. My Christian Faith
84. V S N
85. M L S
86. T ? F
87. A B C D E
88. A B C D
89. M S R
90. T ? F
91. T ? F
92. T ? F
93. T ? F
94. T ? F
95. T ? F
96. T ? F

I. What I Do
97. A B C D E
98. A B C D E
99. A B C D E
100. A B C D E
101. A B C D E
102. A B C D E
103. A B C D E
104. A B C D E
105. A B C D E
106. A B C D E
107. A B C D E
108. A B C D E
109. A B C D E

J. School
110. A B C D E F
111. M S N
112. M S N
113. M S N
114. A B C D

K. Right and Wrong
115. R ? W
116. R ? W
117. R ? W
118. R ? W
119. R ? W
120. R ? W

L. Male-Female Relationships
121. A B C D E F
122. A B C D E F
123. Y N
124. Y N
125. A B C
126. A B C
127. A B C D E

M. My Church
128. A B C D E
129. V S L N
130. A B C D E
131. A B C
132. Y ? N

N. My Feelings About My Church
133. 9 8 7 6 5 4 3 2 1
134. 9 8 7 6 5 4 3 2 1
135. 9 8 7 6 5 4 3 2 1
136. 9 8 7 6 5 4 3 2 1
137. 9 8 7 6 5 4 3 2 1
138. 9 8 7 6 5 4 3 2 1

O. What I Want From My Church
139. 5 4 3 2 1
140. 5 4 3 2 1
141. 5 4 3 2 1
142. 5 4 3 2 1
143. 5 4 3 2 1
144. 5 4 3 2 1
145. 5 4 3 2 1
146. 5 4 3 2 1
147. 5 4 3 2 1
148. 5 4 3 2 1
149. 5 4 3 2 1
150. 5 4 3 2 1

P. How Well My Church Is Doing
151. 5 4 3 2 1
152. 5 4 3 2 1
153. 5 4 3 2 1
154. 5 4 3 2 1
155. 5 4 3 2 1
156. 5 4 3 2 1
157. 5 4 3 2 1
158. 5 4 3 2 1
159. 5 4 3 2 1
160. 5 4 3 2 1
161. 5 4 3 2 1
162. 5 4 3 2 1

TALLY SHEET

Subgroup (if applicable):_____

Date: _____

Tally team: _____

Identification numbers of answer sheets tallied: _____

Directions:

The tally sheet is used to compile the responses from the answer sheets in order to consolidate the survey findings on the summary sheet. To use this tally sheet, follow these steps:

● Divide the answer sheets among two-person tally teams. Be sure to give each team only sheets from one subgroup if you plan to calculate data for subgroups. (See page 19 for an explanation of subgroups.)

● Fill out the top of this page by indicating the subgroup represented, the names of the tally team members, the num-

bers written on your answer sheets and the data.

● Have one person read the answers aloud while the second person records the responses in the column marked "Tally answers." Carefully follow this procedure for the entire test. Except where noted, if a person did not answer a question, do not mark anything.

● When you have recorded the answers from all the answer sheets, total the numbers in the last column for each line.

● For more detailed instructions on using this tally sheet, see page 19.

General Information

Question	Response	Tally answers	Total
1. Sex	F		
	M		
2. Grade	7		
	8		
	9		
	10		
	11		
	12		

A. What I Want in Life

Question	Response	Tally answers	Total
3. Arts	V		
	S		
	N		
4. Family	V		
	S		
	N		
5. Make parents proud	V		
	S		
	N		
6. Make own decisions	V		
	S		
	N		
7. Help people	V		
	S		
	N		
8. Feel safe	V		
	S		
	N		
9. Feel good about myself	V		
	S		
	N		
10. Popular	V		
	S		
	N		
11. Fun	V		
	S		
	N		

Question	Response	Tally answers	Total
12. My feelings	V		
	S		
	N		
13. Money	V		
	S		
	N		
14. God	V		
	S		
	N		
15. No hunger	V		
	S		
	N		
16. Good job	V		
	S		
	N		
17. Nice things	V		
	S		
	N		
18. Important life	V		
	S		
	N		
19. School performance	V		
	S		
	N		
20. No war	V		
	S		
	N		
21. Sports	V		
	S		
	N		
22. Different	V		
	S		
	N		
23. Friends	V		
	S		
	N		
24. Do my own thing	V		
	S		
	N		

Question	Response	Tally answers	Total
25. Church	V		
	S		
	N		
26. Look good	V		
	S		
	N		

B. What I Worry About

Question	Response	Tally answers	Total
27. Treat me	V		
	S		
	N		
28. Kill myself	V		
	S		
	N		
29. Good job	V		
	S		
	N		
30. Sexual things	V		
	S		
	N		
31. Kids like me	V		
	S		
	N		
32. Lose friend	V		
	S		
	N		
33. Hurt me	V		
	S		
	N		
34. Die soon	V		
	S		
	N		
35. Nuclear bomb	V		
	S		
	N		
36. Drink/ drugs	V		
	S		
	N		

Question	Response	Tally answers	Total
37. Parents die	V		
	S		
	N		
38. Hungry/ poor	V		
	S		
	N		
39. Beat up	V		
	S		
	N		
40. Body growing	V		
	S		
	N		
41. Parent drinks	V		
	S		
	N		
42. School	V		
	S		
	N		
43. Looks	V		
	S		
	N		
44. Trouble	V		
	S		
	N		
45. Violence	V		
	S		
	N		
46. Divorce*	V		
	S		
	N		
	No response		

*If this question is left blank, make a mark next to "No response."

C. My Family

Question	Response	Tally answers	Total
47. Freedom	A		
	B		
	C		
	D		
	E		

Question	Response	Tally answers	Total
48. Time	A		
	B		
	C		
	D		
	E		
49. Not yell	A		
	B		
	C		
	D		
	E		
50. Talk	A		
	B		
	C		
	D		
	E		
51. Interest	A		
	B		
	C		
	D		
	E		
52. Responsibility	A		
	B		
	C		
	D		
	E		
53. I love you	A		
	B		
	C		
	D		
	E		
54. Trust	A		
	B		
	C		
	D		
	E		
55. Love	A		
	B		
	C		

Question	Response	Tally answers	Total
56. Projects together	A		
	B		
	C		
57. Talk religion	A		
	B		
	C		
	D		
	E		
58. Mother talk	A		
	B		
	C		
	D		
	E		
59. Father talk	A		
	B		
	C		
	D		
	E		

D. How I Feel About Myself

Question	Response	Tally answers	Total
60. Like self	V		
	S		
	N		
61. Who I am	V		
	S		
	N		
62. Understand	V		
	S		
	N		
63. Purpose	V		
	S		
	N		
64. Body	V		
	S		
	N		

E. My Future

Question	Response	Tally answers	Total
65. Marry	E		
	G		
	F		
	P		
	N		
66. College	E		
	G		
	F		
	P		
	N		
67. Happy in 10 years	E		
	G		
	F		
	P		
	N		
68. Church when I am 40	E		
	G		
	F		
	P		
	N		
69. AIDS	E		
	G		
	F		
	P		
	N		
70. Nuclear war	E		
	G		
	F		
	P		
	N		

F. My Friends

Question	Response	Tally answers	Total
71. Number	A		
	B		
	C		
	D		
	E		

Question	Response	Tally answers	Total
72. Make friends	A		
	B		
	C		
	D		
	E		
73. Better friends	A		
	B		
	C		
	D		
	E		
74. Best friends	T		
	F		
75. Often lonely	A		
	B		
	C		
	D		
76. Do wrong	A		
	B		
	C		
	D		
	E		
77. Parents like my friends	A		
	B		
	C		
	D		
	E		

G. Where I'd Go for Help

Question	Response	Tally answers	Total
78. School trouble	A		
	B		
	C		
	D		
	E		
79. Feelings	A		
	B		
	C		
	D		
	E		

Question	Response	Tally answers	Total
80. Drugs	A		
	B		
	C		
	D		
	E		
81. Sex questions	A		
	B		
	C		
	D		
	E		
82. Feeling guilty	A		
	B		
	C		
	D		
	E		
83. Life decision	A		
	B		
	C		
	D		
	E		

H. My Christian Faith

Question	Response	Tally answers	Total
84. Importance of religion	V		
	S		
	N		
85. More important now	M		
	L		
	S		
86. God loves me	T		
	?		
	F		
87. God exists	A		
	B		
	C		
	D		
	E		

Question	Response	Tally answers	Total
88. Resurrection	A		
	B		
	C		
	D		
89. How I act	M		
	S		
	R		
90. God stop loving	T		
	?		
	F		
91. Pray	T		
	?		
	F		
92. Worship	T		
	?		
	F		
93. Read Bible	T		
	?		
	F		
94. Poverty/ hunger/ war	T		
	?		
	F		
95. Tell about Jesus	T		
	?		
	F		
96. Helping	T		
	?		
	F		

I. What I Do

Question	Response	Tally answers	Total
97. Beer party	A		
	B		
	C		
	D		
	E		

Question	Response	Tally answers	Total
98. Shoplift	A		
	B		
	C		
	D		
	E		
99. Cheat	A		
	B		
	C		
	D		
	E		
100. Vandalize	A		
	B		
	C		
	D		
	E		
101. Lie	A		
	B		
	C		
	D		
	E		
102. Beat up	A		
	B		
	C		
	D		
	E		
103. Alcohol in 12 months	A		
	B		
	C		
	D		
	E		
104. Alcohol in 30 days	A		
	B		
	C		
	D		
	E		
105. Pot/hash in life	A		
	B		
	C		
	D		
	E		

Question	Response	Tally answers	Total
106. Five drinks	A		
	B		
	C		
	D		
	E		
107. Cocaine in life	A		
	B		
	C		
	D		
	E		
108. Help others	A		
	B		
	C		
	D		
	E		
109. TV time	A		
	B		
	C		
	D		
	E		

J. School

Question	Response	Tally answers	Total
110. Home-work	A		
	B		
	C		
	D		
	E		
	F		
111. Enjoy school	M		
	S		
	N		
112. Try my best	M		
	S		
	N		
113. Trouble	M		
	S		
	N		

Question	Response	Tally answers	Total
114. Cut school	A		
	B		
	C		
	D		

K. Right and Wrong

Question	Response	Tally answers	Total
115. Sex at 16	R		
	?		
	W		
116. Discriminate	R		
	?		
	W		
117. Cheating	R		
	?		
	W		
118. Lying	R		
	?		
	W		
119. Drink at 16	R		
	?		
	W		
120. Shoplifting	R		
	?		
	W		

L. Male-Female Relationships

Question	Response	Tally answers	Total
121. Date	A		
	B		
	C		
	D		
	E		
	F		

Question	Response	Tally answers	Total
122. Kiss	A		
	B		
	C		
	D		
	E		
	F		
123. Talk	Y		
	N		
124. In love	Y		
	N		
125. Opposite sex	A		
	B		
	C		
126. Think sex	A		
	B		
	C		
127. Intercourse	A		
	B		
	C		
	D		
	E		

M. My Church

Question	Response	Tally answers	Total
128. Adults know	A		
	B		
	C		
	D		
	E		
129. Help answer	V		
	S		
	L		
	N		
130. For help	A		
	B		
	C		
	D		
	E		

Question	Response	Tally answers	Total
131. Important	A		
	B		
	C		
132. Recommend	Y		
	?		
	N		

N. My Feelings About My Church

Question	Response	Tally answers	Total
133. Kids important	9		
	8		
	7		
	6		
	5		
	4		
	3		
	2		
	1		
134. Church friends	9		
	8		
	7		
	6		
	5		
	4		
	3		
	2		
	1		
135. Learn	9		
	8		
	7		
	6		
	5		
	4		
	3		
	2		
	1		

Question	Response	Tally answers	Total
136. Questions	9		
	8		
	7		
	6		
	5		
	4		
	3		
	2		
	1		
137. Exciting	9		
	8		
	7		
	6		
	5		
	4		
	3		
	2		
	1		
138. Caring	9		
	8		
	7		
	6		
	5		
	4		
	3		
	2		
	1		

O. What I Want From My Church

Question	Response	Tally answers	Total
139. Bible	5		
	4		
	3		
	2		
	1		

Question	Response	Tally answers	Total
140. Christian	5		
	4		
	3		
	2		
	1		
141. Special	5		
	4		
	3		
	2		
	1		
142. Grow	5		
	4		
	3		
	2		
	1		
143. Friends	5		
	4		
	3		
	2		
	1		
144. Know adults	5		
	4		
	3		
	2		
	1		
145. Help others	5		
	4		
	3		
	2		
	1		
146. Right/ Wrong	5		
	4		
	3		
	2		
	1		

Question	Response	Tally answers	Total
147. Values about sex	5		
	4		
	3		
	2		
	1		
148. Values about drugs	5		
	4		
	3		
	2		
	1		
149. Fun	5		
	4		
	3		
	2		
	1		
150. Big issues	5		
	4		
	3		
	2		
	1		

P. How Well My Church Is Doing

Question	Response	Tally answers	Total
151. Bible	5		
	4		
	3		
	2		
	1		
152. Christian	5		
	4		
	3		
	2		
	1		
153. Special	5		
	4		
	3		
	2		
	1		

Question	Response	Tally answers	Total
154. Grow	5		
	4		
	3		
	2		
	1		
155. Friends	5		
	4		
	3		
	2		
	1		
156. Adults care	5		
	4		
	3		
	2		
	1		
157. Help others	5		
	4		
	3		
	2		
	1		
158. Right/ wrong	5		
	4		
	3		
	2		
	1		
159. Values about sex	5		
	4		
	3		
	2		
	1		
160. Values about drugs	5		
	4		
	3		
	2		
	1		

Question	Response	Tally answers	Total
161. Fun	5		
	4		
	3		
	2		
	1		
162. Big issues	5		
	4		
	3		
	2		
	1		

SUMMARY SHEET

Total group size: _____

Subgroup (if applicable): _____

Subgroup size: _____

Date: _____

Directions

The summary sheet is designed to translate and condense the raw data from the tally sheet into useful information about your group. Use the following procedure to analyze the data:

■ Trying to calculate the percentages for each response to every question would be overwhelming. The summary sheet highlights the most important responses to each question, thus condensing the data from the survey to a more manageable size. Therefore, it is not necessary to calculate the information in the shaded areas. However, if you want additional data, calculate it in the appropriate shaded column.

■ Transfer the numbers from the last column of the tally sheet to the column marked "Total responses."

■ If the Total responses column calls for the sum of two or more responses, add the responses together before recording them.

■ In the lines not shaded, calculate the percentage using this formula:

who chose this response ÷ total # of respondents × 100 = percentage

For example, if 54 people took your survey and 22 people marked "V" on question 3, then: $22 \div 54 \times 100 = 41\%$. Fill in this number on the appropriate line under the column marked "Percent."

■ Questions 133 to 138 and 151 to 162 call for averages rather than percentages. To calculate averages, follow the directions given at the beginning of each section.

■ See page 21 for more detailed instructions on using the summary sheet.

General Information

Question	Total responses	Percent
1. Sex	F	% are female
	M	% are male
2. Grade	7	% are in seventh-grade
	8	% are in eighth-grade
	9	% are in ninth-grade
	10	% are in tenth-grade
	11	% are in eleventh-grade
	12	% are in twelfth-grade

A. What I Want in Life

Question	Total responses	$\dfrac{\text{Total responses}}{\text{Total group size}} \times 100 =$	Percent
3. Arts	V		% say it is "very important to be good in music, drama or art."
	S		
	N		
4. Family	V		% say it is "very important to have a happy family life."
	S		
	N		
5. Make parents proud	V		% say it is "very important to make my parents proud of me."
	S		
	N		
6. Make own decisions	V		% say it is "very important to make my own decisions."
	S		
	N		
7. Help people	V		% say it is "very important to do things that help people."
	S		
	N		
8. Feel safe	V		% say it is "very important to feel safe and secure in my neighborhood."
	S		
	N		

A. What I Want in Life (Continued)

Question	Total responses	$\dfrac{\text{Total responses}}{\text{Total group size}} \times 100 =$	Percent
9. Feel good about myself	V		% say it is "very important to feel good about myself."
	S		
	N		
10. Popular	V		% say it is "very important to be popular at school."
	S		
	N		
11. Fun	V		% say it is "very important to have lots of fun and good times."
	S		
	N		
12. My feelings	V		% say it is "very important to understand my feelings."
	S		
	N		
13. Money	V		% say it is "very important to have lots of money."
	S		
	N		
14. God	V		% say it is "very important to have God at the center of my life."
	S		
	N		
15. No hunger	V		% say it is "very important to have a world without hunger or poverty."
	S		
	N		
16. Good job	V		% say it is "very important to get a good job when I'm older."
	S		
	N		
17. Nice things	V		% say it is "very important to have things as nice as other kids have."
	S		
	N		
18. Important life	V		% say it is "very important to do something important with my life."
	S		
	N		

A. What I Want in Life (Continued)

Question	Total responses	$\dfrac{\text{Total responses}}{\text{Total group size}} \times 100 =$	Percent
19. School performance	V		% say it is "very important to do well in school."
	S		
	N		
20. No war	V		% say it is "very important to have a world without war."
	S		
	N		
21. Sports	V		% say it is "very important to be really good at sports."
	S		
	N		
22. Different	V		% say it is "very important to be different from other teenagers I know."
	S		
	N		
23. Friends	V		% say it is "very important to have friends I can count on."
	S		
	N		
24. Do my own thing	V		% say it is "very important to do whatever I want to do when I want to do it."
	S		
	N		
25. Church	V		% say it is "very important to be part of a church."
	S		
	N		
26. Look good	V		% say it is "very important to have hair and clothes that look good to other kids."
	S		
	N		

B. What I Worry About

Question	Total responses	$\dfrac{\text{Total responses}}{\text{Total group size}} \times 100 =$	Percent
27. Treat me	V		% say, "I worry very much about how my friends treat me."
	S		
	N		
28. Kill myself	V		% say, "I worry very much that I might kill myself."
	S		
	N		
29. Good job	V		% say, "I worry very much that I might not be able to get a good job when I am older."
	S		
	N		
30. Sexual things	V		% say, "I worry very much that someone might force me to do sexual things I don't want to do."
	S		
	N		
31. Kids like me	V		% say, "I worry very much about how well other kids like me."
	S		
	N		
32. Lose friend	V		% say, "I worry very much that I might lose my best friend."
	S		
	N		
33. Hurt me	V		% say, "I worry very much that one of my parents will hit me so hard that I will be badly hurt."
	S		
	N		
34. Die soon	V		% say, "I worry very much that I may die soon."
	S		
	N		
35. Nuclear bomb	V		% say, "I worry very much that a nuclear bomb might be dropped on our country."
	S		
	N		

B. What I Worry About (Continued)

Question		Total responses	$\dfrac{\text{Total responses}}{\text{Total group size}} \times 100 =$	Percent
36. Drink/drugs	V			% say, "I worry very much about all the drugs and drinking I see around me."
	S			
	N			
37. Parents die	V			% say, "I worry very much that one of my parents might die."
	S			
	N			
38. Hungry/poor	V			% say, "I worry very much about all the people who are hungry and poor in our country."
	S			
	N			
39. Beat up	V			% say, "I worry very much that I might get beaten up at school."
	S			
	N			
40. Body growing	V			% say, "I worry very much about whether my body is growing in a normal way."
	S			
	N			
41. Parent drink	V			% say, "I worry very much about how much my mother or father drinks."
	S			
	N			
42. School	V			% say, "I worry very much about how I'm doing in school."
	S			
	N			
43. Looks	V			% say, "I worry very much about my looks."
	S			
	N			
44. Trouble	V			% say, "I worry very much that my friends might get me in trouble."
	S			
	N			

B. What I Worry About (Continued)

Question	Total responses	Total responses / Total group size × 100 =	Percent
45. Violence	V		% say, "I worry very much about all the violence in our country.
	S		
	N		
46. Divorce*	V		% of those whose parents are married say, "I worry very much that my parents might get a divorce."
	S		
	N		

*Individuals whose parents are already divorced were instructed to skip this question. Subtract the number who left it blank from the total group size before figuring percentage.

C. My Family

Question	Total responses	Total responses / Total group size × 100 =	Percent
47. Freedom	A + B		% agree or strongly agree with the statement, "I wish my parents would give me more freedom."
	C		
	D + E		% disagree or strongly disagree with the statement, "I wish my parents would give me more freedom."
48. Time	A + B		% agree or strongly agree with the statement, "I wish my parents would spend more time with me."
	C		
	D + E		% disagree or strongly disagree with the statement, "I wish my parents would spend more time with me."
49. Not yell	A + B		% agree or strongly agree with the statement, "I wish my parents would yell at me less often."
	C		
	D + E		% disagree or strongly disagree with the statement, "I wish my parents would yell at me less often."
50. Talk	A + B		% agree or strongly agree with the statement, "I wish my parents would talk to me more about their views on important issues such as sex and drugs."
	C		
	D + E		% disagree or strongly disagree with the statement, "I wish my parents would talk to me more about their views on important issues such as sex and drugs."

C. My Family (Continued)

Question	Total responses	$\dfrac{\text{Total responses}}{\text{Total group size}} \times 100 =$	Percent
51. Interest	A + B		% agree or strongly agree with the statement, "I wish my parents would be more interested in the things I care about."
	C		
	D + E		% disagree or strongly disagree with the statement, "I wish my parents would be more interested in the things I care about."
52. Responsibility	A + B		% agree or strongly agree with the statement, "I wish my parents would give me more responsibility."
	C		
	D + E		% disagree or strongly disagree with the statement, "I wish my parents could give me more responsibility."
53. I love you	A + B		% agree or strongly agree with the statement, "I wish my parents would say, 'I love you,' more often."
	C		
	D + E		% disagree or strongly disagree with the statement, "I wish my parents would say 'I love you,' more often."
54. Trust	A + B		% agree or strongly agree with the statement, "I wish my parents would trust me more."
	C		
	D + E		% disagree or strongly disagree with the statement, "I wish my parents would trust me more."
55. Love	A		% say, "It is very true that there is a lot of love in my family."
	B		
	C		
56. Projects	A		% say, "My family does projects together to help other people at least once a month or more."
	B		
	C		
57. Talk religion	A + B + C		% say, "My family talks together about God, the Bible or other religious things at least once a week."
	D		
	E		

C. My Family (Continued)

Question	Total responses	$\dfrac{\text{Total responses}}{\text{Total group size}} \times 100 =$	Percent
58. Mother talk	A + B		% say, "I hear my mother talk about her religious faith at least twice a week."
	C		
	D		
	E		
59. Father talk	A + B		% say, "I hear my father talk about his religious faith at least twice a week."
	C		
	D		
	E		

D. How I Feel About Myself

Question	Total responses	$\dfrac{\text{Total responses}}{\text{Total group size}} \times 100 =$	Percent
60. Like self	V		% say, "On the whole, I like myself."
	S		
	N		
61. Who I am	V		% say, "I spend a lot of time thinking about who I am."
	S		
	N		
62. Understand	V		% say, "Nobody understands me."
	S		
	N		
63. Purpose	V		% say, "I believe my life has a purpose."
	S		
	N		
64. Body	V		% say, "I feel good about my body."
	S		
	N		

E. My Future

Question	Total responses	$\frac{\text{Total responses}}{\text{Total group size}} \times 100 =$	Percent
65. Marry	E + G		% say there is an "excellent or good chance I will someday be married and have children."
	F		
	P		
	N		
66. College	E + G		% say there is an "excellent or good chance I will go to college."
	F		
	P		
	N		
67. Happy in 10 years	E + G		% say there is an excellent or good chance I will be happy 10 years from now."
	F		
	P		
	N		
68. Church when I am 40	E + G		% say there is an "excellent or good chance I will be active in church when I am 40."
	F		
	P		
	N		
69. AIDS	E + G		% say there is an "excellent or good chance myself or someone close to me will get AIDS."
	F		
	P		
	N		
70. Nuclear war	E + G		% say there is an "excellent or good chance the world will be destroyed by a nuclear war sometime in the next 10 years."
	F		
	P		
	N		

F. My Friends

Question	Total responses	$\dfrac{\text{Total responses}}{\text{Total group size}} \times 100 =$	Percent
71. Number	A		% say, "I have no close friends."
	B		
	C		
	D + E		% say, "I have six to ten (or more) close friends (not relatives)."
72. Make friends	A + B		% agree or strongly agree with the statement, "I wish I could be better at making friends."
	C		
	D		
	E		
73. Better friend	A + B		% agree or strongly agree with the statement, "I wish I could be better at being a friend to others."
	C		
	D		
	E		
74. Best friends	T		% say, "Some of my best friends belong to this church."
	F		
75. Often lonely	A + B		% say, "I feel lonely quite often or every day."
	C		
	D		
76. Do wrong	A + B		% say, "My friends often or very often try to get me to do things I know are wrong."
	C		
	D		
	E		
77. Parents like my friends	A		% say, "My parents like all of my friends."
	B		
	C		
	D		
	E		% say, "My parents don't like any of my friends."

G. Where I'd Go for Help

Question	Total responses	$\dfrac{\text{Total responses}}{\text{Total group size}} \times 100 =$	Percent
78. School trouble	A		% would seek help from *parents* if having trouble in school.
	B		% would seek help from *peers* if having trouble in school.
	C		% would seek help from an *adult friend or relative* if having trouble in school.
	D		% would seek help from a *minister or youth worker* if having trouble in school.
	E		% would *not seek help* if having trouble in school.
79. Feelings	A		% would seek help from *parents* if wondering how to handle feelings.
	B		% would seek help from *peers* if wondering how to handle feelings.
	C		% would seek help from an *adult friend or relative* if wondering how to handle feelings.
	D		% would seek help from a *minister or youth worker* if wondering how to handle feelings.
	E		% would *not seek help* if wondering how to handle feelings.
80. Drugs	A		% would seek help from *parents* if friends started using drugs or alcohol.
	B		% would seek help from *peers* if friends started using drugs or alcohol.
	C		% would seek help from an *adult friend or relative* if friends started using drugs or alcohol.
	D		% would seek help from a *minister or youth worker* if friends started using drugs or alcohol.
	E		% would *not seek help* if friends started using drugs or alcohol.
81. Sex questions	A		% would seek help from *parents* if having questions about sex.
	B		% would seek help from *peers* if having questions about sex.
	C		% would seek help from an *adult friend or relative* if having questions about sex.
	D		% would seek help from a *minister or youth worker* if having questions about sex.
	E		% would *not seek help* if having questions about sex.

G. Where I'd Go for Help (Continued)

Question	Total responses	$\dfrac{\text{Total responses}}{\text{Total group size}} \times 100 =$	Percent
82. Feeling guilty	A		% would seek help from *parents* if feeling guilty about something.
	B		% would seek help from *peers* if feeling guilty about something.
	C		% would seek help from an *adult friend or relative* if feeling guilty about something.
	D		% would seek help from a *minister or youth worker* if feeling guilty about something.
	E		% would *not seek help* if feeling guilty about something.
83. Life decision	A		% would seek help from *parents* if deciding what to do with life.
	B		% would seek help from *peers* if deciding what to do with life.
	C		% would seek help from an *adult friend or relative* if deciding what to do with life.
	D		% would seek help from a *minister or youth worker* if deciding what to do with life.
	E		% would *not seek help* if deciding what to do with life.

H. My Christian Faith

Question	Total responses	$\dfrac{\text{Total responses}}{\text{Total group size}} \times 100 =$	Percent
84. Importance of religion	V		% say, "Religion is very important in my life."
	S		
	N		
85. More important now	M		% say, "Religion is more important to me now than it was a year ago."
	L		
	S		
86. God loves me	T		% say, "I am sure God loves me just as I am."
	?		
	F		
87. God exists	A + B		% say, "I am sure or mostly sure God exists."
	C		
	D		
	E		

H. My Christian Faith (Continued)

Question		Total responses	Total responses / Total group size × 100 =	Percent
88. Resurrection	A			% declare a belief in Jesus Christ and the Resurrection.
	B			
	C			
	D			
89. How I Act	M			% say, "Most of the time my religious beliefs influence how I act at school and with friends."
	S			
	R			
90. God stop loving	T			% believe, "God will stop loving me if I do a lot of wrong things."
	?			
	F			
91. Pray	T			% believe God wants them to pray.
	?			
	F			
92. Worship	T			% believe God wants them to worship.
	?			
	F			
93. Read Bible	T			% believe God wants them to read the Bible.
	?			
	F			
94. Hunger/poverty/war	T			% believe God wants them to help get rid of hunger, poverty and war.
	?			
	F			
95. Tell about Jesus	T			% believe God wants them to tell other people about Jesus.
	?			
	F			
96. Helping	T			% believe God wants them to spend time helping other people.
	?			
	F			

I. What I Do

Question	Total responses	$\frac{\text{Total responses}}{\text{Total group size}} \times 100 =$	Percent
97. Beer party	A		
	B		
	C + D + E		% have been to parties three or more times in the past year where kids their own age were drinking alcohol.
98. Shoplift	A		
	B + C + D + E		% have shoplifted once or more during the past year.
99. Cheat	A		
	B + C + D + E		% have cheated on a school test once or more in the past year.
100. Vandalize	A		
	B + C + D + E		% have damaged or destroyed property at least once in the past year.
101. Lie	A		
	B + C + D + E		% have lied to their parents at least once in the past year.
102. Beat up	A		
	B + C + D + E		% have hit or beaten up another kid at least once in the past year.
103. Alcohol in year	A		
	B + C + D + E		% have drunk alcohol alone or with peers at least once in the past year.
104. Alcohol in month	A		
	B + C + D + E		% have drunk alcohol alone or with peers at least once in the past month.
105. Pot/hash in life	A		
	B + C + D + E		% have used marijuana or hashish at least once in the past year.
106. Five drinks	A		
	B + C + D + E		% have had five or more drinks in a row on one or more occasions in the past two weeks.
107. Cocaine in life	A		
	B + C + D + E		% have used cocaine or crack at least once in their lifetime.
108. Help others	A		
	B + C + D + E		% have spent three or more hours helping people outside their family without payment.

I. What I Do (Continued)

Question	Total responses	$\frac{\text{Total responses}}{\text{Total group size}} \times 100 =$	Percent
109. TV time	A		
	B		
	C		
	D+E		% watch three or more hours of television on an average school day.

J. School

Question	Total responses	$\frac{\text{Total responses}}{\text{Total group size}} \times 100 =$	Percent
110. Homework	A+B		% spend no more than one hour a week on homework.
	C		
	D		
	E+F		% spend at least five hours per week on homework.
111. Enjoy school	M		
	S		
	N		% rarely or never try their best at school.
112. Try my best	M		
	S		
	N		% rarely or never try their best at school.
113. Trouble	M		% are in trouble most of the time at school.
	S		
	N		
114. Cut school	A		
	B+C+D		% have skipped at least one school day in the past month.

K. Right and Wrong

Question	Total responses	$\dfrac{\text{Total responses}}{\text{Total group size}} \times 100 =$	Percent
115. Sex at 16	R		
	?		
	W		% disapprove of sexual intercourse for two unmarried 16-year-olds who love each other.
116. Discriminate	R		
	?		
	W		% disapprove of racial discrimination shown by trying to keep a minority family from moving into a neighborhood.
117. Cheating	R		
	?		
	W		% disapprove of cheating on a school test.
118. Lying	R		
	?		
	W		% disapprove of lying to their parents.
119. Drink at 16	R		
	?		
	W		% disapprove of 16-year-olds drinking a couple of beers at a party.
120. Shoplifting	R		
	?		
	W		% disapprove of stealing a shirt from a store.

L. Male-Female Relationships

Question	Total responses	$\dfrac{\text{Total responses}}{\text{Total group size}} \times 100 =$	Percent
121. Date	A		% have not dated at all in the past year.
	B		
	C		
	D + E + F		% have dated six or or more times in the past year.

L. Male-Female Relationships (Continued)

Question	Total responses	$\frac{\text{Total responses}}{\text{Total group size}} \times 100 =$	Percent
122. Kiss	A		% have not kissed an opposite sex peer.
	B		
	C		
	D		% have kissed an opposite sex peer six or more times in the past year.
123. Talk	Y		% have difficulty talking with an opposite sex peer.
	N		
124. In love	Y		% say they are in love with an opposite sex peer.
	N		
125. Opposite sex	A		% say they usually like to do things with opposite sex peers.
	B		
	C		
126. Think sex	A		% say they think about sex very often.
	B		
	C		
127. Intercourse	A		% say they have never had sexual intercourse.
	B		% say they have had sexual intercourse once.
	C + D		% say they have had sexual intercourse two or more times.
	E		

M. My Church

Question	Total responses	$\frac{\text{Total responses}}{\text{Total group size}} \times 100 =$	Percent
128. Adults know	A		% say no adults in the church know them well.
	B		
	C		
	D + E		% say six or more adults in the church know them well.

M. My Church (Continued)

Question	Total responses	Total responses / Total group size × 100 =	Percent
129. Help answer	V		% say the church is a great help in answering their questions about life.
	S		
	L		
	N		% say the church is no help at all in answering their questions about life.
130. For help	A		% say there are no adults in the church that they would seek out to help with an important question about life.
	B		
	C		
	D+E		% say there are six or more adults they would seek out to help with an important question about life.
131. Important	A		% say the church is very important to them.
	B		
	C		
132. Recommend	V		% say they would recommend their church to an unchurched friend.
	?		
	N		

N. My Feelings About My Church

Instead of calculating percentages for questions 133 to 138, calculate the average rating given for each statement. To do this, multiply by nine the number of times 9 was chosen; by eight, the number of times 8 was chosen; etc. Then add together all the responses to the statement and divide by the total number of responses.

Question	Total responses		Average rating
133. Kids important	9X	=	
	8X	=	
	7X	=	
	6X	=	
	5X	=	
	4X	=	
	3X	=	
	2X	=	
	1X	=	
	Total	=	
	÷		
		(total # of responses)	
	=	————————— —the average rating on a scale of 1 to 9 given to the statement, "Kids are important in my church."	
134. Church friends	9X	=	
	8X	=	
	7X	=	
	6X	=	
	5X	=	
	4X	=	
	3X	=	
	2X	=	
	1X	=	
	Total	=	
	÷		
		(total # of responses)	
	=	————————— —the average rating on a scale of 1 to 9 given to the statement, "I have many friends in my church."	

N. My Feelings About My Church (Continued)

Question	Total responses		Average rating
135. Learn	9X	=	
	8X	=	
	7X	=	
	6X	=	
	5X	=	
	4X	=	
	3X	=	
	2X	=	
	1X	=	
	Total	=	

÷

_____
(total # of responses)

= _____ —the average rating on a scale
of 1 to 9 given to the statement, "I learn a lot in my church."

Question	Total responses		Average rating
136. Questions	9X	=	
	8X	=	
	7X	=	
	6X	=	
	5X	=	
	4X	=	
	3X	=	
	2X	=	
	1X	=	
	Total	=	

÷

_____
(total # of responses)

= _____ —the average rating on a scale
of 1 to 9 given to the statement, "Questions are invited in my
church."

N. My Feelings About My Church (Continued)

Question	Total responses		Average rating
137. Exciting	9X	=	
	8X	=	
	7X	=	
	6X	=	
	5X	=	
	4X	=	
	3X	=	
	2X	=	
	1X	=	
	Total	=	
	÷		
	(total # of responses)		
	=		—the average rating on a scale 1 to 9 given the statement, "It's exciting in my church."
138. Caring	9X	=	
	8X	=	
	7X	=	
	6X	=	
	5X	=	
	4X	=	
	3X	=	
	2X	=	
	1X	=	
	Total	=	
	÷		
	(total # of responses)		
	=		—the average rating on a scale of 1 to 9 given to the statement, "Everyone cares about me in my church."

O. What I Want From My Church

Instead of calculating percentages for questions 139 to 150, calculate the average rating given for each statement. To do this, multiply by five the number of times 5 was chosen; by four, the number of times 4 was chosen; etc. Then add together all the responses to the statement and divide by the total number of responses.

Question	Total responses		Average rating
139. Bible	5X	=	
	4X	=	
	3X	=	
	2X	=	
	1X	=	
	Total	=	
	÷		
		(total # of responses)	
	=		—the importance on a scale of 1 to 5 of learning about the Bible.
140. Christian	5X	=	
	4X	=	
	3X	=	
	2X	=	
	1X	=	
	Total	=	
	÷		
		(total # of responses)	
	=		—the importance on a scale of 1 to 5 of learning what it means to be a Christian.
141. Special	5X	=	
	4X	=	
	3X	=	
	2X	=	
	1X	=	
	Total	=	
	÷		
		(total # of responses)	
	=		—the importance on a scale of 1 to 5 of learning what's special about themselves.
142. Grow	5X	=	
	4X	=	
	3X	=	
	2X	=	
	1X	=	
	Total	=	
	÷		
		(total # of responses)	
	=		—the importance on a scale of 1 to 5 of helping my religious faith grow.

O. What I Want From My Church (Continued)

Question	Total responses		Average rating
143. Friends	5X	=	
	4X	=	
	3X	=	
	2X	=	
	1X	=	
	Total	=	
	÷		
	(total # of responses)		
	=		—the importance on a scale of 1 to 5 of making good friends.
144. Adults care	5X	=	
	4X	=	
	3X	=	
	2X	=	
	1X	=	
	Total	=	
	÷		
	(total # of responses)		
	=		—the importance on a scale of 1 to 5 of getting to know adults who care about me.
145. Help others	5X	=	
	4X	=	
	3X	=	
	2X	=	
	1X	=	
	Total	=	
	÷		
	(total # of responses)		
	=		—the importance on a scale of 1 to 5 of having opportunities to help other people.
146. Right/wrong	5X	=	
	4X	=	
	3X	=	
	2X	=	
	1X	=	
	Total	=	
	÷		
	(total # of responses)		
	=		—the importance on a scale of 1 to 5 of learning how to make decisions about what is right and wrong.

O. What I Want From My Church (Continued)

Question	Total responses		Average rating
147. Values about sex	5X	=	
	4X	=	
	3X	=	
	2X	=	
	1X	=	
	Total	=	
	÷ _____ (total # of responses)		
	= _____		—the importance on a scale of 1 to 5 of learning about sex and sexual values.
148. Values about drugs	5X	=	
	4X	=	
	3X	=	
	2X	=	
	1X	=	
	Total	=	
	÷ _____ (total # of responses)		
	= _____		—the importance on a scale of 1 to 5 of learning about alcohol and other drugs, and what my values about them should be.
149. Fun	5X	=	
	4X	=	
	3X	=	
	2X	=	
	1X	=	
	Total	=	
	÷ _____ (total # of responses)		
	= _____		—the importance on a scale of 1 to 5 of having lots of fun and good times.
150. Big issues	5X	=	
	4X	=	
	3X	=	
	2X	=	
	1X	=	
	Total	=	
	÷ _____ (total # of responses)		
	= _____		—the importance on a scale of 1 to 5 of learning more about what a Christian should do about big issues such as poverty and war.

P. How Well My Church Is Doing

Instead of calculating percentages for questions 151 to 162, calculate the average rating given for each statement. To do this, multiply by five the number of times 5 was chosen; by four, the number of times 4 was chosen; etc. Then add together all the responses to the statement and divide by the total number of responses.

Question	Total responses		Average rating
151. Bible	5X	=	
	4X	=	
	3X	=	
	2X	=	
	1X	=	
	Total	=	
	÷		
	(total # of responses)		
	=		—the average rating on a scale of 1 to 5 given to the question, "How well does your church help you learn about the Bible?"
152. Christian	5X	=	
	4X	=	
	3X	=	
	2X	=	
	1X	=	
	Total	=	
	÷		
	(total # of responses)		
	=		—the average rating on a scale of 1 to 5 given to the question, "How well does your church help you learn about what it means to be a Christian?"
153. Special	5X	=	
	4X	=	
	3X	=	
	2X	=	
	1X	=	
	Total	=	
	÷		
	(total # of responses)		
	=		—the average rating on a scale of 1 to 5 given to the question, "How well does your church help you learn what's special about you?"

P. How Well My Church Is Doing (Continued)

Question	Total responses		Average rating
154. Grow	5X	=	
	4X	=	
	3X	=	
	2X	=	
	1X	=	
	Total	=	
	÷		
	(total # of responses)		
	=		—the average rating on a scale of 1 to 5 given to the question, "How well does your church help your religious faith grow?"
155. Friends	5X	=	
	4X	=	
	3X	=	
	2X	=	
	1X	=	
	Total	=	
	÷		
	(total # of responses)		
	=		—the average rating on a scale of 1 to 5 given to the question, "How well does your church help you make friends?"
156. Adults care	5X	=	
	4X	=	
	3X	=	
	2X	=	
	1X	=	
	Total	=	
	÷		
	(total # responses)		
	=		—the average rating on a scale of 1 to 5 given to the question, "How well does your church help you get to know adults who care about you?"
157. Help others	5X	=	
	4X	=	
	3X	=	
	2X	÷	
	1X	=	
	Total	=	
	÷		
	(total # of responses)		
	=		—the average rating on a scale of 1 to 5 given to the question, "How well does your church help you help other people?"

P. How Well My Church Is Doing (Continued)

Question	Total responses		Average rating
158. Right/Wrong	5X	=	
	4X	=	
	3X	=	
	2X	=	
	1X	=	
	Total =		
	÷ _____ (total # of responses)		
	= _____		—the average rating on a scale of 1 to 5 given to the question, "How well does your church help you learn about what is right and wrong?"
159. Values about sex	5X	=	
	4X	=	
	3X	=	
	2X	=	
	1X	=	
	Total =		
	÷ _____ (total # of responses)		
	= _____		—the average rating on a scale of 1 to 5 given to the question, "How well does your church help you learn about sex and sexual values?"
160. Values about drugs	5X	=	
	4X	=	
	3X	=	
	2X	=	
	1X	=	
	Total =		
	÷ _____ (total # of responses)		
	= _____		—the average rating on a scale of 1 to 5 given to the question, "How well does your church help you learn about alcohol and other drugs, and what your values about them should be?"

P. How Well My Church Is Doing (Continued)

Question	Total responses		Average rating
161. Fun	5X	=	
	4X	=	
	3X	=	
	2X	=	
	1X	=	
	Total	=	
	÷ _____ (total # of responses)		
	= _____		—the average rating on a scale of 1 to 5 given to the question, ''How well does your church provide lots of fun and good times?''
162. Big issues	5X	=	
	4X	=	
	3X	=	
	2X	=	
	1X	=	
	Total	=	
	÷ _____ (total # of responses)		
	= _____		—the average rating on a scale of 1 to 5 given to the question, ''How well does your church help you learn about what a Christian should do about big issues such as poverty and war?''

Practical Programming Resources for Your Youth Ministry

TRAINING VOLUNTEERS IN YOUTH MINISTRY

Video Kit

Give your volunteer youth workers a deeper understanding of youth ministry. You'll get expert, in-depth education with the **Training Volunteers in Youth Ministry** video kit. The nation's top authorities on youth ministry and teenagers provide solid, practical information. Your complete kit includes four 30-minute videotapes and 120-page leaders guide packed with tons of volunteer-building help . . .

> Video 1: Youth Ministry Basics
> Video 2: Understanding Teenagers
> Video 3: Building Relationships
> Video 4: Keys for Successful Meetings

You'll use this valuable resource again and again, sharpening the skills of your volunteer team. Design a training plan to meet your needs using helpful tips from the leaders guide. You'll discover how to find, motivate and keep volunteers. Plus, get ready-to-copy worksheets to enhance your training program. Strengthen your youth ministry team with practical, affordable youth ministry training.

ISBN 0931-529-59-X, $98

WHY TEENAGERS ACT THE WAY THEY DO

Dr. G. Keith Olson

What makes your teenagers tick?

- Why does Ann seem unable to take responsibility?
- How did Tim develop strong leadership skills?
- Why does Johnny act like a klutz—always injuring himself?
- Why does Karen always put herself down?

Why Teenagers Act the Way They Do helps you unravel the mystery of personality development. You'll discover how each young person is unique with different wants, needs and urges. Learn ways to turn your teenagers' weaknesses into strengths. Get hundreds of suggestions to improve your ministry—and ways to build solid relationships with parents. Positive, practical suggestions to help them understand and cope with their own teenagers. Together, you'll help your young people mature into Christian adults.

ISBN 0931-529-17-4, $15.95

INVOLVING YOUTH IN YOUTH MINISTRY

Thom and Joani Schultz

Develop your young people as leaders with this practical approach to youth ministry. Under your guidance, they'll learn valuable skills. Planning. Self-discipline. Time management. Problem-solving and more.

You'll learn successful strategies to help you . . .

- Motivate your members
- Evaluate your present program
- Share your workload
- Develop an effective team of adult volunteers
- Train young people to plan and do their own meetings and special events
- Involve youth in peer ministry and more

Build a stronger, close-knit group with this youth-based ministry plan.

ISBN 0931-529-20-4, $9.95

Strengthen Your Youth Ministry

PARENTING TEENAGERS

Video Kit

Offer parents needed support for coping with their teenagers—through practical video training.

Your complete kit includes four 30-minute VHS videos and 144-page leaders guide packed with helpful information and ready-to-copy worksheets. Help parents discover . . .

     Video 1: What Makes Your Teenager Tick?
     Video 2: Parenting: How Do You Rate?
     Video 3: Communicating With Your Teenager
     Video 4: Your Teenager's Friends and Peer Pressure

Give parents of teenagers the insights, encouragement and support they need to survive the tough teenage years.

ISBN 0931-529-60-3, $98

TRAINING TEENAGERS FOR PEER MINISTRY

Dr. Barbara B. Varenhorst with Lee Sparks

Expand your ministry effectiveness. Teach your young people how to be skillful care-givers. Use this easy-to-follow program to enable kids to minister effectively to their friends. The activity-rich format equips young people with important life skills . . .

- Making responsible decisions
- Effective listening
- Respecting confidences
- Knowing how to deal with typical teenage concerns, such as family problems, sexual concerns, death and dying

Teach your young people how to turn their faith into real caring by training your teenagers for peer ministry.

ISBN 0931-529-23-9, $8.95

WORRY, WORRY, WORRY: SCHOOL, WAR AND OTHER SCARY STUFF

Katie Abercrombie

Now you can help young people grapple with their biggest fears. Offer kids an action-packed study series that helps them get a grip on their worries:

- How they look
- Their future
- Nuclear war
- Keeping friends
- Violence and crime
- Losing a parent

You'll lead kids through 13 lively sessions using the step-by-step outlines in your detailed leaders guide. Get the resource that builds faith as it teaches young people how to deal positively with their fears.

ISBN 0931-529-48-4 (leaders guide), $9.95
ISBN 0931-529-49-2 (student book), $3.95

More Ministry-Building Resources

FAST FORMS FOR YOUTH MINISTRY

Compiled by Lee Sparks

Here's a lifesaver for busy youth workers. **Fast Forms for Youth Ministry** gives you ready-to-copy forms, schedules, checklists and letters to save you time and effort. In just minutes, you'll have ready-to-use documents that took hours to produce and perfect. Each form is designed to help you better organize and manage your ministry. You'll find hundreds of uses for . . .

- Planning checklists
- Evaluation forms
- Sample letters and more

Make your ministry more effective with this practical, useful tool.

ISBN 0931-529-25-5, $11.95

YOUTH MINISTRY CARE CARDS

Here's a quick, colorful and low-cost way to build attendance and give affirmation. **Youth Ministry Care Cards** are inspiring post cards your kids will love to get. Each card includes a meaningful Bible verse and zany cartoon.

Affirmations—positive, encouraging messages to let your kids know you're thinking about them.

Attendance Builders—unforgettable reminders to attract more kids to your meetings, retreats and special events.

Each 30-card pack contains 6 different messages.

Affirmations ISBN 0931-529-28-X, $3.95/pack
Attendance Builders ISBN 0931-529-36-0, $3.95/pack

THE YOUTH MINISTRY RESOURCE BOOK

Edited by Eugene C. Roehlkepartain
Foreword by Dr. Martin E. Marty

Get a gold mine of youth ministry information. This handy desk top reference gives you the most up-to-date information available on . . .

- **Young people and the youth culture . . .**
  Learn what recent research reveals about today's teenagers.
- **Youth ministry in America . . .**
  Who's doing what? Profiles of 339 youth ministry organizations.
- **The youth ministry profession . . .**
  Get all the inside information on your profession.
- **Youth ministry resources . . .**
  Find out where to get a wealth of resources on hundreds of topics.

Build effective youth ministry programs with this easy-to-use treasury of youth ministry data.

ISBN 0931-529-22-0, $16.95